ENCYCLOPAEDIA OF SPECIAL EDUCATION - IX

SLOW LEARNERS
THEIR PSYCHOLOGY AND INSTRUCTION

By

Dr. G. Lokanadha Reddy
Dean, School of Education and
HRD and Dean Academic Affairs
Dravidian University
Kuppam - 517 426
Chittoor Dist, AP State
(India)

Dr. R. Ramar
Headmaster
S.S.H.N. Hr. Secondary School
Muhavur - 626 111
Tamil Nadu
&

Dr. A. Kusuma
Dept. of Human Development &
Family Studies
Sri Padmavathi Mahila Visvavidyalayam
Tirupati (A.P.)
(India)

DISCOVERY PUBLISHING HOUSE PVT. LTD.
NEW DELHI-110 002

First Published - 1997

Reprinted – 2025

ISBN: 978-93-5056-518-6 (Set)
ISBN: 978-81-7141-399-7

Slow Learners: *Their Psychology and Instruction*

Published by:
DISCOVERY PUBLISHING HOUSE PVT. LTD.
4383/4B, Ansari Road, Darya Ganj
New Delhi-110 002 (India)
Phone: +91-11-23279245; 23253475; 43596065
E-mail: discoverybooksindia@gmail.com
discoverypublishinghouse@gmail.com
namitwasan9@gmail.com
web: www.discoverypublishinggroup.com

Printed at:
Infinity Imaging Systems
Delhi

Foreword I

This book is written to enlighten the practitioners and researchers in the field of education in general and special education in particular. The problem that plagues every teacher is how to provide appropriate instruction to slow learners—the learners in the lowest rung of the ladder - who are found in every class room at every grade level. The very fact that this group, hitherto ignored, constitutes about 18% of the total student population, warrants our immediate attention to realise the goal of providing an amount of education suitable to their capacities and put them in the appropriate position in the nations work-force i.e., human capital formation.

The authors of this book seem to have set out to give the intellectual grounding and practical strategies to the present and tomorrow's teachers to make them to be more effective instructors of slow learners. The development of the past few decades show that the teacher's behaviour have a profound impact on student achievement. To exercise a better impact of them on student learning, the teachers must have both a deep understanding of sound principles of psychology and a clear sense of how these principles can be applied to the field of education in general and to the process of teaching - learning in particular. This insight is adequately provided to the teachers by this book. The first half of the book mainly concentrates on concept, problems and developments of slow learners. The second half of the book presents strategies for instructional activities viz., planning courses, presenting lessons and adapting instruction to meet the needs of slow learners. In short, the goal of this book is to give guidelines to the teachers to circumvent slow learning problems of students.

The authors deserved to be congratulated for their excellent efforts in preparing this book which is expected to be well received by its users of all kinds.

Prof. S. Padmanabhaiah
Head and Dean
Faculty of Education
S.V. University
Tirupati (A.P.)

Foreword II

Society expects much from its schools, both in terms of general education and vocational training. The school plays a pivotal role in human resource development. The task of the teachers in schools is a challenging one. Teaching is one of the toughest jobs there is because a teacher has to do many things. He must be a good leader, an effective speaker, a quick diagnostician, a tactful diplomatic and a firm but fair disciplinarian. The authors of this book have embarked on an endeavour to communicate what they know about slow learners, about their learning problems, and, most importantly about how to teach slow learners, to people who are now or will soon be doing one of the most important jobs in the world—teaching the next generation.

Effective teaching is intelligent application of psychological principles to solve the practical problems encountered in teaching learning process. Teaching slow learners is an arduous task. But their problems, challenges, progress and success are much fascinating to watch and to participate in. This book will be of immense value to the teachers right from primary level to university level as well as to the students at B.Ed. and M.Ed. levels and the research scholars. The information that this book contains on psychology and instruction of slow learners will help the present as well as the coming generations of teachers to do the best possible job with the slow learning children.

The aforesaid target groups will find this book very useful to gain an insight into the learning problems of slow learners, teacher effectiveness and methodologies of teaching slow learners. I hope this book will give the teachers the intellectual and practical skills needed to do one of the most challenging jobs in the world - teaching the slow learners.

Prof. P. Ramasamy
Vice Chancellor
Alagappa University
Karaikudi,
Tamilnadu

CONTENTS

I Concept of Slow Learners

Chapter Outline

Chapter Objectives

This chapter outlines concept of slow learners. After reading the chapter the reader should be able to:

- Understand the concept of slow learners
- Distinguish the slow learners from under achievers and learning disabled
- List out the characteristics of slow learners
- Describe the causes of slow learning
- Realise the importance of teachers' role in teaching slow learners

The experience of educators confirms that there are many children who are so backward in basic subjects that they need special help. These pupils have limited scope for achievement. They have intelligence quotients between 76 and 89 and they constitute about 18 percent of the total school population. These students do not stand out as very different from their classmates except that they are always slow on the uptake and are often teased by the other students because of their slowness. They are quite well built physically but rather clumsy and uncoordinated in movement. They are no trouble in school. Although much of the work is too difficult for them, they are patient and co-operative. Some of them are much more limited in their capabilities and some have additional handicaps in physical, environmental, emotional, which impede their school progress and personal development. They need special help in the form of special class in ordinary school. Most of the slow learners struggle along in ordinary classes failing to have the special attention which they need.

Their ability to deal with abstract and symbolic materials, [i.e. language, number and concepts] is very limited and their reasoning in practical situation is inferior to that of average students. These pupils differ slightly from normal students in learning ability. They are also unable to deal with relatively complex games and school assignments. They need much external stimulation and encouragement to do simple type of work. These students who are known to be slow to 'catch on' are called slow learners.

Burt [1937] has rightly pointed out that the term 'backward' or 'slow learner' is reserved for those children who are unable to cope with the work normally expected of their age group. In teaching backward children, the mental age is often taken as a guide to the levels of attainment to be expected of pupils. Thus, if a child's mental age is 10 years, we assume that his attainment age should also be at the 10 year level. On the contrary, if his attainment age falls below his mental age he is considered a slow learner. Jenson [1980] states that students with IQ 80 to 90 who are traditionally labelled 'dull normal' are generally slower to 'catch on' to whatever is being taught if it involves symbolic, abstract or conceptual subject matter. In the early grades in school, they most often have problems in reading and arithmetic and are labelled 'slow learners'. But it is really not that they learn so slowly as that they lag behind in developmental readiness to grasp the concepts that are within easy reach of the majority of their age mates. So they may be called rather 'slow developers' than slow learners.

The handicaps of those children who are blind, deaf, or physically handicapped are readily apparent to the observer but the handicaps of the slow learners are not always so obvious. Their handicap is related to their power of thinking and their ability to learn. They are therefore not so able as most children to meet the normal demands of education and life in modern society. Many of them will be absorbed into the life of the community as adults and will contribute usefully without drawing undue attention to themselves. The period at which their limitations are so obvious is that of the school years. In the school certain skills such as verbal intelligence, the capacity for abstract, and conceptual thinking are valued. Education reflects the requirements of a community for minimum attainment in reading, writing and simple calculation in it's members and comparisons of attainments in these are most obvious at school. Slow learners lag behind in developing these skills at early grade itself and they find it very difficult to cope with their class mates. These students have learning difficulties which tend to increase if the teaching is not suitably geared to their slower rate of progress, and modified to achieve the most effective ways of learning.

Hence there is a greater need for special educational measures for the slow learners to ensure maximum progress they are capable of in the traditional three R's, and, no less important, in other developments such as practical, personal and social which are very valuable in adult life. We have to give them special attention on humanitarion grounds so that they can overcome the unhappiness and personal inadequacy that are the concomitants of severe educational and social failures. Other utilitarian reasons also justify the need for special attention to slow learners in the school. First, the country needs the fullest development of its human resources, not only in those capable of development of higher skills but also in those capable of routine tasks which are equally essential for the maintenance of the social organisation. Secondly, the cost of mental ill health and delinquency which can result from educational failure may well be greater in the long run than the cost of developing adequate means of special educational treatment in childhood.

The experience of schools confirms that there are many children who are so backward in basic subjects that they need special help. The backward children can be classified into three broad categories. The first category consists of those students who are very backward because of retarded mental developments which are often accompanied by additional handicaps, such as physical deficiencies, ill-health, limited verbal experiences at home and emotional disturbances. Their educational problems are so acute that they need special educational treatment outside the ordinary school. The second category consists of under achievers whose ability is not quite so limited but who nevertheless have more difficulty in learning than average children. Absence from school, unfortunate personal circumstances, or inadequate environmental conditions further limit their progress. Failure to recognize and provide for their problem is one of the main contributory causes of their backwardness. The third category consists of the slow learners who have very limited cognitive ability. The causes of their failure range from specific perceptual difficulties to emotional maladjustments. These students need some form of special or remedial teaching to make a marked progress.

According to Kirk [1962] the slow learners, average and gifted students can be classified according to their rate of learning. He also strictly refused to equate slow learnrs with mentally retarded because the former is capable of achieving a reasonable degree of academic success even though at a slower rate than the average student. As an adult, a slow learner usually becomes self supporting, independent and socially adjusted, but in the early stage, he adapts himself to regular classroom programmes which fit in with his slower learning ability. These slow learners are markedly different from under achievers and learning disabled.

Difference between Slow Learner and Under Achiever:

Though the slow learners and the under achievers fail to score or attain what is expected of them, there is a marked difference between the two. Slow learners are those students who are generally unable to do the work normally expected of their age group. They are the students who find it very difficult to keep pace with their age/class mates. They are unable to do the work of the class in which they are placed or even the class below that. There are others whose ability is not quite so limited but who nevertheless have more difficulty in learning than average students. Absences from school, unfortunate personal circumstances, or inadequate environmental conditions have often further limited their progress. Such students are termed as under achievers. Their attainment is not in tune with their capability. It is below the expected level of achievement. Their achievement is not on par with their ability. In short, their educational attainment falls below their capability. While the inadequate performance of the slow learners can be attributed to their low mental ability, there are various other causative factors as mentioned above for the inadequate performance of under achievers who possess potentiality, which the slow learners lack.

Difference Between Slow Learners and Learning Disabled

Though both the slow learners and the learning disabled have learning difficulties, there is still difference between the two. A slow learner is one who is unable to do the work of the class in which he is placed or even the class below that. He is not upto the attainment levels of the various subjects which are normal for his age or grade. Kirk [1963] defines learning disabled as those children who have disorders in development in language, speech reading, and associated communication skills needed for social interaction. He further noted that he did not include as learning disabled those children whose primary handicap was generalised mental retardation or sensory impairment like blindness or deafness.

Federal Register [1977] defines specific learning disablity as a disorder in one or more of the basic psychological processes involved in understanding or in using language, spoken or written, which may manifest itself in an imperfect ability to listen, think, speak, read, write, spell or to do mathematical calculations. The term includes such conditions as perceptual handicaps, brain injury, minimal brain disfunction, dyslexia, and developmental aphasia. The term does not include children having learning problems which are primarily the result of visual, hearing, or motor handicaps, of mental retardation, of emotional disturbance, or of environmental, cultural, or economic disadvantage. Slow learning comes under learning problem and it is concerned with the lower learning rate of the children. The second part of the definition of specific learning disability clearly points out that slow learning does not fall under the purview of learning disability. At the same time, it is to be admitted that there are certain common characteristics between slow learners and learning disabled.

Characteristics of Slow Learners

Taking the aforesaid factors into consideration, characteristics of slow learners can be systematically listed out.

a) Limited Cognitive Capacity

Schonell [1942] defines general intelligence as an inborn, all-round mental power which is but slightly altered in degree by environmental influences although its realisation and direction are determined by experience. Intelligence is viewed not merely as an unfolding or maturing of this innate potentiality but also as something that grows and develops in the course of the child's active experience of his environment. This is what the slow learners lack. Due to limited cognitive capacity, slow learners fail to cope with learning situations and to reason abstractly. Rational thinking becomes practically impossible for them.

Slow Learners experience difficulty with the complex mental operation of reasoning. They are usually slower to observe the features of things and to perceive relationships between things in their experience. So they are very poor in the process of developing concepts or general ideas which underlie a great deal of school work, especially in language and number. At the most, they can succeed in rote learning. They evince interest in learning where relationships are clearly demonstrated. With regard to retentive memories they require more practice and revision when compared with normal students. Also, they are poor in employing cognitive strategies which are very essential to facilitate retention processes. These strategies reflect planned and goal directed behaviour and involve cognitive control processes known as executive function, that focus on the retrieval of information from long term memory [Flavell, 1977]. The executive function helps us to organise, direct, and supervise the cognitive resources needed to process information. It is a " how to " search mechanism or organisation programme that directs the retrieval of information based on the reconstruction and refinement of environmental input. Executive function is the self conscious planning and executing of cognitive processes in a manner appropriate for the task demands; that is, it enables us to recognise and mobilise the cognitive tools available for remembering and recalling information [Neisser, 1967]. Executive function helps to provide a format for understanding how we retrieve information. [Swanson and Watson, 1982]. Memory development is tied to our over all knowledge development and improves with the qualitative changes in mental operations as children progress to higher levels of cognitive development [Liben, 1977; Piaget & Inhelder, 1973]. Slow Learners do not have adequate cognitive development since they possess limited cognitive capacity. Due to this limited cognitive capacity they are unable to keep pace with their age group.

b) Poor Memory

Memory is a complex process and is not fully understood, although some researchers have established theories that seem to explain the various observable facets of memory. Flavell [1977] and Flavell and Wellmen [1977] define memory as a series of cognitive processes, including recognition and recall, knowledge, cognitive strategies and metamemory. Each of these processes has an influence on learning. Atkinson and Shiffrin [1968] consider memory from the view point of a flow-through model. In the flow-through model, information is stored in sensory register for a brief time before it is transferred to stort-term memory and long-term memory. But the slow learners have a poor memory power.

Burt [1946] remarks that of all the special mental disabilities that hamper educational progress, the most frequent is a weakness in what may be termed long term memory. Slow learners need to go over material more times before it is fixed in their minds. The efficiency of initial learning is important as well as actual retention and recall; these are all influenced by attitudes, interests and emotional states. But slow learners are unable to retain information in memory storage for a long time and recall the information when it is needed. One of the causes of poor memory in slow learners is weakness in attention.

Attention is the cognitive process that enables us to attend to selected features of environmental stimuli that are detected by the sensory system. Attention can be divided into two components as selective attention and sustained attention. These processes are complementary functions and occur simultaneously. Selective attention involves experiencing environmental events through our sensory input channels. This is accomplished by an orienting reaction that activates appropriate regions of the brain to the source of environmental stimuli, selective attention occurs with the use of attentional strategies that are based on previous experiences and help to organise environmental information. These strategies, which include scanning and searching, are information acquisition routines that represent consistent patterns of focussing on the environment to extract information systematically [Garwood,1983]. Scanning is the ability to survey all environmental information. Searching, on the other hand, enables us to focus on specific or relevant environmental information that matches a mental model based on previous experience.

Sustained attention involves directing cognitive activities towards specific tasks. It includes attention span, which helps to establish optimal conditions for cognitive processing and is based on an indication of the complexity of the task and the intensity of the cognitive processes devoted to the task. Attentional strategies also include sustaining focus on relevant stimuli and shifting focus to new stimuli. Attentional strategies are affected by individual differences and cognitive styles that affect how we approach new experiences. These individual differences include reflective and impulsive approaches in responding to task demands and distractibility and persistance in remaining on task. Slow Learners lack concentration and they are known for distraction and short span of attention. So they are very poor in attentional strategies for a clear perception of concept. What is to be learned must be attended to and its main features observed. Failure in this may be due to factors in the child such as restlessness and distractibility. Motivation may be poor. Attention may be poor because the material to be learned is unsuitable - too difficult or outside the child's experience. It may be that it is presented in a way that does not facilitate accurate perceptions of it. One way in which remembering can be improved is by ensuring that as many useful associations are made as possible for meaningful associations are of great importance for slow learners for accurate perceptions of the concept.

A clear perception is the pathway to better memory. Perception is the cognitive process that identifies, organises and translates sensory data into meaningful information. The product of perception is figural information which is a direct representation of the physical and observable characteristics of our experiences, that is, inferences about how things feel, smell and taste. Meaning is distributed to figural information only when it is associated with environmental events and contents. Perceptual processes include discrimination, co-ordination and sequencing. Discrimination allows us to differentiate among distinctive features within the sensory system, coordination allows the integration of information from two or more information sources, and sequencing enables us to recognise spatial and temporal stimulus sequences and patterns

[DeRuiter & Wansart, 1982]. But the slow learners experience difficulties in these areas of perceptual processing.

c) Distraction and Lack of Concentration

Research works of Curtis, K. and Shaver, J.P. (1980) reveal that the attention span of the slow learners is relatively short. Also, they lack concentration. They can not concentrate on the instruction of the teacher which is mostly verbal exposition for more than thirty minutes at a stretch. They need short and frequent lessons for better perceptions. Modular approach or personalised system of instruction can cater to the needs of slow learners. Media application in the instructional process can draw and sustain their attention for a little longer time and promote concentration also. To overcome distractibility and to promote concentration, multimedia instructional strategy will be very suitable for slow learners. Research studies [Soundararaja Rao and Rajaguru, 1995] reveal that when the learning materials are presented through concrete situations, the slow learners's attention and concentration do not differ significantly from that of a normal student. They are able to concentrate on enjoyable and successful work for a considerable time. The degree to which the work is suited to the slow learners's capacity, and engages interest and activity is important. The slow learner's physical condition and his expectations of success or failure are also influential. In addition, the ability to concentrate seems to be, to some extent, a product of experience and training. Creative and practical activities seem to promote the development of good attention and of work habits.

d) Inability to Express Ideas

Tansley and Gulliford (1962) state that schools give considerable thought to the ways of achieving good standards in reading and writing, but important as reading and writing are, it must not be forgotten that they are only subsidiary skills in language. Children's ability to express themselves orally and to comprehend what is said to them is more important. This is where the slow learners are lacking. Slow learners have difficulty in finding and combining words, their immaturity and emotional reluctance being one of the chief reasons for their backwardness in expression. They often have recourse to gestures or to action rather than words.

With slow learners the difficulties are in knowing what to say, or if they know what to say in finding ways of saying it. A small vocabulary is one of the chief weaknesses. The lack of a work, or the frequent inability to call it up when needed, results in hesitations, new starts and round about ways of saying things. Expression is often lacking in order, sequence and selectivity. The difficulty in knowing what to select to say is a common enough weakness in expression. Also, the errors in the language usage of the slow learners are, of course, frequent. This can be attributed to the fact that what the slow learner hears out of school is in continual opposition to what he hears in school. He lacks imagination and foresight. He is not able to foresee the consequences in the future. To express ideas one must be good at communication which involves listening as well as talking. But, slow learners are poor at remembering messages and listening to instructions. As a result, they are unable to express ideas with clarity.

Causes of Slow Learning

Even though there are various causative factors for slow learning, only some important ones are discussed below. An insight into the causative factors of slow learing will enable the teachers to identify and combat slow learning at early stage itself. The earlier they are identified, the sooner remedial instruction can be imparted. It is not that all the factors are at work in case of all the slow learners. One or more factors or the interaction between these factors may cause slow learning in case of each slow learner. The following are the prominent causative factors.

a) Poverty

Poverty happens to be the primary factor causing slow learning in a developing country like India. Poverty affects children in two ways (i) by impairing student's health and (ii) by reducing their learning capacity. Poverty produces many mental and moral deprivations which ultimately speak upon the performance of students. "A sound mind in a sound body" is a tenet.

Only when the body is sound, the mind can work to its capacity. Our brains can remain sharp and alert, ready for any sort of information processing, only when we have good health which is usually affected by poverty. Poverty affects physical as well as mental health and this leads to intellectual dullness. Wealth plays a prominent role in acquiring general knowledge through enriched experience.

A child from a sophisticated family has a variety of avenues to explore and he gets enough materials to meet his requirements. He gets education, toys and books which are congenial to acquire general knowledge to improve his education background. Thus his mind is slowly conditioned and trained up to increase his learning rate over the years. On the contrary, a child from an impoverished family does not get enough opportunity to live a full life. Since the poor students have no access to such avenues it is not possible for them to sharpen their brain or to increase their learning rate at early stage. Poverty in itself does not necessarily cause slow learning but may create conditions and susceptibilities which may facilitate the onset of slow learning. However, poverty is not the sole cause of slow learning. We have to investigate into other causes to gain first hand knowledge about slow learners.

b) Intelligence of Family Members

Another potent factor that influences the learning of an individual is the level of intelligence of his parents as well as family members. It has its own impact on the learning of children. The educated parents are very keen on the intellectual development of their children. They start teaching and training their children before they are admitted to K.G. Classes. Also, they are able to provide the children with educational toys and books which all facilitate the learning of the children. Further, they themselves do intensive parent tutoring in reading and arithmetic. In this manner they train up their children to increase the learning rate. It is true that educated and intelligent parents can provide educational experiences and materials to their children according to their own intellectual level.

But if the parents are not intelligent or sophisticated, they can not take positive steps towards upliftment of their children.

They seldom evince interest in the intellectual development of their children. Neither learning material nor parent tutoring is provided to the children of illiterate parents. As a result, the children of impoverished families do not get adequate opportunities to train up their minds in order to increase their rate of learning. Without knowing arithmetic or alphabets they enter L.K.G. or First standard, whatever the case may be. Such children, when they come to school for the first time, see others far ahead of them and it gives them an inferiority complex which culminates in losing self confidence. These ultimately lead them to intellectual dullness which facilitates onset of slow learning. Children coming from affluent families which have high socio-economic status are not usually slow learners. Most of the slow learners are from indigent families. Research evidences also confirm this fact.

c) Emotional Factors

All students are likely to have emotional problems at some point in their school career. The slow learners have such serious and long lasting emotional problems that these hamper very much their learning process. These emotional problems of slow learners result in poor academic achievement, poor interpersonal relationship, and poor self-esteem. An Important area for personal, social and emotional development for children is self-concept or self-esteem. This aspect of their development will be strongly influenced by experiences at home, with peers, and at school. Self concept includes the way we perceive our strengths, weaknesses, abilities, attitudes and values. Its developments begin at birth and is continually shaped by experience. Lack of positive self-concept can severely damage a child's social development.

Slow Learners who are usually withdrawn, immature, low in self-image, or depressed are easily disturbed. Typically, such students have few friends or no friends at all, or may play with children much younger than themselves. They have elaborate fantasies or daydreams, and may have either very low self- images or grandiose visions of themselves. The slow learners are very much withdrawn. Withdrawn and immature students almost always suffer from a lack of social skills. Social skills training programmes have been quite effective in improving the social behaviour of withdrawn, friendless students, and in increasing their acceptance by their classmates (Gottlieb and Layser, 1981; Gresham, 1981; Strain and Kerr, 1981)

When children begin school life, they tend to judge themselves on specific accomplishments rather than on a general sense of truth (Damon and Hart, 1982; Harter, 1982). You can understand this when you see that even the smallest failure can cause a child to feel worthless. A child's social as well as emotional development during the primary grades is shaped by three influences. First in importance are parents and family. Second is the peer group. Third is the school experience (Coopersmith, 1975). Emotional factors contribute a lot towards the slow learning of children. Psychologists have confirmed this through various research findings. When a child comes to school, he brings his emotional world with him. Tension and conflict that the child experiences exercise a negative influence on learning. So, the tensions at home, the relationship between the siblings and parents themselves have an adverse effect on the learning of children, not to mention the frustration which he sustains from his family and the external world. In autocratic homes the children develop fear and frustration which hinder effective learning. Fear and anxiety generated by the teacher's attitude also will emotionally disturb the children. When the children are emotionally upset, tension and frustration set in which cause onset of slow learning.

d) Personal Factors

Besides all the aforesaid factors, there are some personal factors which are also responsible for slow learning. Physical deformities, pathological body conditions, and defects in sight, hearing and speech may pave the way for slow learning. These develop complex in children which adversely affects their learning. Personal factors include long illness or long absence from school and lack of confidence in self. Naturally when they remain absent from school for a long period due to illness or some other reason, they can not keep pace with their class mates and they will lag behind. This will ultimately affect their self confidence and create conditions and susceptibilities which may facilitate the onset of slow learning. It has been pointed out that children, who lack self confidence are slow learners.

Slow learning caused by physical attributes can be easily tackled provided diagnosis and remedial measures are made at early stage itself. It is needless to say that it is earlier the better. A careful examination of eyes, ears, throat, speech organs and the central nervous system is very essential. Services of consultants, Paediatricians, opthalmologists, audiologists, neurologists and speech therapists should be effectivey made use of. There are children with visual defects other than loss of acuity. There are some hearing defects which may only be revealed by audiometric examination. Similarly, brain damage can not be confirmed without a neurological examination or electro-encephalography. It is not only better but also cheaper to diagnose these defects in early stage itself so that clinical remedy can be ensured before the defects become worse and cause other consequences. There are also children whose physical development and muscular co-ordination are so retarded that they need immediate remedial measures. There are also some others who are malnourished because either feeding is poor or the metabolic processes are faulty. The slow learning problem of such children can be surmounted by ensuring special diet and treatment by nutrition experts.

Teacher for Slow Learners

Most of the backward countries are backward not because of inadequate supply of physical and financial resources but because of acute shortage of skilled personnel and technicians. Education promotes and develops an openness of mind, tolerance, co-operation, ability to adjust to the changes. Above all, it lays stress on the qualities of courage and endurance and encourages a vigorous and relentless pursuit of truth and free enquiry. Education enhances the understanding of the behaviour of interrelationships among the tangible and the intangible phenomena surrounding and imparts skill to translate the knowledge into action and makes the most beneficial use of them. So it is necessary that we enable the slow learners to make the most beneficial use of education. The question of whether to place the slow learners and other backward children in the special school or in the normal school sparked an academic debate which raged in the first half of the century. Now a decisive conclusion has been arrived at in this regard. Except those students who because of their physical impairments need special education in special schools, others should be placed in the normal school where they will have better exposure and better interaction which will ameliorate their learning process. So the teachers in the ordinary schools have to shoulder this onerous task of tackling the problems of the slow learners found in ordinary schools.

Now there is a growing interest in the problem of backward students in ordinary schools and an increased awareness of the size of the problem. Research evidences of Stella (1993) Reddy and Ramar (1994, 1995), Janakkumar (1996), Natarajan (1996), Rajaguru (1994) confirm this. But we dont have provision adequate to the need. There is an emphasis on starting those special classes with manageable number of pupils, but these are often first victims of staff shortages. It is more true so in case of the schools in the Govt sector. Though we have some really dedicated teachers in the private sector, their number is not encouraging. There is often an acute shortage of teachers who are interested in backward children and knowledgeable about the methods of dealing with them. There is a need for all the teacher trainees to have some instruction in the methods of the early steps of reading and number during training. They must be apprised of the methods of helping children who can not keep up with their age group. So it is always better to introduce a paper exclusively on special education for the teacher trainees at B.Ed level and this paper may be prescribed for indepth study at M.Ed level. Since most of the teachers are only B.Ed holders, it becomes very essential to include special education paper in the B.Ed syllabus. For the secondary grade teacher trainees also, a separate unit on individual differences from the instruction point of view should be included in the psychology paper. The teachers trained in this manner will be better prepared to identify the slow learners and to tackle their problems.

This book is written to communicate what we know about slow learners about their learning problems, and most importantly, about how to modify classroom instruction to slow learners so that optimum human resource development can be ensured in course of time. Teaching is one of the toughest jobs, there is because a teacher must do many things well. A teacher taking special classes for the slow learners, must be a good leader, an effective speaker, a quick diagnostician, a tactful diplomat, a firm but fair disciplinarian and above all a good humanitarian. These teachers must know their subjects, and even more importantly, know the craft of driving home the concepts to the bosoms of the slow learners. They have to be "on" all the time, and they should not leave their jobs behind when they go home at the end of the day.

Yet dedicated teachers love what they do. They do the duty regardless of what others say and without laying any claim to its fruits. Society may not always give these teachers the respect they deserve, nor pay them adequately, nor provide them with the facilities they need to do their job well. But it always gives them its children, and they do the job well with the limited resources available at their disposal. Let us hope that other teachers also will fall in line and together we can bend our energy to overcome the problems of all backward students in our committed task of human resource development. Let us face it, children are fun. It is more true so in case of slow learners. Their changes, challenges, endeavour, their successes are fascinating to watch and to participate in. As Robert Slavin rightly remarked, teachers matter, and they know they matter.

Summary

Slow learners are the students who are unable to cope with the work normally expected of their age group. They have intelligence quotients between 76 and 89 and they constitute about 18% of the student population. Their ability to deal with abstract and symbolic materials is very limited and their reasoning in practical situation is inferior to that of average students. These students slightly differ from normal students in learning ability. It is not really that they learn so slowly as that they lag behind in developmetal readiness to grasp the concepts that are within easy reach of the majority or their age group. So they may be called rather "slow developers" than slow learners.

Slow learners are markedly different from under achievers. While the inadequate performance of slow learners can be attributed to their low mental ability, there are various other causative factors for the inadequate performance of under achievers who possess potential which the slow learners lack.

Limited cognitive capacity, poor memory distraction and lack of concentration, inability to express ideas and emotional instability are the chief characteristics of the slow learners. These characteristics are invariably found in all slow learners. These characteristic features will be very useful to identify the slow learners.

Poverty, intelligence of family members, emotional factors and personal factors are the important causes of slow learning. All these factors cause slow learning but the degree may vary from factor to factor in case of each slow learner. If the factors are properly dealt with, the problem of slow learning can be easily tackled.

Teachers entrusted with the task of teaching slow learners should be committed to the task assigned to them. They should carry on the work regardless of what others say with a high degree of dedication. Even though the society does not always give the teachers the respect they deserve, it always gives them children. It is satisfying to teach slow learners. Their changes, their challenges, their successes are fascinating to watch and to participate in.

REFERENCES

1. Atkinson, R.C., and Shiffrin R.M., (1968) 'Human Memory : 1A Proposed System and its Component Processes'. In K. Spence and Spence (Eds), *The pshycology of learning and motivation*, Vol.2, Academic Press, New York.

2. Bill R. Gearheart (1985) 'Learning Disabilities, Educational Strategies' . Times Mirror, Mosty college publishing, Missouri, U.S.A.

3. Burt, C. (1946) 'The Backward child ' U.L.p, London.

4. Chintamani Kar (1992) 'Exceptional Children: Their Psychology and Education' Sterling Publishers Private Ltd, New Delhi.

5. Curtis, K. and Shaver, J.P (1980) 'Slow Learners and the study of Contemporary Problems, *Social Education*, 44, 4, pp, 302-38 April.

6. De Ruiter, J. and Wansart, W. (1982) 'Psychology of Learning Disabilities'. Rockville, MD: Aspen.

7. Federal Register (1977) Definition and Criteria for Defining students as Learning Disabled'. U.S. Government Printing Office, Washington D.C.

8. Flavell, J.H. (1977) 'Cognitive Development'. Englewood Cliffs, Prentice Hall New Jersey.

9. Flavell, J.H. and Wellman, H.M. (1977) 'Metamemory' In R.V. Vail and J.W. Hagen (Eds) *Perspectives on the Development of Memory and Cognition*, Lawrence Erlbaum, Hillsdale, NJ.

10. Garwood, S.G. (1983) 'Educating Young Handicapped Children' Aspen Systems, Rockville, Md.

11. Gottlieb, J., and Leyser, Y. (1981) 'Friendship between Mentally Retarded and Non-retarded Children'. In S. Ashen and J. Gottman (Eds) The *Development of Children's Friendship*, Cambridge University Press, Cambridge.

12. Gresham, F. (1981) 'Social Skills Training with Handicapped Children: A Review '. *Review of Educational Research*, 51, 139 - 76.

13. Jenson, A.R. (1980) 'Bias in Mental testing', Methuen and Co. Ltd, London.

14. Kirk, S. (1963) 'Proceedings of the Annual Meeting of the Conference on Exploration into the Problems of the Perceptually Handicapped Child '. vol. 1, Chicago.

15. Kirk, SA (1972) 'Educating Exceptional children' Houghton, Mifflin, Boston.

16. Liben, L.S. (1977) 'Memory from a Cognitive Development Perspective: A Theoretical and Empirical Review'. *In W.F Overton and J.M. Gallagher (Eds) knowledge and development: vol. 1. Advances in Research and Theory*, Plenum, New York.

17. Neisser, U. (1977) 'Cognitive Psychology'. Appleton-Century-Crofts, New York.

18. Piaget, J., and Inhelder, B. (1969) 'The Psychology of the Child'. Basic Books, New York.

19. Robert Slavin (1986) 'Educational Psychology - Theory into Practice' Prentice Hall of India Private Ltd, New Delhi.

20. Schonell, F.J. (1942) 'Backwardness in Basic Subjects'. Oliver and Boyd, London.

21. Strain, P. and Kerr M.M. (1981) 'Mainstreaming of Children in Schools'. Academic Press, New York.

22. Swanson, H.C., and Watson, B. (1982) 'Education and Psychological Assessment of Exceptional Children: A Cognitive Apprach to Solving Real Life Problems'. Jossey- Bass, San - Francisco.

23. Tansley, A.E., and Gulliford, R. (1962) 'The Education of Slow Learning Children'. Routledge and Kegan Paul Ltd, London.

2 Identifying Slow Learners

Chapter Outline

Chapter Objectives

This chapter delineates various modes of identifying slow learners. After reading this chapter you should be able to:

- List out the needs for ready identification
- Describe the three phase process for identifying slow learners
- Apply various intelligence tests and personality tests to identify and confirm the slow learners
- Assess slow learning on the basis of learning rate and Sandra's check-list

Children of to-day are the citizens of tomorrow; they are going to be the pillars of the country. Hence it is essential to ensure that each pillar is as strong as the other. Morover, we cannot bring about optimum human resource development without uplifting the slow learners who constitute about 18% of the total student population. There is every possibility that each classroom has some slow learners. It is more true so at primary and high school levels. They come to school regularly; but they are likely to become drop-outs if their needs are not adequately met. From psychological point of view, it would be more beneficial to identify the slow learners as early as possible. The earlier they are identified, the sooner they can be subjeced to remedial instruction.

From the survey works conducted so far it is observed that it is some, how easier to identify more severely handicapped children than the mildly handicapped ones. But, a teaching expert can easily make out any deviation in the classroom behaviour pertaining to learning difficulties of children. The teacher is the right person, by virtue of his position and his frequent interaction with the students, to adjudge the learning rate of his students. Manifestation of certain drawbacks and learning difficulties will naturally draw the attention of the teacher towards such slow learning children. Also, the teacher has primary knowledge about the fact which spells out clearly that the slow learners require more time and more help to acquire the pre determined skills than the average children. Hence, the earlier we identify the slow learners; the better we can combat slow learning.

Need For Early Identification

Early identification and prevention are basic goals of intervention programmes for any category of problem or backward students. For slow learners these goals present peculiar difficulties - yet it is not without promise. The difficulties are related to identifying the *specific* causes of slow learning, the particular promise is that the slow learners so much respond to special remedial instruction that preventive efforts and remedial measures seem to have a chance of success. Because children's behaviour is quite responsive to conditions in the social environment and can be shaped by adults, the potential for primary prevention

- preventing serious behaviour problems from occurring in the first place - would seem to be great. But as Bower (1981) notes, the task of primary prevention is not that simple. For one thing, the tremendous amount of money and personnel needed for training in child management are not available. For another, even if the money and the personnel could be found, professionals would not always agree on what patterns of behaviour should be prevented or on how undesirable behaviour could be prevented from developing (Kazdin, 1987).

If the slow learning is due to the specific cause of emotional disturbance of the child, an early identification and required intervention will be very fruitful. Research evidences also confirm this. Early intervention with preschoolers, whether they are aggressive or withdrawn, has the potential to make many such children 'normal' - that is, indistinguishable from their peers - by the time they are in the elementary grades (Lovaas, 1987; Strain, Steele, Ellis and Timm, 1982). Slow learning caused by physical attributes can be easily overcome if the problem is identified at early stage before it becomes worse or leads to complication. There are some students who stand out as being obviously extremely backward due to poor physcial co-ordination, their clumsy manipulation, and their very retarded speech. When these physical attributes are set right, slow learning can be tackled by providing physiotherepy and proper training. Identifying and intervening at early stage will be more feasible and fruitful. Though the slow learners come to school regularly they are likely to become drop outs if their needs are not adequately met. Only earlier identification can ensure effective intervention which will diminish wastage and stagnation to a considerable extent. From psychological point of view also it would be better to identify the slow learners earlier. Add these arguments stress the importance of identifying the slow learners at an early stage and also the operating causative factors so that required remedial measures can be taken up not only to alleviate the causative factor but also to ameliorate their learning process. The earlier, the better is the golden rule here.

A Three Phase Process

Psychologists and educationists have devised various tools

and techniques to identify slow learners. Tansley and Gulliford (1962) have laid down four different measures whereas Chintamani Kar (1992) has propogated seven measures to identify slow learners. But, identifying the slow learners on the basis of a three phase process will be more feasible and more reliable. The three phases are:

i. Initial Identifying phase

ii. Scientific Confirmatory phase

iii. Counter - Check phase

i. Initial Identifying Phase

To identify the slow learners initially the following techniques are very useful.

(a) Observation Technique

(b) An Educational Assessment

(c) A Social History of the Child in his family and Cultural Setting.

The aforesaid three techniques can be used separately or in any mode of combination to identify the slow learners. The speciality of these techniques is that the teacher does not require any testing tool to identify the slow learners.

On the contrary, he can easily identify the slow learners by means of his careful observation of the child. Also, a critical educational assessment of the child and knowing the social history of the child can easily bring the slow learners into the focus of the teacher. Since all the records required for making an educational assessment of the child are at his disposal, the teacher can easily complement the findings of his observation with educational assessment of the child. A deep insight into each technique is essential for properly identifying the slow learners.

a) Observation Technique

This is the most convenient and practically the foremost technique to identify slow learners. Observation of children's behaviour by the teacher as well as experts helps in identifying slow learners. This can be done under simple as well as controllable conditions. While making observation of the children's behaviour, a strict vigil should be kept to study their reactions to various situations. A child's behaviour can be observed not only in the classroom, but also on the playground, home and in the group. Observation can be done by just scrupulously watching the child at close quarters and by moving along with the child. How he grasps the instructional presentation, how he responds in the classroom and in the school premises should be noted down and analysed properly. It should be kept in mind that the observer should have the capacity for analysing and interpreting the information he gets from his observation. Observation technique is very congenial for ascertaining the curricular, co-curricular, extra-curricular and recreational interest of the children. In educational programmes such as recitation of a memory poem or reproduction of an essay or passage or testing comprehension can easily bring to light the slow learners. But observation technique alone will not suffice for reliable identification for there is a possible chance to confuse an under achiever with a slow learner. So, there is a need to complement observation technique with other technique or techniques.

b) An Educational Assessment

An education assessment provides a detailed description of the child in the school setting, giving information about:

1. The child's level of attainment in the basic subjects in terms of what he can do, what his special difficulties appear to be, and what steps have already been tried, e.g. whether remedial measures have been attempted, and if so, by what method and with what result. Evaluation of deficiencies in school achievement is possible through scholastic tests. These tests can throw light on areas like arithmetic, reading, spelling, composition, writing language and comprehension. General and specific problems of children can be easily singled but by the psychologists and the teachers through scholastic tests, and causes of anomalies can also be evaluated properly.
2. The child's level of language development and speech.

Slow learners are usually found to be wanting in this respect.

3. Standards of achievement in other areas of curriculum, e.g. in art, practical subjects, physical education.
4. Emotional and social behaviour as displayed both in and out of the classroom.
5. Interest in and attitude towards school.
6. Previous school history with particular reference to attitude towards school, changes of school and re-gularity of attendance.
7. The child's interest and background knowledge.
8. Degree of parental co-operation, lack of parental co-operation has been found to facilitate the onset of slow learning.

All the above measures can be undertaken by the teacher with the records available at his disposal. These bring to light not only the slow learning of the children but also signify the causes for that.

c) A Social History of the Child in his family and Cultural Setting

Most discussions about backward children lead to the point when the importance of the home as a powerful factor in the child's response to school is agreed upon. Efforts should be made to find out about birth conditions, age of passing the 'milestones', stages in speech development, illness and accidents and any marked irregularities in development. Details about the family history, particularly with reference to mental or physical illnesses that may have a bearing on the child's condition and the facts about the cultural and economic factors in the home should also be gathered and noted down. Then family attitudes and relationships should be assessed. This is a most important aspect to assess, for the emotional climate of the home, the attitude towards the child, and the way difficulties in development have been met can be poweful determinants of the child's capacity to learn. The aforesaid three techniques used sequentially or simultaneously will enable the teacher to identify the slow learners more reliably.

ii. Scientific Confirmatory Phase

The slow learners identified in the first phase should be subjected to certain scientific confirmatory tests for better reliability and accuracy. Further, these tests help the teacher to discriminate between the slow learners and other backward children like under achievers. Many standardised tests which can be administered as scientific confirmatory tests are now available. They are

a. Terman - Merrill Scale
b. Wechsler - Intelligence Scale
c. Other Intelligence tests in Common Use
d. Ravens Progressive Matrices
e. Personality Test
f. Psychometric and psychological Test
g. Medical Examination

Administering one or more than one of the above tests to the identified slow learners we can easily confirm whether we have correctly identified the slow learners. These tests will be very useful to differentiate a slow learner from other backward children as stated earlier. A thorough knowledge of these tests is essential for those who are entrusted with the task of instructing the slow learners.

a) Terman - Merrill Scale

Intelligence tests are designed to provide a general indication of individual's aptitude in many areas of intellectual functioning. Intelligence itself is seen as the ability to deal with abstractions, to learn, and to solve problems (Estes, 1982; Sternberg 1982, 1986), and tests of intelligence focus on these skills. The most frequently used verbal test is the New Revised Standard - Binet Scale, commonly called the Terman - Merill Scale, after its authors. It was developed in 1937. The items in the scale are of a variety of types : for example, vocabulary; verbal reasoning and comprehension; memory for sentences; words and digits; description and interpretation of pictures; copying shapes and patterns by drawing. Although there are some practical tests, it is mainly a verbal test. The tests are fringed into two age-levels and the examiner proceeds from a year group of tests which are answered correctly (the basal age) through to a year group in which all the tests are failed. Each test passed obtains two months of mental age and the total is added to the basal age. This total is the mental age and the IQ is then calculated by the formula:

$$IQ = \frac{\text{Mental Age}}{\text{Chronological Age}} \times 100$$

Example : Chronological Age (C.A.) = 11 - 6

	No. of sub-test							Year	Months
	1	2	3	4	5	6			
Year VI	+	+	+	+	+	+	Basal Age	6	0
Year VII	+	-	+	+	+	+	5 passes		10
Year VIII	+	-	+	-	-	-	2 passes		4
Year IX	+	-	+	-	-	-	2 passes		4
Year X	-	+	-	-	-	-	1 passes		2
Year XI	-	-	-	-	-	-	0 passes		0
								7	8

$$IQ = \frac{M.A}{CA} \times 100 = \frac{7 - 8}{11 - 6} \times 100 = 67$$

An IQ of 100 means essentially normal, above hundred is above normal, and below 100 is below normal. Those who are found to possess IQ from 75 to 90 are classified as slow learners. If the IQ is less than that they can be classifed as mildly regarded. This is confirming the slow learners on the basis of their IQ. However, it must be borne in mind that IQ is, in fact, no substitute for the knowledge that can be gained from observation of the child's learning and thinking in the classroom. It must be taken as only the beginning of our study of his intellectual capacities and must always be considered in relation to all the other information which can be acquired - about his health and physical development, his emotional and social maturity, his keenness to learn and his attitude towards school. This fact also serves as a sufficient condition for employing the three phase process to identify slow learners.

b) Wechsler Intelligence Scale

IQ tests measure intelligence by assessing a variety of skills thought to be aspects of intelligence. Sternberg (1986) hypothesises that there are three distinct types of intellectual abilities, which he calls intelligence, wisdom and creativity. He argues that individuals can be strong in any of these areas without necessarily being strong in all. The most widely used measure of IQ for school age children is the Wechsler Intelligence Scale for children Revised or WISC - R (Wechsler, 1974). The WISC-R yields a score for verbal IQ, one for performance (non verbal) IQ, and a total score. This is a definite advantage which WISC-R has over the Standard Binet test and it has contributed to its rapid acceptance. Wechsler Scales are helpful in making certain types of predictions in the evaluation of minority cultural groups, particularly bilingual children, and of those who have been culturally or educationally deprived.

Many Psychologists are now using the Wechsler Intelligence Scale for children which provides verbal, performance and Full Scale Quotients. Wechsler Intelligence Scale is an individual test which combines both verbal and non-verbal material. In the verbal scale, there are tests of vocabulary, information, verbal similarities, comprehension, and a short test of simple number thinking. In the performance scale, there are tests of picture completion and arrangement, block designs, object assembly and coding. The treatment of the scores is such that the child's level of functioning on the verbal and performance scales and also on the sub-tests within each scale may be compared. Thus WISC-R can be used, along with other information, for assessment of students who are experiencing difficulties in school.

Other Intelligence Tests in Common use

There are other tests of intelligence which can be used in certain instances. *The Columbia Mental Maturity Scale* is such a test which has been widely used. It requires approximately 20 minutes, much less time than the Stanford , Binet or one of the Wechsler tests requires and it can be used with children of ages 3 1/2 years through 9 years 11 months. It is a nonverbal response -to-drawings test that requires only a pointing response.

Quite contrary to this, *The Slosson Intelligence Test for Children and Adults* is a highly verbal test, and it has grown in popularity is recent years. it has been used in some learning disability programmes also for identification purposes, but its verbal nature makes its use with culturally different groups unacceptable. These tests are unacceptable if results are used to indicate mental retardation. However, if it is used to indicate normal ability, and all that is required is establishment of below average, average and above average intelligence for further classification of students according to their mental ability, it is considered acceptable.

The Kaufman Assessment Battery for Children (k-ABC) is a new test which was introduced in 1983, and its initial acceptance appears to be excellent. The K - ABC is designed to assess both intelligence and achievement and was specifically designed for use in the assessment of learning disabled and other exceptional children. It is for use with children of ages 2 1/2 to 12 1/2 years and provides four global scales: (1) sequential processing, (2) simultaneous processing, (3) mental processing composite, a combination of (1) and (2) that provides a global estimate of intellectual functioning, and (4) achievement. It also includes a special non-verbal scale for use with hearing, speech, or language-disordered students and non English speaking students. For Indian students it would be non appropriate to administer a non verbal test which they could take with relative ease.

d) Ravens Progressive Matrices

The Standard Progressive Matrices, sets A,B,C,D and E designed by J.C. Raven is a test of a person's capacity at the time of the test to apprehend meaning figures presented for his observation, see the relationship between them, conceive the nature of the figures completing each system of relations presented, and by so doing, develop a systematic method of reasoning.

The scale consists of 60 problems divided into five sets of 12 each. In each set the first problem is as nearly as possible self evident. The problems which follow become progressively more difficult. The order of the tests provides the standard training in the method of working. The five sets provide five opportunities for grasping the method and five progressive assessments of a person's capacity for intellectual activity. To ensure sustained interest and freedom from fatigue, the figures in each problem are boldly presented, accurately drawn and, as far as possible, pleasing to look at. The scale is intended to cover the whole range of intellectual development from the time a child is able to grasp the idea of finding a missing piece to complete a pattern, and to be sufficiently long to assess a person's maximum capacity to form comparisons and reason by analogy without being unduly exhausting or unwieldy. The score obtained by adults tend to cluster in the upper half of the scale, but there are enough difficult problems to differentiate satisfactorily between them. While administering the scale, every one is given exactly the same series of the problems in the same order and is asked to work at his own speed, without interruption, from the beginning to the end of the scale. A person's total score provides an index of his intellectual capacity. Here, those who secure below 15/60 or fall below 25th percentile point can be classified as slow learners. This RPM has been effectively used in Indian setting by Sundaraja Rao and Rajaguru (1995).

(e) Personality Tests

Psychologists have made attempts through personality tests to throw light on the emotional characteristics of children as well as temperamental traits. Certain personality traits like persistence, sensitiveness, concentration, emotional stability, assertiveness etc., have a direct bearing on specific backwardness. Thematic Apperception Test (TAT), Rorschach Ink Blot Test (RIBT) Word Association Test (WAT), Free Association Test and some psychoanalytical procedures are very helpful to psychologists and teachers to identify the slow learners. The teacher's assessment of children's traits for personality can be very profitably used for diagnostic and productive purposes. A brief account about two of the above tests is given below just to highlight how to make use of the tests to identify slow learners.

The Rorschach Ink blot test

Drever (1964) defines projective technique as the interpretations of situations and events, by reading into them our own experience and feeling. It is also simply defined by English and English (1958) as the process of perceiving objective stimuli in line with personal interests, desires and fears or expectations. On the basis of this assumption Hermann Rorschach, a Swins psychologist developed ink blot test in 1921. Although ink blots had been used in the past to elicit responses from individuals Rorschach was the first person to grasp fully the potential for the use of these responses for personality assessment. The material of the Rorschach consists of ten ink blots printed on malt - surfaced white cards approximately 14 cm x 17 cm. The cards are presented in standard order. The subject is allowed to turn a card as he pleases but he is not allowed to keep the card at an unusual distance greater than his own arm's length. All the responses are taken down verbatim.

It is claimed by Klopfer and Kelly (1942) that information regarding the following may be elicited from the Rorschach responses of a subject.

i. The degree and mode of intellectual control with which the subject tries to regulate his experiences and actions.

ii. The responsiveness of his emotional energies to stimulations from outside and prompting from within.

iii. His mental approach to given problems and situations.

iv. His creative and imaginative capacities and the use he makes of them.

v. A general estimate of the intellectual level and the qualitative features of his thinking.

vi. A general estimate of the degree of security and anxiety.

vii. The relative degree of maturity in the total development of personality.

A critical review of the responses made by the subjects gives us a reasonable assessment about the subjects personality and intellectual capacity on the basis of which backward students including slow learners can be easily identified.

The Thematic Apperception Test (TAT)

The TAT was devised by Murray and Morgan (1938). The chief value of the TAT resides in its power to evoke fantasies. Ever since projective techniques have been recognised, the Rorschach has held an unassailable position of prominence. Its nearest rival is Thematic Apperception Test. The standard TAT consists of twenty cards eleven of which are used irrespective of the sex and age of the subject. For the nine remaining presentations, alternatives exist which can be chosen sometimes according to sex, sometimes according to age. In two cases (cards 12 and 13) there are three alternatives. The basic idea of the TAT is simpler, contrived than that of the Rorschach. The task required of the subject is to tell stories relating to a series of pictures. In so doing, it is believed that, he will reveal something of himself, in a more direct way that it is possible with the Rorschach. The stories told by the subjects with provide us with the base for assessment of their personality and intellectual level on the basis of which we can identify problem students, slow learners etc:

f) Psychometric and Psychological Tests

For diagnostic purposes, psychometric tests of sensory nature can be used. These tests are primarily used for better appraisal, analysis and evaluation of specific skills of backward children. These tests serve as vital means for psychologists to discover the exact nature of errors made by the backward children. There are also other psychological tests which can be used to assess the span of attention, auditory perception, steadiness, memory and reasoning powers. These tests not only disclose the slow learners but also they underline the causative factors of slow learning.

g) Medical Examination

Though Medical Examination cannot be strictly equated with the above tests, it has its own credence and scientific base. A medical examination should be more than the usual school medical examination. A careful examination of eyes, ears, throat, speech organs and the central nervous system is certainly called for. Today consultants are more accessible and the services of pediatricians, ophthalmologists, audiologists, neurologists, and speech therapists should be used freely. If the slow learning is caused by any of the above factors, certainly remedial treatment can be given and ultimately the learning rate can be increased. There are children whose physical development and muscular co-ordination are so retarded that remedial measures are necessary, e.g. remedial physical education, physiotherapy. Others are malnourished because either feeding has been poor or the metabolic processes are faulty. Such children may need special diets and treatment by nutrition experts to overcome their learning disability.

iii. Countercheck Phase

The slow learners identified and then confirmed by scientific confirmatory test can be once again counter-checked either on the basis of rate of learning as suggested by Kirk (1962) or on the basis of Sandra's Checklist as recommended by Chintamani Kar (1992).

Countercheck by Rate of Learning

Kirk (1962, 1971) took rate of learning as the basis for identifying slow learners. According to him, the slow learners, gifted and the average children can be classified according to their rate of learning. In 1968 Bloom proposed that rather than providing all students with the same amount of instructional time and allowing learning to differ, perhaps we should require that all or almost all students reach certain level of achievement by allowing time to differ. That is, Bloom suggests that we give students as much time and instruction as necessary to bring them all to a reasonable level of learning. Suppose we expect 80 percent mastery level. Then we can assess learning rate in the following manner.

A specific passage from science or social science may be taught by the teacher. Then the students may be instructed to make a thorough study of passage. To ascertain their mastery, some 20 to 25 objective type test items can be framed based on the passage dealt with. Then the teacher should note down how much time each student takes to get 80 per cent score. The time taken by each student to attain 80% mastery level will signify his rate of learning. Naturally slow learners will take more time to attain the specified mastery level than average and gifted students.

Sandra's Checklist

Sandra's checklist is very useful to countercheck the slow learners. It contains 69 behaviour symptoms arranged under five characteristics patterns. it was primarily mean for identifying specific problem of mild retardates who constitute a significant group of slow learners. A single characteristic pattern has no meaning at all. But a group of characteristics provides a clue to analyse certain learning problems of the child. The teacher has to countercheck whether the identified and then confirmed slow learner exactly or somewhat fits in for the behaviour symptoms arranged under each of the five characteristics patterns. All the five characteristics patterns with the important behaviour symptoms are given below categorywise.

1. **Characteristics of Cognitive Learning Problems**

   i. The slow learners learn at a slower rate and they face difficulty in retaining what they have learned.

   ii. The slow learners prefer concrete learning to abstract learning.

   iii. Transfer of learning becomes impossible for slow learners.

   iv. They lack judgement and common sense and they are highly distractible.

   v. They gain from direct teaching and do not acquire skills incidentally.

   vi. A slow learner is an underachiever and has a very short span of attention.

2. **Characteristics of language and Language - Related Problems**

   i. Verbal expressions for slow learners are difficult.

   ii. Oral reading is more difficult than silent reading.

   iii. Slow learners face articulation problems.

   iv. Proper expression of thoughts becomes difficult for them.

3. Characteristics of Auditory Perceptual Problems

i. Slow learners face trouble in writing from dictation. They usually leave common prefixes and suffixes while writing.

ii. Slow learners fail to understand verbal directions. So they are unable to give proper reply, when a question is asked.

iii. They prefer visually presented materials to orally presented matierial.

iv. Identification of different sounds becomes difficult for them. They also find difficulty in distinguishing between similar sounding words (e.g., Tap-Tip, Pen-pin etc.)

v. Slow learners usually give inappropriate answers to verbal questions. They also fail to learn the art of counting by memory.

4. Characteristics of Visual - Motor Problems

i. Slow learners are easily distracted by visual stimuli. They have awkward movements.

ii. They find it difficult to discriminate between colour, size and shape relationship and are unable to recall to memory the objects that they see.

iii. They have a very poor handwriting and face difficulties in motor work. Very often they complain about physical problems. Recognition of common objects becomes a problem for them.

iv. Slow learners prefer part learning to whole learning and find oral learning tasks easier.

5. Characteristics of Social and Emotional Problems

i. Slow learners do not have the stamina to sit in a class for long periods.

ii. They are lovers of solitude and are not gregarious. They fail to make friends and are not at all sociable.

iii. Slow learners become aggressive towards their friends and peers on trivial matters and they are afraid and self-conscious. They daydream in excess compared to normal children.

iv. Nail-biting is another interesting characteristic of slow learners. Sometimes they also engage themselves in anti-social activities.

v. Their mood changes frequently and their achievement is below expectancy.

vi. They prefer not to work in a group and have inappropriate and excessive verbalisation.

Summary

Children of to day are the citizens of tomorrow; they are going to be the pillars of the country. Hence it is essential to ensure that each pillar is strong as the other. From psychological point of view, it would be more beneficial to identify the slow learners as early as possible. The earlier they are identified, the sooner they can be subjected to remedial instruction.

Though the psychologists and educationists have devised various means to identify slow learners, identifying slow learners on a three phase process would be more feasible and reliable. The three phases are initial identifying phase, scientific confirmatory phase and countercheck phase.

The initial identifying phase makes use of the techniques such as observation technique, an educational assessment and a social history of child in his family and cultural setting. The aforesaid three techniques can be used separately or in any mode of combination to identify the slow learners. The speciality of these techniques is that the teacher does not require any testing tool to identify the slow learners.

In the scientific confirmatory phase intelligence tests, personality tests, psychometric and psychological tests and medical examination can be effectively used to identify slow learners. Though Terman - Merrill scale and WISC - R are widely used all over the world, Ravens Progressive Matrices has been successfully used in Indian setting to identify slow learners.

The slow learners intially identified and confirmed by a scientific confirmatory test can once again be counterchecked on the basis of rate of learning as suggested by Kirk or on the basis of Sandra's. Checklist as recommended by Chintamani Kar.

REFERENCES

Bill R. Gearheart (1985) 'Learning Disabilities : Education Strategies'. Times Mirror / Mosby College Publishing, Toronto.

Bower, E.M. (1981) 'Early Identification of Emotionally Handicapped Children in School '. Chas, C. Thomas, Spring field.

Catherine Voelker Morsink (1984) 'Teaching Special Needs Children in Regular Classrooms'. Little, Brown and Company Boston.

Chintamani Kar (1992) 'Exceptional Children - Their Psychology and Education'. Sterling Publishers Private Ltd, New Delhi.

Daniel P. Hallahan and James M. Kauffman (1981) 'Exceptional Children'. Printice Hall. Inc, Englewood Cliffs, New Jersey.

Drever, J. (1964) A Dictionary of Psychology, Revised by Wallerstein Harmondsworth, Penguin.

English, H.B., and English, A.A.A (1958) 'Comprehensive Dictionary of Psychological and Psychoanalytical Terms'. Longmans, London and New york.

Estes, N.K. (1982) 'Learning Memory and Intelligence'. In R.J. Sternberg (Ed) *Handbook of Human Intelligence,* Cambridge University Press, New York.

Kazdin, A.E.(1987) 'Conduct Disorders in Childhood and Adolescence', Sage Publications, Beverlly Hills, C.A.

Kirk, S.A.(1972) 'Educating Exceptional Children' (2nd Ed.), Houghton, Mifflin, Boston.

Lovaas, O.I.(1987) 'Behavioural Treatment and Normal Educational and Intellectual Functioning in Young Austic Children'. *Journal of Consulting and Clinical Psychology,* 55, 3-9.

Robert Slavin (1986) 'Educational Psychology - Theory into Practice' Printice Hall of India, New Delhi.

Sternberg, R.J. (1982) 'Reasoning, Problem Solving and Intelligence', In R.J. Sternberg (Ed) Handbook of Human Intelligence Cambridge University Press, New York.

Sternberg, R.J (1986) 'Intelligence, Wisdom and Creativity: Three is better than One'. Educational Psychologist, 21,175 -190.

Strain, P.S., Steel, P., Ellis, T., and Timm, M. (1982) 'Long-term Effects of Oppositional Child Treatment with Mothers as Therapists and Therapist Trainers'. Journal of Applied Behavioural Analysis, 15, 163 -169.

Tansley, A.E., and Gulliford, R. (1962) 'The Education of Slow Learning Children'. Routeledge Kegan Paul Ltd, London.

Terman, L.M, and Merrill, M. (1937) Measuring Intelligence, Harrap.

Wechsler, D.A, (1949) 'Intelligence Scale for Children', Psychological Corporation. New York.

Wechsler, D.A. (1955) 'Wechsler Adult Intelligence Scale'. Psychological Corporation, New York.

3 Intellectual Development of Slow Learners

Chapter Outline

Chapter Objectives

This chapter outlines the intellectual development of slow learners. After reading this chapter you should be able to:

- List out the factors affecting the intellectual development of Slow learners
- Describe the development of slow learners at various Developmental stages
- Understand the memory of slow learners
- Calculate Intelligence Quotient and mental Age
- Develop an insight into the relationship between intelligence and attainment

Slow learners are known for limited intellectual development. This limited intellectual development of slow learners is a vital factor to be taken into account in considering what methods of learning and teaching should be employed and what standards may be achieved. Since low intelligence is a unique characteristic of slow learners, we have to analyse what is meant by intelligence and the significance of test results. Schonell (1942) defines general intelligence as an inborn, all round mental power which is but slightly altered in degree by environmental influences although its realisation and direction are determined by experience. But there has been a good deal of controversy about the relative effects of inheritance and environment on intelligence with rather fruitless attempts to measure the exact contribution of each. In recent years the concept of intelligence is gaining ground which rather bypasses this controversy about the effects of nature and nurture. The innate basis of intelligence is admitted, but intelligence is viewed not merely as an unfolding or maturing of this innate potentiality but also something that grows and develops in the course of the child's active experience of his environment. Some people experience substantial changes in their estimated IQ often because of schooling or other environment influences (Petty and Field, 1980).

The question of the effect of environment and experience on the growth of intelligence is a matter of immense interest to teachers of slow learners. Many slow learners grow up in adverse circumstances which hamper rather than foster the development of intelligence. Mckenzie (1977) and Schickedanz (1982) emphasise that even before entering school, children begin to build an understanding of written language. This knowledge follows a course of development similar to that of spoken language. From seeing print, children make guesses about how it works. This process works best when children have many books, magazines and other printed materials available. But very poor families rarely provide as good opportunities for the incidental learning as average and good homes do. Children in such families seldom get opportunities to play with toys and other materials, through which many productive ways of thought and activity are developed. In such homes, there are no books; no picture books in early childhood to extend knowledge and vocabulary;

no story telling which promotes children's knowledge in language and in understanding of the ways of the world. There is no constructive conversation to develop the thinking ability. They don't organise any trip away from the immediate surroundings, no holiday at new locations. Such deficiencies serve enough to limit, to some extent, the development of concepts and the abilitiy to think which we measure in intelligence testing.

Factor Affecting Intellectual Development

There are various factors which determine the intellectual development of children and the teachers dealing with slow learners should be well aware of these vital factors which have a direct bearing on the intellectual development of slow learners. They are

1. Poverty of the home
2. Intelligence of parents & family members
3. Socio-economic status of the family
4. Physical attributes
5. The effects of early adverse experiences
6. The effects of educational experiences

Poverty of the Home

Intellectual development generally refers to the development of memory, reasoning and judgement, attention and moral concept, imagination, power of understanding and intelligence. But the aforesaid aspects are very much affected by the poverty of the home in which the child is reared up. The children in the poor homes don't get the right type of exposure and interaction which are essential to sharpen reasoning and judgement and to develop power of understanding. The early pleasant experiences at home ignite the spark of imagination and it boosts up attention and memory. But the children in the poor families are often deprived of this kind of required exposure and interaction. Further, the cumulative effects of these make the children of such families dull in the long run. They eventually become slow learners.

Intelligence of Parents and Family Members

Intelligence of parents and family members play a vital role in the intellectual development of the backward children. The manner in which the parents interact with their children strongly influences the children's development. Moreover, it is parents who have the earliest and the strongest influence on a child. When the parents and family members are educated they, by way of social interaction and individual behaviour, provide a right type of environment for the children to develop concept formation and to develop their reasoning and critical thinking skills. The family discussion, the hobby at home, even the games played at home and above all the journals and magazines available in the educated families first attract the attention of the children in those families giving them some sporadic spark to develop reasoning and judgement. But the cumulative effects of all these amenities ultimately culminate in the intellectual development of the children. That's why the children from educated families are not slow learners. There may be a few exceptional cases on either side but we can not generalise on the basis of exceptional cases.

Socio-Economic Status of the Family

During early childhood a child's social life changes in relatively predictable ways. The social network grows from an intimate relation with parents or other guardians to include other family members, non related adults and peers. Social interactions extend from home to neighbourhood and from nursery school to formal school.

Socio economic status of the family plays a pivotal role in the intellectual development of children. It so happens that sometimes the family members especially parents may not be educated at all but they may be affluent. They may be traders or running a profitable business. Or they may be landlords possessing various kinds of lands in terms of acres. These people are able to afford for the education of their children. Also, these parents have a knack for imitation. They want that their children should get everything that a child in an educated circles gets. So they bring for their children games materials, toys, gadgets, etc. which all facilitate intellectual development. Further, since they can not coach up their children, they arrange for private tuition for which they are prepared to spend any amount of money. So the children from these families get all facilities available in the educated families except elite social interaction at home and they ultimately don't lag behind in the intellectual development. That is why the slow learners are mostly from poor families.

Physical Attributes

Besides all the aforesaid factors, there are some other personal attributes which all more or less affect the intellectural development of children. Physical attributes include physical deformities, pathological bodily conditions and defects of sight, hearing, and speech which may create conditions and susceptibilities which may retard or hamper intellectual development. Similarly, mental deprivation and long illness or long absence from school may also be responsible for hindering intellectual development of children. When the students have these physical problems they can not be attentive at all. When there is no proper attention, they cannot understand properly. Without understanding there is no room for reasoning and critical thinking. Eventually, they end up without making correct concept formation. As a result, their intellectual development is very much hampered. And they ultimately become slow developers or slow learners. Similarly when the children come to school after long illness or long absence they find it very difficult to cope with their classmates and this develops in them a complex which ultimately retards their intellectual development.

The Effects of Early Adverse Experiences

Hebb (1949) has suggested that there are two meanings of the word Intelligence. He refers to these two meanings as Intelligence A and Intelligence B. Intelligence A is the innate potentiality for development, which probably amounts to the possession of a good brain and a good neural metabolism'. Intelligence B is the quality and level of functioning that has develped; it has been acquired in the course of experience. The question of the effect of environment and experience on the growth of intelligence is a matter of obvious interest to teachers of backward children. Many educationally subnormal children grow up in circumstances which limit rather than foster the development of Intelligence B and this must be remembered as well as the probability that they have a poor Intelligence A. Very poor homes rarely provide as good opportunities for the incidental learning as average or good homes do. So it is essential that we ensure pleasent and informative experiences to the children at early age. A healthy environment provides intellectual stimulation in the early years which is very significant for children's mental development. Emotional relationship is also important in determining the child's attitude to himself and the vitality of his response to his environment. Mental growth may be limited by restricted living condition by parents' attitudes or by emotional upsets which prevent children being fully active in relation to their environment. The early adverse experiences cause slow learning in course of time. So to overcome slow learning at early stage itself, it becomes necessary to remove the child from the unsatisfactory environment or to remove the adverse experiences of the child.

Cognitive development is shaped by early experience and later development can be predicted from early experiences (Kagan, 1976; Kagan et al, 1979). However, many researchers question the degree to which early experiences determine later development (Samcroff, 1975; Clarke and Clarke, 1976; Goldhaber, 1979; Kagan, 1976; Kagan et al, 1979; Thomas, 1981). Their research has shown that young children who are deprived of appropriate early experiences can catch up if given supportive environments later (Clarke and Clarke, 1976). Such findings do not imply that early environments are unimportant but they do indicate that both early and later experiences affect development. The effect of experience on development is presumed to be more at early stage. Hence it is essential to ensure that the children do not have much adverse experiences which hamper their intellectual development.

The Effects of Educational Experiences

Several studies on subnormal children bring to light the fact that there is a relatively marked tendency for IQS to decline while the child is in unfavourable school and home conditions. Also, the length and type of schooling may have an appreciable effect on the level of intelligence reached and the kind of mental abilities developed. A school which has trained teachers in special education and which can make use of many media attributes can enhance the intellectual development of slow learners. They are the students who yearn for some pleasant experiences. So it is essential that the teachers handling those children should refrain from using harsh words or censure. A pleasant smile, a few encouraging words will develop the self concept of slow learners and they will, in turn, develop self confidence which will, ultimately, tell upon their performance. Since most of the slow learners are in the mainstream they deserve this kind of treatment lest they should develop complex. A teacher should, under no circumstances, laugh at their slower rate of learning or make a comparison with an endowed student. The teacher should never fail to ensure that a congenial atmosphere is prevalent for the smooth learning of slow learners. Frequent use of media in the instructional process can ensure a favourable as well as pleasant experience to the slow learners in the school. Moreover, the teacher may extend his service to the slow learners in the evening after class hours so that individual attention can be paid and the slow learners can learn at their own pace availing the guidance services of the teachers. If the teacher and the administrator ensure such favourable conditions to slow learners, they can overcome their problem of slow learning in the long run.

The instructional programme for all students, the slow learners as well as the gifted should reach the highest possible level. The ultimate objective of education in a free society is to produce citizens who are critical thinkers, wise consumers, thoughtful participants, and productive contributors. Survival in the high technology society of the future will require a high level of knowledge, a capacity for self-management, and a positive attitude about the need for life long learning. This type of education is very essential for the slow learners. It can be facilitated by teachers who encourage creative thinking enable students to succeed in discovery learning, and design co-operative learning experiences. This type of instruction is appropriate not only for students with high ability, but also for students with low ability like slow learners. However, it requires careful teacher planning and monitoring. But a dedicated resourceful teacher can rise to the occasion with ease. What matters much is his commitment to the cause of slow learners.

Slow Learners at Various Developmental Stages

Piaget divided the cognitive development of children and adolescents into four stages: sensori motor, preoperational, concrete operational, and formal operational. He believed that all children pass through these stages in order, and no child can skip a stage, although different children pass through the stages at somewhat different rates. Each stage is marked by the emergence of new intellectual abilities that allow people to understand the world in increasingly complex ways. It is interesting to see how far slow learners get in these stages.

Sensorimotor Stage (Birth to Two Years)

This stage is called sensorimotor because during it babies and young children explore their world by using their senses and their motor skills. This stage is marked by reflexes - natural responses that people are born with, formation of concept of "object permanence" and gradual progression from reflexive behaviour to goal directed behaviour. It is very interesting to note that this stage need not concern us much from slow learners' point of view. It is a stage from birth to about eighteeen months when the child simply learns to pattern his sense impressions of the world around him and to act in a variety of ways in relation to it. Hence this stage is not much of educational importance with regard to slow Learning.

Preoperational Stage (Two to Seven Years)

While infants can learn about and understand the world only by physically manipulating objects, the preschooler has greater ability to think about things and can use symbols to mentally represent objects. During this preoperational stage children's language and concepts develop at an incredible rate. Yet, much of their thinking remains egocentric and centered.

Symptoms of slow learning can be traced in this stage when the child makes his first attempts at conceptual thinking. But the slow learners below the ages of 10 or 11 years are still in this stage even though they are supposed to have entered the concrete operational stage. They are more easily led astray by particular, irrelevant features in which they perceive. In the understanding of the causes of events, these children are still in the intuitive stage. Similarly, their judgements about behaviour are likely to be based on personal feeling and attitudes rather than on any real idea of rules or moral principles. The slow learners due to lack of understanding linger a bit longer in this stage which hampers educational progress and causes slow learning.

Concrete Operational Stage (Seven to Eleven Years)

During the elementary school years the cognitive abilities of children undergo dramatic changes. The thinking of an elementary student is therefore quite different from that of a preschooler. Elementary school children have no longer difficulties with conservation problems. One fundamental difference between the preoperational and concrete operational children is that the younger child, who is in the preoperational stage, responds to perceived appearances, while the older, concrete operational child responds to inferred reality. It is no coincidence that throughout the world children start formal schooling at an age close to the beginning of the concrete operational stage. Most of what children are taught in school requires the skills that appear in this stage. During the concrete operational stage the children can form concepts and see relationships between things. They are no longer quite so egocentric, but are beginning to see things from another's perspective.

In this stage it is easier to identify the slow learners. While the children in the concrete operational stage are supposed to see relationship between things, the slow learners find it very difficult to see the relationship between things. They are slower to perceive and use possible associations. Thus slow learners can be found lacking in the development stage. However, while differences between the preoperational and concrete operational stages are dramatic, concrete operational children still do not think like adults. They are very much rooted in the world as it is, and have difficulty with abstract thought.

Formal Operational Stage (Eleven Years to Adulthood)

Sometimes around the onset of puberty children's thinking begins to develop into the form characteristic of adults. The preadolescent begins to think abstractly and to see possibilities beyond the here and now. These abilities continue to develop into adulthood. With the stage of formal operational thought comes the ability to deal with potential or hypothetical situations so that the "form" is now separate from the "content". The adolescent who has reached the stage of formal operations is likey to proceed quite systematically, varying one factor at a time. The abilities that make up formal operational thought - thinking abstractly, testing hypotheses, and forming concepts that are independent of physical reality are critical in the learning of higher order skills. But a slow learner of 11 years hardly enters this stage. At this stage he is still found in the preceding stage only. Slow Learners do not reach this stage of logical abstract thinking at the age of 11 or 12. What we can hope to do is to provide the best conditions for their development from the intuitive stage into the stage of concrete operations where simple reasoning is possible about things and events which they can perceive and imagine. This will eventually lead to logical abstract thinking, a vital skill of formal operational stage. At the very least, therefore, it is reasonable to suppose that providing children with rich opportunities for experience, and encouraging their mental activity in relation to it, is a step in the right direction.

Memory

Memory is a very complex cognitive process and viewed orginally as a storage bin component in which information is stored and retrieved when needed. This view of memory is relatively passive and does not consider a child's active involvement in processing and remembering information. To day memory is viewed as a dynamic process that enables us to take complex environmental information and to transform and organise it in a manner that permits storage and retrieval at a later time. What we refer to as memory is, of course, not one power of the mind but involves several different processes. The efficiency of the initial learning is important as well as actual retention and recall; these are all influenced by attitudes, interests and emotional states. There is no doubt that slow learners have poorer power of retention than average students, but it would be a mistake to assume, as there is sometimes a tendency to do, that the remedy lies only in increasing the amount of repetition. The poor retention may be due to the quality of initial learning rather than the amount of time spent going over the same material.

One of the most frequent complaints about the backward children is the weakness of their memory. As Burt remarks, 'Of all the special mental disabilities that hamper educational progress, the most frequent is a weakness in what may be termed long distance memory. Short-term memory is a component of memory where limited amounts of informations can be stored for a few seconds. It is the part of the memory where information currently being thought about is stored. On the contrary, long-term memory is a component of memory where large amount of information can be stored for a long time. But the slow learners are very weak in long-term memory. So to hold information in memory they should be trained to use rehearsal and schemata in their learning.

They need to go over the material more times before it is fixed in their minds, and more frequent revision is required to prevent forgetting. Slow learners have so markedly poor powers of memory, that they forget from one page to the next word that they have already learnt. They are often unable to remember the simplest number facts in spite of having plenty of practice with interesting apparatus. At the same time it is very essential to remember here that the slow learners are often able to remember other things reasonably well, sometimes to the point of being specially knowledgeable about footballers, makes of cars or aeroplanes, names, birds, animals etc. Without strengthening their memory and retention we cannot aim at any comprehensive intellectual development in slow learners. Hence it becomes indispensable to think of the ways and means to strengthen the memory of slow learners. For that the teacher has to develop a psychological insight into the factors that hamper their retention. Once the contributing factors are identified, required remedial measures can be taken up to boost up the retention power of slow learners. Some of the common causative factors and the ways to overcome the particular problem are briefly discussed below.

One of the causes of poor memory in slow learners is weakness in attention. What is to be learnt must be attended to and its main features observed. Failures in this may be due to factors in the child such as restlessness and distractibility. When there is lack of attention, he can not ensure retention. Calfee (1976) suggests that there are three aspects of attention. These are alertness, noticing details of the world around us and being sensitive or receptive to stimuli; relativity, the ability to block out some stimuli and be sensitive to others; and concentration, the ability to focus thoughts on one task. But the slow learners are generally weak in all these aspects of attention. It is, therefore, the foremost duty of the teacher to draw and sustain the attention of the slow learners. Since they are known for restlessness the teacher should make them feel at home. At any cost the teacher should not give room for prevalence of such classroom environment or learning condition which makes the slow learners feel dejected and neglected. If they feel so their attention will go from bad to worse. Also, the teacher should reduce their distractibility by growing their attention by making use of media attributes and by ensuring their participation in the class room interaction. A sympathetic attitude on the part of the teacher, encouraging words and teacher's knack to appreciate the child when he makes a right response occasionally will imbibe in slow learners an interest in the instruction. When the interest is created it will pave the way for focussed attention and ultimately prolonged retention.

Sometimes external factors other than the personal factors may be responsible for the poor attention of slow learners. Attention may be poor because the material to be learned is unsuitable - too difficult or outside the child's experience or it may be due to the fact that it is presented in a way that does not facilitate accurate perceptions of it. Apart from the personal factors dealt with in the preceding paragraph, the teacher should be very wary about the external factors affecting the attention of the slow learners. There is one more reason why the teachers should be extra careful about the external factors. It is becuase these two external factors fall under the purview of the teacher who can exercise full control over these factors. Since the slow learners are poor in abstract thinking they cannot learn anything which is outside their experience. It simply leads to inattention or restlessness. So the teacher has to ensure that a new concept to be taught is within his experience and he should relate it with the earlier concept already in his mind. Then only the concept will find a place in the slow learner's long term memory. To facilitate accurate perceptions of the new concept the teacher should take every possible effort to make a concrete presentation of the instructional content. Since good memory plays a key role in the intellectual development of slow learners the teacher should take care of these causative factors failing which the intellectual development of slow learners will be highly retarded.

Slow learners are very poor in understanding relationship and association between things. As a result, they find it very difficult to remember the concepts for a long time. Most of the newly acquired information do not find a place in their long term memory. This causes in them inability to remember and recall information when they are required. Their rate of forgetting is not only more but also fast. So the teacher has to tackle this problem to promote the intellectual development of slow learners. One way in which remembering can be improved is by ensuring that as many useful associations are made as possible. One of the reasons for the poor memories of slow learners is that they are slow to perceive and use possible associations. The teacher must therefore pay special attention to getting children to see links which bright children see for themselves, and encourage various modes of learning the material so that several associations are possible. The associations which can be used are between the word and its visual pattern; the word and its auditory pattern as it is spoken or sounded; the word and the kinaesthetic memory of writing it. All these must be mutually linked and with the meaning of the word. A network of associations such as this can be added to by linking the work to other groups. For example, teaching right, light, sight, fight, etc. together in spelling or phonetics enables the association of similarity to play some part in the learning and recall. Meaningful relationships as between light and night may also be used. Wherever possible several links should be used to improve the chances of recall. At the same time care must be taken to ensure that associations are not so elaborate that the child gets confused. So it is very essential to present the material in such a way that it facilitates the making of generalisations. Thus meaningful associations are of great importance. It is a fallacy to think that because slow learners are limited in intelligence, they can only learn by rote memorisation. They can also make meaningful learning where the existing association and relationships between things are made known to them and then they need more repetition, revision and practice to ensure retention. A committed teacher can easily tackle these causative factors and he can improve the memory of slow learners. Once it is done, it will bring about the intellectual development of slow learners in course of time.

The Intelligence Quotient

The intelligence quotient is a ratio of chronological age to mental age multiplied, by 100. It is calculated by administering intelligence test to individuals. The tests are grouped into age levels and the examiner proceeds from a year group of tests which are answered correctly (the basal age) through to a year group in which all the tests are failed. Each test passed obtains two months of mental age and the total is added to the basal age. This total is the mental age, and the IQ is then calculated by the formula:

$$IQ = \frac{\text{Mental age}}{\text{Chronological age}} \times 100$$

The usefulness of the IQ in the assessment procedure, its undoubted value in drawing attention to certain individual differences and its apparent simplicity and objectivity, have tended sometimes to give the IQ by iteself more importance than it merits. The students whose IQ falls between 75 and 89 are called slow learners. But there is no agreement among researchers regarding the range of IQ of slow learners. According to Tansley and Gulliford the range is from 70 to 85, according to Jensen the range is from 80 to 90, and according to Chintamani Kar the range is from 75 to 89. Similarly, the percentage of slow learners and subnormal children also varies from researcher to researcher. According to Burt it is 15 percent, according to Schonell it is 17 per cent and according to Scottish Council for Research in Education it is 24 per cent. The reason that IQ scores are important is that they are highly predictive of school performance (Demyer, 1975). By about age six, IQ estimates tend to become relatively stable, and most people's IQs remain about the same into adulthood (Hopkins and Bracht, 1975).

The origins of intelligence have been debated for decades, and still cause emotional confrontations. Some psychologists (Such as Jensen, 1969) are of the view that intelligence is overwhelmingly a product of heredity, while others (such as Kamin, 1975) firmly believe that intelligence is mostly influenced by environment and question whether IQ tests are valid indicators of intelligence at all. Most investigators believe that both heredity and environment play an important part in intelligence (Schiff et al, 1982; Scarr and Mc Cartney, 1983). Infact, IQ by itself, does not provide much information beyond indicating the child's standing relative to other children of his age. It does not tell us how that child is different from other children with the same score, how he is likely to react in different situations, nor how successful his future adjustment will be. It is, infact no substitute for the knowledge that can be gained from observation of the child's learning and thinking in the classroom. IQ should be taken as the beginning of our study of his intellectual capacities and this must be always considered in relation to all other information which can be required about his health, physical development, his emotional and social maturity, his keenness to learn and his attitude towards school.

The intelligence quotient is one way of expressing the child's score on the test. But we have to consider whether it is a reliable meausre. The child's mood of happiness or unhappiness and his feeling of security or insecurity at the time of the intelligence test play a decisive role in influencing the child's score on the test. Hence when a comprehensive plan is made to gear up the intellectual development of the slow learners, the teacher should take the IQ only as the beginning and he should consider other vital factors like health, physical development, his emotional and social maturity, his keeness to learn and his attitude towards school. Moreover, measuring intelligence can not be as simple and accurate as measuring height.

The Mental Age

Just as a person's physical age is indicated in terms of years like 8, 9, 10, 14 or 15 years etc., the word mental age is used for indicating a person's stage of mental development. This term 'mental age' was used even before Binet but then it was not so popular. Hence the credit for the use of this term goes to Binet. The mental age refers to the average mental ability of some children of the same age.

The mental age is the test age and it is a way of expressing the child's score on the test. It is a misleading inference that a mental age of six implies a six-year-old's mentality. The child may have indeed passed the tests which the average six year old passes but he may well have passed the tests in several different age groups. In some children the scatter of passes through the age groups is wide; in other cases, children pass only a few tests beyond the basic year groups of tests. Two children may get the same score by virtue of very different mental achievements on the test. It is, therefore, very essential that we look beyond the actual test score and notice the abilities and levels of functioning of which it is an average. We have to think not only of the altitude of intelligence, i.e high or low, but also of its breadth, i.e. the different abilities in which it is manifested.

A further objection to too liberal an interpretation of the mental age is that a slow learner with a low mental age is different in many respects from a young normal child with the same mental age. For instance, a ten year old with a mental age of six will differ from a normal six year old in physical development and skills; his interests and experience may be more like those of his age group although their range and his understanding of them will be poorer. He is less curious, spontaneous and active; the quality of his learning and remembering will be poor. Moreover, the wrong habits of learning and thinking and the earlier incidence of failures make him very different from the normal child whose behaviour has been less modified by such experience. It is therefore essential for the teacher who teaches the slow learners to think not only of the altitude of intelligence but also its breadth. This will give the teacher a better insight into the problems of slow learning and a better preparedness to surmount the problem of slow learning.

The Relationship Between Intelligence and Attainment

In teaching backward children, the mental age is often taken as a guide to the levels of attainment to be expected of pupils. Thus, if a child's mental age is 10 years we assume that his attainment age should also be at the 10 year old level. If his reading age is two years below his mental age he is considered retarded and special efforts must be made to get him 'working to capacity' or 'up to expectation'. It is not generally expected that children should get attainment ages in advance of their mental ages. We don't expect them to be working above their capacity, if capacity for learning is defined in terms of scores on a verbal test of intelligence. Yet it is not unusual that we find children whose reading age exceeds their mental age. For this disparity, there is no need to suspect the intelligence test as inaccurate, or that the child's reading is mechanical without good comprehension - the result of over emphasis on word recognition skills. Both these explanations may be applicable to some cases but there is every possibility that the results are valid and reliable. First, the child's determination, good motivation and a high degree of interest may result in surprisingly good attainments in some cases. After all, learning in school does not depend on intellectual ability alone. Second, a child may have special abilities like 'ear for', 'eye for' etc which enable him to do well in certain subjects. Lastly, the very nature of test construction and statistical errors in test measurements lead to attainment ages scattering above and below mental ages.

The question of over-achievement came to limelight following the publication by Pidgeon and Yates of evidence that in a normal sample of children, the proportion who are over achieving is almost as great as the proportion of those who are under achieving. This evidence, together with shift in emphasis in view of intelligence has generated some new thinking about the relationship between educational attainment and intelligence. Further, investigations are very much needed in this regard.

Under these circumstances some practical implications do emerge immediately. One is that, while we expect attainment and intelligence test results to approximate, anything like an exact numerical equivalence should not be expected. There is no reason why some children should not have attainment ages above their mental ages. This is not a signal for exercising academic pressure but it is for intensifying the attention to all the other factors which promote educational progress - the quality of learning, social and emotional factors in the child. Conclusions such as 'not working to capacity' should not be made simply in terms of apparent differences between intelligence and attainment test ages. A broader view of learning capacity should be taken.

Summary

Slow learners are known for limited intellectual development which should be taken into account in considering what methods of learning and teaching should be employed and what standards may be achieved.

The question of the effect of environment and experience on the growth of intelligence is a matter of immense interest to the teachers of slow learners.

The various factors that have a direct bearing on the intellectual development of slow learners are poverty of the home, intelligence of parents and family members, socio-economic status of the family, physical attributes, the effects of early adverse experiences and the effects of educational experiences.

Slow learners do not differ from other children at sensory motor stage. Early symptoms of slow learning come to surface at pre-operational stage and in the next two stages of cognitive development the slow learners stand apart from others since onset of slow learning becomes explicit by now.

One of the chief complaints about slow learners is the weakness of their memory. Poor memory of slow learners may be due to their weakness in attention and / or poor motivation by the teacher. Attention may be poor because the material to be learned is unsuitable - too difficult or outside the child's experience. Or, it may be due to poor presentation which does not facilitate accurate perception of the concept. Remembering can be improved by ensuring that as many useful associations are made as possible and by signifying the meaningful relationships between things.

The intelligence quotient is one way of expressing the child's score on the test. But IQ by itself does not provide much information beyond indicating the child's standing relative to other children of his age. So the teacher should take the IQ only as the beginning and he should consider other vital factors like health, physical development, his emotional and social maturity, his keenness to learn and his attitude towards school.

The mental age is the test age and it is a misleading inference that a mental age of six implies a six year old's mentality. We have to think not only of the altitude of intelligence i.e. high or low, but also of its breadth, i.e. the different abilities in which it is manifested.

Mental age is often taken as a guide to the levels of attainment to be expected of pupils. If a child's mental age is 10 years we assume that his attainment age should be at the 10 year level. But we find over achievement and under achievement. Proportion of over achievement is as great as the proportion of under achievement. A broader view of learning capacity should be taken.

REFERENCES

Bill R. Gearheart (1985) 'Learning Disabilities: Educational Strategies'. Times Mirror, Mosby College Publishing, Missouri, USA.

Calfee, R.C. (1976) 'Sources of Dependency in Cognitive Processes'. In D. Klahr (Ed) *Cognition and Instruction*, Eribaum, Hillsdale, New Jersey.

Catherine Voelker Morsink (1984) 'Teaching Special Needs Students in Regular Classrooms'. Little, Brown and Company, Boston.

Chaube, S.P (1983) 'Educational Psychology'. Lakshmi Narain Agarwal, Agra.

Chintamani Kar (1992) 'Exceptional Children: Their Psychology and Education'. Sterling Publishers Private Ltd, New Delhi.

Clarke, A.M., and Clarke, A.D.B. (1976) 'Early Experience: Myth and Evidence'. The Free Press, New York.

Daniel P. Hallahan and James M. Kauffman (1991) 'Exceptional Children: Introduction to Special Education, Prentice. Hall, Inc, Englewood, Cliffs, New Jersey.

De Myer M.K. (1975) 'The Nature of Neuro Psychological Disability in Autistic Children'. *Journal of Autism and Childhood Schizophrenia*, 5, 109 - 128.

Goldhaber, D(1979) 'Does the Changing View of Early, Experience Imply a Changing View of Early Development?' In L.G. Hatz (Ed) *Current Topic in Early Childhood Education*, vol. 2, pp 117 - 140, Norwood, New Jersey .

Hopkins, K.D., and Bracht, G. H. (1975) 'Ten Year Stability of Verbal and Non-verbal IQ Scores'. *American Educational Research Journal*, 12, 469-477.

Kagan, J.(1976) 'Emergent Themes in Human Development', *American Scientist*, 64, 186 - 196.

Kagan et al (1979) 'A Cross Cultural Study of Cognitive Development' *Monographs of the Society for Research in Child Development*, 44, No. 5

Mc Kenzie, M(1977) 'The Beginnings of Literacy. *Theory into Practice*, 16, 315 - 324.

Pelty, M.F., and Field, C.J.(1980) 'Fluctuation in Mental Test Scores'. *Educational Research*, 22, 198 - 202.

Robert Slavin (1986) 'Educational Psychology: Theory into Practice'. Prentice Hall of India, Pvt. Ltd., New Delhi.

Sameroff, A. (1975) 'Early Influences on Development : Facts and Fancy'. *Merill - Palmer Quarterly*, 21, 267 - 294.

Schiekedanz, J.A. (1982) 'The Acquisition of Written Language in Young Children'. In B. Spodek (Ed) *Handbook of Research in Early Childhood Education*, pp 242 - 263, Free Press, New York.

Schonell, F.J. (1949) 'Backwardness in Basic Subjects'. Oliver and Boyd, London.

Tansley, A.E. and Gulliford, R. (1962) 'The Education of Slow Learning Children'. Routeledge and Kegan Paul, London.

Thomas, A. (1981) 'Current Trends in developmental Theory'. *American Journal of Orthopsychiatry*, 51, 580 - 609.

4 Emotional Development of Slow Learners

Chapter Outline

Chapter Objectives

This chapter deals with the emotional development of slow learners. After reading this chapter you should be able to:

- Describe the emotional needs of The slow learners
- List out the factors Influencing the emotional development of slow learners
- Make a reasonable assessment and measurement of emotional development
- List out the characteristics of emotionally disturbed slow learners.
- Devise measures to help the maladjusted slow learners
- Describle how emotional development of slow learner is a joint responsibility of the parents and teachers.

Emotions play an important role in determining whether our relations with other people are pleasant and joyful or sad and painful. These emotions affect not only our personal and social adjustment but also our physical health. Our behaviour is controlled by emotions which are dynamic internal adjustment that operate for the satisfaction and welfare of the individual. The term emotion is derived from the Latin word 'emovere' which means 'to move out'. According to Drever emotions are stirred up conditions of the organism involving internal and external changes in the body. Young defines emotion as a disturbed state of organism which originates in the psychological situation and includes viceral changes due to increased activity of the autonomic nervous system. Smiling, laughing, weeping, fear, anger, worry, joy grief, surprise, sympathy, pity or compassion, emphathy are some emotions. Emotion involves three components. They are feelings, impulses and physical and physiological reactions.

There is a subtle difference between emotion and feeling. Generally, emotion is connected with the pleasantness or umpleasantness of a feeling and in a way emotion is regarded as a feeling. For instance, fear, anger, love, joy, grief are sometimes termed as feelings and they are emotions as well. But emotion has more intensity than feeling has. Our entire body gets affected by emotion. Some of the body glands and nerves produce a special secretion during emotion. Infact, feeling is a part of emotion and emotion is something more than mere feeling. 'The more' implies secretion from inner body glands and its effect, and attitude to become active in certain direction. Emotional maturity is related to age. People usually attain emotional maturity along with their physical maturity. We can not think of any intellectual development or all round development of a person without proper emotional development in him. Emotional development refers to an individual's ability how he has control over his emotions or feelings.

Emotional Needs of Slow Learners

It would be improper to assume that, just because the slow learners are limited in intelligence, their emotional life is also similarly limited. They may not be capable of a varied and subtle expression of emotions but they do have the same basic needs as normal children. It is very obvious that the experience of love, approval, security and personal attention can have a considerable effect on the personal growth of even severely subnormal children. The basic emotional needs of children have been variously stated but only a few essential ones are discussed below in relation to slow learners. To ameliorate the emotional development of the slow learners, a psychological insight into the basic emotional needs and the factors influencing emotional development is a must for a teacher entrusted with the task of teaching slow learners.

i) The Need for Security

Children need the security of a stable family; the security of a familiar place in which to live and work; the security of familiar people whose attitude and behaviour are consistent and predictable; and the security of the known routine. A sense of security is a must for emotional stability. It is necessary that the boy has a pleasant experience at home and in the school. Only the parents and teachers can create a conducive environment in which he feels secured. This will avert, to a great extent, creeping in of any sort of emotional problem. Ensuring security to the child is the milestone in his emotional development.

ii) The Need for Giving and Receiving Affection

Research evidences confirm how vitally important it is for children to have someone who loves them, and who watches and encourages each step they take in growing up. The inadequate satisfaction of this need is apparent in slow learners who are continuously seeking the close attention and approval of the teacher. Even senior students go into a childish sulk or do work well below their best, when they harbour a grievance that the teacher is giving more attention to another student. Children who have been deprived throughout childhood of the full attention and affection of parents will often look upon the teacher as a parent substitute. So it becomes all the more necessary for the parents and teachers to be affectionate towards the children and to have pleasant interaction with them so that the children can develop better social interaction and transactions.

Most of the emotional problems arise because the social interaction and transactions between the child and the social environment are inappropriate. From this it can be understood that the problem is not just in the child's behaviour or just in the environment. When the child gives and receives affection, he does not feel neglected and it pares the way for an appropriate social interaction and transaction between the child and the social environment.

iii) Need For Acceptance by Other Children

Even a normally adjusted child becomes distressed by the temporary rejection of his playmates. The backward students who have never learned the elementary techniques of making friendship and getting on with the group, become desperate and dejected when they are rejected by their playmates. Most of the slow learners remain isolated because they have had little experience of mixing with others. The isolated child may withdraw still further or, alternatively, try to get approval and acceptance from the group by boasting, showing off, and dare devil behaviour. Kazdin (1989) notes that children usually do not see themselves as having behaviour or emotional problems. They tend to attribute their difficulties to external factors-parents, teachers, playmates, or incidents or conditions beyond their control. Parents and teachers are responsible for socialising children. So it is the primary duty of the parents and teachers to ensure that the child is accepted by his playmates or peer group in the social environment and school environment respectively. This will facilitate the emotional development of the child in the long run.

iv) Recognition and Self-esteem

Every child wants to feel successful and get recognition for what he can do. Since slow learners have fewer talents with which to satisfy their needs, it is most important that the school should provide many ways and means for successful achievement. Whenever the slow learners gain some degree of success, which is of course very rare, the teacher must make use of the opportunity to praise or reward the slow learners so that his praise will serve as an incentive for them for making more endeavour in the right direction. After all, what they want from the teacher is recognition. If the need is not satisfied in worthwhile ways in school, it may be satisfied outside the school, possibly in delinquent ways. Scores of characteristics are associated with the area of emotional disturbance. These include poor academic achievement, poor interpersonal relationship and poor self-esteem (Kneedler, 1984). This makes the role of teacher more important. A little pain on the part of the teacher will result in optimal gain for the slow learners.

v) The Need for Independence and Responsibility

The urge to become increasingly independent, self-reliant and responsible is a marked feature of normal development. But since the slow learners have emotional problems they are more dependent on other people and have more limited capacities for shouldering responsibility. Yet they get immense satisfaction when they do accomplish a step forward in independence. Opportunities for learning to become more independent and responsible are, of course, vitally important for their future. Such opportunities must be created for them by the parents at home and by the teacher in the school so that the slow learners can develop social skills and self-reliance which are very essential for his adult life.

vi) The Need for New Experience and Activity

The normal child has a strong urge to explore and findout. He is prepared to welcome the challenge of new situations and new learning. But the slow learners are less spontaneously currious, and tend to prefer the security of the known and familiar. However, they do show a similar pleasure in new experience and in activity. Since their mental and social handicaps tend to limit the satisfaction of this need, a variety of activities and interests in school become all the more necessary. The teacher must provide for work experience in the school in which the slow learners can sometimes do as good as normal child. Such successful and useful activities make him more confident and prepare him, in a way, for adult life.

The growth of personality and the achievement of mental health mostly depend upon the satisfaction of these needs at each stage from infancy to adolescence. Security and affection are the essential needs of infancy and if these have not been fully met, as in the case of many slow learners, there will be a poor foundation for the later building-up of personality. Further, the security and affection provided in the school can go a long way to make up for the lack of them in the child's own home life. The needs for acceptance by the peer group, for recognition and for independence become increasingly important as the child gets older, and are essentially relevant to developing the qualities children should have if they are to be successful when they leave school.

These needs are also important in relation to the child's motivation for learning. The success of learning and teaching in school does not depend on the quality of the teaching materials and the methods used. The learner must want to learn. The process of learning must provide one way of satisfying his emotional needs. While there are many ways in which we can motivate children's learning, the basis of good motivation is in the satisfaction of emotional needs that are mentioned above. For instance, children learn something in order to:

i) gain adults' approval and retain their affection;

ii) be like other children and be able to join in activities with them;

iii) achieve success and get recognition for it;

iv) satisfy the need for play and activity.

In other words, good motivation depends on a good teacher pupil relationship, the enjoyment of group participation, on feelings of success and mastery and on employing the child's natural interest in activities. Research into the causes of educational failure, whether in bright or dull pupils, has made us realise that anything which interferes with the fulfilment of these basic emotional needs can result in a lowered capacity for learning. Teaching, therefore, means not only providing them with the right books and using the best methods but also meeting the basic emotional needs.

Factors Influencing the Emotional Development of Slow Learners

The causes of emotional problems have been attributed to four major factors. They are biological disorders and diseases, pathological family relationship, negative cultural influences, and undesirable experiences at school. Although in the vast majority of the cases there is no conclusive empirical evidence that any of these factors is directly responsible for disordered behaviour, it is apparent that some may give a child a predisposition to exhibit problem behaviour, and others may precipitate or trigger it. That is, some factors such as genetics influence behaviour over a long period of time and increase the likelihood that a given set of circumstances will trigger maladaptive responses. Other factors may have a more immediate effect and may trigger maladaptive responses in an individual who is already predisposed to problem behaviour.

Another concept important in all theories of emotional or behavioural disorder is the idea of contributing factors. It is extremely unusual to find a single factor or cause that has led directly to disordered behaviour. Usually several factors together contribute to the development of a problem. In almost all cases the question of what specifically has caused a child to have a behavioural disorder can not be answered; no one really knows. A thorough knowledge of the causative factors is very essential for the teachers so that they can devise or modify their instructional strategy and approach accordingly to overcome the problems.

i) Biological Factors

Behaviour may be influenced by genetics, neurological, or biochemical factors, or by combinations of these, Certainly there is a relationship between body and behaviour and it would therefore seem reasonable to look for a biological causal factor of some kind for certain emotional / behavioural disorder. There are differences between bright and dull pupils especially in those aspects of emotional life which are modified by or dependent on intelligence. Slow learners, for example, like young children, tend to live more for the present moment without foreseeing the consequences of impulses. As adolescents and adults, they will be less able to think out solutions to their emotional and social problems. Much therefore, depends on the development of positive attitudes and proper channelling of emotions during school life.

All children are born with a biologically determined behavioural style, or temperament. Although children's inborn temperaments may be changed by the way they are reared, some believe that children with difficult temperaments are predisposed to develop emotional disorders (Thomas and Chess, 1984). Other biological factors besides temperament, disease, malnutrition, and brain trauma, for example - may predispose children to develop emotional problems(New Comb and Bentler, 1989). However, except in rare instances, it is not possible to determine that these factors are direct causes of problem behaviour. There is convincing evidence that genetic factors contribute to schizophrenia (Plomin, 1989), although even when there is severe and profound disturbance, the role of specific biological factors often remains a mystery (Kauffman, 1989, Prior and Werry, 1986).

We find uneven development in slow learners in different aspects of growth - physical, intellectual and emotional. Where the discrepancies are considerable, it is important that they must be recognised and taken into account. Physically a fourteen year old slow learner can be as well developed as the majority of the boys of his age. He may have reached puberty. Intellectually, he may have the reasoning ability of a ten or eleven-year-old.

Emotionally, his reactions to frustration and his need for attention may be like those of a pre-school child. Disparities of this kind present a problem to the boy himself as well as to his teachers, for the child it may mean that he has impulses with which he is intellectually and emotionaly incapable of controlling. For the teacher, it means that expectations for responsibility, co-operation and behaviour will be very different from those appropriate to most boys of his age and size (Tansley and Gulliford, 1962).

Slow development is another potent biological factor. Emotional development is rather slower in slow learners. An average child beginning school soon acquires sufficient emotional control to settle to the tasks of formal learning. But the slow learners need a much longer period of informal activity and the support of a sympathetic teacher to reach that stage. While normal children will be sufficiently mature by the age of eight or nine slow learners require a continued informal approach to learning, as well as special efforts to help them grow up emotionally.

ii) Family Factors

Effect of home influence on emotional development of child is unique. Nature of home and up bringing plays a vital role in emotional development of a child. It is impossible to realise fully the countless ways in which a child has been influenced in the years before he came to school - by the ways in which he has been loved or rejected, rewarded or punished, accepted as he is or urged to be something he cannot be. Nothing can be done about the past but knowing something of the child's past history may at least make us a little more tolerant of him.

The family is of first importance in creating a sense of security. Some family causes of insecurity are obvious enough, such as parental separations or disharmony, permanent or temporary break-ups in the family, long illness or unemployment. Empirical research on family relationships indicates that the influence of parents on their children is no simple matter, and that deviant children may influence their parents as much as the parents influence them. It is increasingly clear that family influences are interactional and transactional and that the effects of parents and children on one another are reciprocal (Patterson, DeBaryshe, and Ramsey, 1989). A child in a family which is outwardly stable may also feel insecure if there is reason for him to believe that he gets an insufficient share of affection or that he is a disappointment to his parents by not being able to live up to their expectations in behaviour or achievement. There may be brighter and more successful brothers and sisters to be compared with. School experience may provide him with some ways of achieving success. If the parents' attitude is crucial, even at this moment it may develop complex in him. He should be made aware that he is loved for his own sake and accepted inspite of his limitations. His small success should be received with approval. If these are done, he will be better able to face his inevitable frustrations whether they be due to his personal difficulties or the taunts of quicker children in the neighbourhood.

A large proportion of slow learners come from poor homes. In some cases the living conditions are very poor. It is easy to brand such homes as bad but we really need to consider in what ways they are bad. Although they may be squalid and hygienically unsatisfactory, they are not always completely inadequate from a mental health point of view. They may provide a measure of secuirity and affection. We have to be. wary of making easy generalisations. In homes where both parents are working, the provision made for the child when he comes home from school and the kind of attention shown by mother when she is at home are what matter. The father's attitude to the child, how he treats him and what he thinks of him are important for proper emotional development of the child.

iii) Cultural Factors

Social and cultural conditions or changes have a marked effect on children's behaviour. Children and their families are embedded in a culture that influences their behaviour (Rogoff and Morelli, 1989). Apart from family and school, many environmental conditions affect adult's expectations of children and children's expectations for themselves and their peers. Values and behavioural standards are communicated to children through a variety of cultural conditions, demands, prohibitions, and models. Several specific cultural influences leap to mind the level of violence in the media - especially television and motion picture - the use of terror as a means of coercion, the availability of recreational drugs and the level of drug abuse, changing standards for sexual conduct, religious demands and restrictions on behaviour, and the threat of nuclear accidents or war.

Undoubtedly, the culture in which children are reared exerts an influence on their emotional, social, and behavioural development. Case studies of rapidly changing cultures bear this out. Other research evidences suggest cultural influences on anxiety, depression and aggression (Chivian et al, 1985; Goldstein, 1983; Hawton, 1986). The level of violence depicted on television and in movies is almost certainly a contributing factor in the increasing level of violence in our society. Particularly troubling is the finding that television violence seems more "real" to disturbed than to nondisturbed children. This finding suggests that disturbed children may be more likely than others to perform aggressive acts after watching televised violence (Sprafkin, Gadow and Dussault, 1986).

From the research findings mentioned above, it can be understood what a crucial role the culture and the media play in the emotional development of children. Adults' expectations of children should be appropriate to the latters' level and stage and it should never be in advance of the stage the children have reached. Over expectations will result in undesirable stress and strain for the children which may ultimately lead to emotional problems or disorder. Media influence can not be underestimated. In some developing countries, television and motion pictures have changed the cultural facet of the society. As a result, there arises a conflict of values which in turn creates conditions and susceptibilities for onset of emotional or behavioural disorder.

iv) School Factors

Many of the emotional problems of slow learners are not directly related to their low level of intelligence so much as to the educational and social consequences of low intelligence. Since they are not able to perform as well as their normal peers, they easily get left on the fringe and are denied full participation with others through which so many social and emotional developments are possible. Their unsatisfying early experiences of school result in developing feelings of inferiority and lack of confidence. Some children may have emotional problems when they begin school, others develop behavioural or emotional disorders during their school years, perhaps in part because of damaging experiences in the classroom itself. Children who exhibit emotional disorder when they enter school may become better or worse according to how they are managed in the classroom. A child's temperament and social competence may interact with classmates' and teachers' behaviour in contributing to emotional problems. When a child with an already difficult temparament enters school lacking the skills for academic and social success he or she is likely to get negative responses from peers and teachers.

The school can contribute to the development of emotional problems in several rather specific ways. Teacher may be insensitive to children's individuality; they may require a mindless conformity to the rules and routines. Discipline in the school may be too lax, too rigid, or inconsistent. Instruction may be offered in skills for which the child has no real or imagined use. The school environment may be such that the misbehaving child is rewarded with recognition and special attention (even if that attention is criticism or punishment), whereas the child who behaves is ignored. Finally, teachers and peers may be models of misconduct - the child may misbehave imitating them (Kauffman, 1989)

Assessment and Measurement

It is much easier to identify emotional problems than it is to define and classify types and causes of emotional disorder. Most children with emotional problems do not escape the notice of their teachers. The most common type of emotional problem - conduct disorder - attracts immediate attention, so there is seldom any real problem in identification. Immature children and those with personality problems may be less obvious, but they are not difficult to recognise. Observation is the most direct method and requires the least amount of inference on the teacher's part (Taylor, 1984). However, although observation can be very helpful in documenting the behaviour under question, a trained professional's judgement is required in deciding the amount, frequency or degree of behaviour that must be present in order for a student to be characterised as "disturbed" or "disordered". Scores of characteristics are associated with the area of emotional disturbance (Kneedler, 1984). The important issue is the degree of the behaviour problem. It is therefore all the more important to make an adequate as well as accurate assessment and measurement of the emotional problems so that appropriate remedial treatment can be provided so as to accentuate emotional devc lopment.

Although formal assessment is more likely to be the major base for identification of students with special needs, informal assessment can also serve as a base for initial educational intervention. Guerin and Maier (1983) state that informal assessment includes "information gathered through observations of everyday student behaviour, through the examination of student products such as paper tests and presentations, and through discussion with students." As for emotional problems, informal assessment will be very helpful to assess the prevalence of the problem and formal assessment will be required only to measure the degree of prevalence. Formal assessment and measurement can be done in certain systematic ways such as -

i) Maintaining weekly diaries
ii) Case conference
iii) The Vineland Social Maturity Scale.
iv) Stott's Bristol Social Adjustment Guides
v) Primer of Sociometry.

i) Weekly Diaries

Teachers may keep a weekly diary in which observations of children's behaviour are recorded. Even though the teachers spend only a short period to record in the diaries, this will be worth the time spent since it compels the teachers to observe and think more carefully about individual children. It is often interesting to note how related are the isolated observations made at different times. In essence, the case study aims at gathering together all the available evidence about the child's physical and psychological growth, and his social setting of school, home and neighbourhood. Then an attempt is made to see these, not as a mere collection of facts, but in terms of the forces that make the child act as he does and this provides an adequate basis for formulating ways to help him.

ii) Case Conference

Some schools make use of case conference for which a regular time is set aside to discuss about one or two children. Medical and psychological records are considered. The class teacher reports on the child's progress and on any special problem. Also, other teachers who teach the child add their observations, and then general discussion follows. The case discussion has various advantages. The comments and questions of colleaques may help the class teacher to see the child in a new light and may suggest alternative methods of teaching or discipline. All the teachers can learn something about the child under consideration and there is therefore a greater unity of approach, which is highly desirable in the case of difficult children. It also makes for continuity of treatment when the child moves up to another teacher. The discussion method is perhaps the most valuable since every teacher learns from other teachers' observations and educational beliefs.

iii) The Vineland Social Maturity Scale

One aspect which should be watched at all ages is growth in social maturity. Children should be gradually developing the ability to look after themselves and to participate in those activities which lead towards ultimate independence as adults. The Vineland Social maturity scale is very helpful to assess the growth in social maturity. It provides a method of assessing the development of personal and social competence. It consists of 117 items of behaviour, grouped according to age levels. The items include self help, locomotion, occupation, communication, self direction and socialisation. It can be applied with other simpler check lists in order to assess the emotional problem manifested by the child. It brings to light not only the social maturity of the child but also the operating emotional problems.

iv) Stott's Bristol Social Adjustment Guides

Stott's Britol Social Adjustment Guides serve as effective means of looking systematically at the behaviour and relationships in the classroom. They are designed to provide a means of assessing which children in a group are showing behaviour serious enough to be characterised as unsettled or maladjusted. The assessment has the advantage that it is based entirely on the teacher's everyday observation of the child in various situations. For the first stage of the assessment, four page forms are available listing descriptions of children's behaviour under the main headings of Attitude to Teacher, Attitude to School work, Games and Play, Attitude to other children, Personal Ways, Physique. The teacher underlines, in each section, phrases which are applicable to the child in question. The completed form is then scored by means of a key and items indicative of unsettlement or maladjustment which are noted on a diagnostic form. The number of items so noted gives some indication of the seriousness of the problem. In addition, the symptoms are grouped according to their type i.e. depression, hostility towards adults or towards other children; anxiety about adult interest and affection etc. This classification helps us to understand in what directions the behaviour is disturbed and how serious is the the disturbance. On the basis of assessment made thus appropriate remedial measures may be thought of by the teacher to overcome the problem.

v) Primer of Sociometry

Another technique that helps to supplement casual observations is sociometry. It is quite simple to apply in the classroom. The technique aims at discovering the friendship and social preferences within a class. The main value of sociometry study is that knowledge of the relationships in the classroom enables the teacher to arrange groups for work and informal activities in a way which promotes social development. This will be especially important in the case of the child who is always on the fringe.

It is to be borne in mind that we should not use any technique casually just because it sounds interesting or looks impressive. It should be used only as a part of our endeavour to understand the children in the class with a view to planning more effectively for them. Use of such techniques should be supported and strengthened by the teacher's study of child development from the books and sources now available. Any method of assessment should not end in fixing a label to the child instead of being seen as a first step to greater understanding and appropriate action.

Characteristics of Students with Emotional Disturbances

The aim of all kinds of assessment and measurement should be to penetrate the surface impressions and to understand the causes of the attitudes and behaviour evinced by children. Common characteristics of slow learners such as laziness, inattention, showing off, aggressiveness may occur for different reasons in different children. We can not handle the individual child's problem in the wisest manner unless we have an insight into the underlying causes. As mentioned earlier, scores of characteristics are associated with the area of emotional disturbance (Kneedler, 1984). The important issue is the degree of the behaviour problem. Virtually any behaviour that is exhibited excessively over a long period of time might be considered an indication of emotional problem.

Quay (1979) surveyed the literature on the reported characteristics of emotional disturbances and noted four general categories or factors, conduct disorder, anxiety withdrawal, immaturity, and socialised aggressive disorder.

Children who fall into the 'conduct disorders category are characterised frequently as disobedient, distractible, selfish, jealous, destructive, impertinent, restive and disruptive. Hyperactivity is also associated with this factor, although this term is sometimes used by itself to describe certain students. The anxiety withdrawal factor includes behaviours identified as fearful, tense seclusive, depressed, hypersensitive, timid and baseful. The "immaturity" factor is characterised by short attention span, preoccupation, inattention, passivity, and poor co-ordination. Quay noted that each of these three factors represents behaviours that are either maladapative or a source of personal distress. The fourth factor, "socialised aggressive disorder", however, seems to be tied more to poor home conditions that model or reward aggressive behaviour. On the basis of these characteristics emotionally disturbed slow learners evince certain frequent pattern of behaviour. An insight into the patterns of behaviour and their causes will enable the teacher to pay special attention to the slow learners and also to modify or devise his instruction so as to suit the learning pace and learning rate of the slow learners.

Some Frequent Patterns of Behaviour and Their Causes

Most of the slow learners evince some certain frequent patterns of behaviour in the school as well as at home. It is these patterns of behaviour which make them markedly different from the normal students. Any teacher handling the slow learners for a reasonable period of time can easily notice these patterns of behaviour by means of their keen observation. But they have to take a little pain and strain on their part to study and assess the underlying causes. A proper understanding of the contributory causes is very essential for the teacher to tackle the behavioural problem as well as to make his instruction more effective. Some of the frequent patterns of behaviour are

i) Laziness

ii) Inattention

iii) Aggressiveness

iv) Immature and withdrawn.

v) Maladjustment.

i) Laziness

Laziness is an evident pattern of behaviour evinced by the slow learners. In some slow learners the laziness seems to have a constitutional basis. They are slower and less energetic than others by nature. A slow temper characterises all their activities. For some slow learners the laziness may be the consequent result of biological factors-glandular dysfunction, poor health, fatique resulting from inadequate sleep and nutrition.

In some other slow learners, laziness may be the result of emotional conditions such as anxiety, conflict, or day dreaming which absorb the children's energy and attention. In yet others, laziness may be a sign of deep rooted sense of failure. They are not buoyed up by the pleasurable and stimulating anticipation of success in any work that they undertake. Prevalence of laziness may be attributed to the fact that a satisfactory way of motivating the child in particular activities has not been found. In our classroom experience we can observe slow learners who are lazy in the classroom scampering off enthusiastically to carftwork or games. A teacher has to ascertain which cause is operating in the particular slow learner first and then he should combat the particular behavioural problem.

ii) Inattention

Another specific pattern of behaviour shown by the slow learners is inattention. Slow learners have, no doubt, a very short span of attention than normal chidren but most of the slow learners are able to concentrate on enjoyable and successful work for a considerable time. The degree to which the work is suited to the child's capacity and engages interest and activity is important. The slow learners who are emotionally unsettled are understandably often restless and distractible. It may be irrelevant for some to concentrate on 3R's work when their fundamental needs for security and affection are not adequately fulfilled. Besides, the ability to concentrate is to some extent a product of experience and training. Those children who are provided with adequate opportunities for absorbing personal and social play are more likely to develop the capacity to persist, and be able to accept the requirements of class routines. Creative and practical activities seem to promote the development of good attention and of work habits.

iii) Aggressiveness

Aggression has been analysed from many different view points. The analyses that have the strongest support is empirical research are those of social learning theorists such as Bandura (1973) and behavioural psychologists such as Patterson (Patterson, De baryshe and Ransey, 1989). Their studies take into account the child's experience and his or her motivation, based on the anticipated consequences of aggression. In brief, they view aggression as 'learned' behaviour and they assume that it will be possible to identify the conditions under which it will be learned.

Children learn many aggressive behaviours by observing parents, siblings, playmates, and people portrayed on television and in movies. Individuals who model aggression are more likely to be imitated if they are high in social status and are observed to receive rewards and escape punishment for their aggression, especially if they experience no unpleasant consequences or obtain rewards by overcoming their victims. If children are placed in an unpleasant situation and they can not escape from the unpleasantness or obtain rewards by aggression, they are more likely to be aggressive, especially if this behaviour is tolerated or encouraged by others. It is not that all the slow learners exhibit aggressive behaviour. As mentioned in first chapter, they are no trouble in the school and they are patient and co-operative. But there are some slow learners, especially those who come from poor homes which have in high measure emotional problems and lack love and affection. For those students if the teacher proves to be more than a substitute for parents, their aggressiveness can be easily tackled and proper emotional development can be expedited.

Teaching aggressive children to be less obnoxious is not an easy task. But social learning theory and behavioural research provide some general guidelines. In general, research does not support the notion that it is wise to let children act out their aggression freely. There are some most helpful techniques which include providing examples for non aggressive responses to aggression-providing circumstances, helping the child rehearse or role-play nonaggressive behaviour, preventing the child from obtaining positive consequences for aggression, and punishing aggression in ways that involve as little counteraggression as possible.

iv) Immature and Withdrawn

All children exhibit immature behaviour or act withdrawn once in a while. Children who are immature and withdrawn are typically infantile in their ways and they are usually reluctant to interact with other people. They are social isolates who have few friends. They seldom play with children of their age. Also they lack social skills necessary to have fun. Some resort to fantasy or day dreaming. Some of them develop fears that are completely out of proportion to the circumstances; some complain constantly of little actes and pains and let their "illness" keep them from participating in normal activities; some regress to earlier stages of development and demand constant help and attention; and some become depressed for no apparent reason (Klein and Last, 1989; Kovacs, 1989).

A particularly important aspect of immature, withdrawn behaviour is depression. Only very recently have mental health workers and special educators begun to realise that depression is a widespread and serious problem among children and adolescents (Forness, 1988, Klein and Last, 1989; kovacs, 1989). Today the psychologists are of common opinion that the nature of depression in children and youths is quite similar to that of depression in adults. The indications of depressions include disturbances of mood or feelings, inability to think or concentrate, lack of motivation and decreased physical well-being. Expression sometimes has a biological cause, and antidepression medications have at times been successful in helping depressed children and youths to overcome their problems. In many cases, however, no biological cause can be found. Depression can also be caused by environmental or phychological factors, such as death of a loved one, separation of one's parents, school failure, rejection by one's peers or a chaotic and punitive home environment. Interventions based on social learning theory-instructing children in social interaction skills and self-control techniques and teaching them to view themselves more positively for example-have often been successful in such cases. These intervention strategies will be very helpful for slow learners most of whom are immature and withdrawn to overcome their problems.

v) Maladjustment

The report of the Underwood Committee on Maladjusted Children describes maladjustment in the following terms: "A child may be regarded as maladjusted who is developing in way that have a bad effect on himself or his fellows and cannot without help be remedied by his parents or his teachers and other adults in ordinary contact with him. It is characteristic of maladjusted children that they are insecure and unhappy, and that they fail in their personal relationship. Receiving is difficult for them as well as giving, and they appear unable to respond to simple measures of love, comfort and reassurance. At the same time they are not readily capable of improvement by ordinary discipline.

The child who is perpectually in trouble, a nuisance in school life annoying to other children and generally unable to adjust to school life is called maladjusted. It is not that all the slow learners are maladjusted. Only a few of them have this maladjustment problem in addition to their slow learning problem. We find maladjustment in those slow learners who have a high degree of emotional problems. The main characteristic of maladjustment is that it spreads into many areas of the child's activity. A iack of adequate home relationship may result in attention seeking or other behaviour which is disliked by other children. The child feels rejected and isolated. and this may lead to annoying behaviour which still further isolates him. At the same time, his insecurity leads to distractibility in school. He fails to make marked progress; he becomes anxious about his failure and this anxiety and frustration make it more difficult for him to learn. He is in a vicious circle. The cumulative effect of all these failures hamper his emotional development and educational progress.

Measures to Help Maladjusted

There are no clear cut remedies for maladjustment which can be described step by step. However, the following general principles can be applied by the teachers to tackle the problems of maladjusted as far as possible. They are

i) Case study

ii) Good teacher child relationship.

iii) Positive discipline

iv) Broad curriculum.

i) Case Study

A case study can be made to discover some of the reasons for the maladjustment. In many cases, knowing the causes will indicate the approach that is needed, and in others, will enable us to afford the child some relief by encouraging him to tell about his anxieties, instead, of bottling them up. At least, knowing some of the reasons why the child behaves as he does makes us more sympathetic and tolerant.

ii) A Good Teacher Child Relationship

The teacher's understanding of the child should lead to the child realising that he is understood. It is rarely possible to give maladjusted children as much attention as they need. But there are many subtle ways in which a child can sense that an adult is anxious to help him such as the extra word of encouragement, the extra help with work, the teacher's willingness to discuss his problems, to trust him and give him some responsibility. A difficulty with relationships is one of the characteristics of maladjusted children, and so a relationship built up with the teacher can be a most effective therapeutic measure. This is not always easy. The withdrawn child takes a long time to respond. The over-active boy so often causes trouble that it is difficult to aviod nagging at him. But a sense of humour in the teacher can be of immense value here. Children can be jollied out of moods; laughter in the class, as long as it is not derisive can dispel feelings of tension and grievance. A good teacher child relationship will considerably enable the children to overcome their problems and it will also create a favourable environment for their gradual emotional development.

iii) Postive Discipline

Underwood (1955) states that maladjusted children are not really capable of improvement by ordinary discipline. A rigid strict class discipline may induce apparent improvement in class but is likely to provoke maladjusted children to other form of difficult behaviour elsewhere, e.g. bullying in the playround, temper tantrums at home, delinquency in the neighbourhood. They need a more permissive discipline so that they do not find themselves up against authority at every turn, or breaking rules which they do not understand and are therefore unable to conform to. The withdrawn child needs a permissive atmosphere to encourage him to 'come out of his shell'. In this way by enforcing positive discipline specific maladjustment problem can be tackled and favourable school environment can be created for their emotional development.

iv) Broad Curriculum

A more permissive atmosphere is easier to maintain if the curriculum includes many outlets for activities and emotional expressions. The freedom and variety of play with younger children; art and craft, physical activity, movement and drama for older ones provide the means for achieving success and outlets for strong emotional energies. Emotional release is an essential feature of any form of therapy.

Emotional Development of Slow Learners - A Joint Responsibility

Emotional development of slow learners is a joint responsibility of parents and teachers. If either of them is negligent or indifferent the slow learner can not have a proper emotional development. The child develops much of his emotions even before he comes to school and his early experiences at home very much influence his emotional development. It makes the responsibility of parents all the more important. It does not mean that the teachers have to play a less important role. Both parents and teachers are equallly responsible for the emotional development of children.

Role of the Parents

A well stable family or a good home is the basic requirement of emotional development. The parents should ensure that the basic emotional needs of the child such as - need for security, need for giving and receiving affection, need for acceptance by others, need for recognition and self esteem, need for independence and responsibility etc. are adequately fulfilled. It is their primary duty to provide the child with pleasant experiences at home so that their emotional development can be influenced to a great extent. The parents should set themselves as good models of behaviour for emulation by children. If the parents themselves have emotional problems, it will create susceptive conditions for the children to develop emotional problems. If the father and mother, although living in the same house, are almost completely entranged, the child is torn by conflicting loyalties as well as upset by the continual tension at home. This will, ultimately, create emotional problems for the child. So the parents should evince a right attitude by accepting the slow learners inspite of his limitations. They should give them love and affection in good measure. Slow learners without serious emotional problems respond well to additional special or remedial instruction and they are able to achieve moderate success. It is important that the parents should realise their role in the emotional development of their children and act accordingly.

Role of the Teacher

When a child comes to school, he brings his emotional world with him. Emotional factors contribute immensely to the slow learning of children. Teachers role is pivotal in the emotional development of slow learners. The slow learners who have emotional problems due to their unpleasant experience at home look upon the teacher for a substitute of their parents and a teacher can do better than parents, if he wills. Since emotional factors serve as an underlying cause of slow learning in some cases, it is the duty of the teachers to enable the students to overcome their emotional problems so that their learning can be geared up. First the teacher has to tackle the two most frequent patterns of slow learners with emotional disturbances i.e. laziness and in attention. For this the teacher has to provide for active participation in the learning process. They have to draw and sustain the attention of the slow learners to ensure active participation. Straight, dry lectures can be boring and bored students quickly stop paying attention to even the most carefully crafted lesson. For this reason, it is important to introduce variety, activity, or humour to enliven the lecture and maintain student attention. For example, use of humour has been found to increase student achievement (Kaplen and Pascoe, 1977), and illustrating the lecture with easily understood graphics can help hold student's attention. On the other hand, too much of variation in the mode of presentation can hurt achievement if it distracts students from the lesson content (Wyckoff, 1973).

Several studies have established that students learn more from lessons that are presented with enthusiasm and expressiveness than from dry lectures (Coates and Smidchens, 1966; Abrami et al 1982; Crocker and Brooker, 1986). It is also apparently helpful for student interest and achievement to vary the types of questions, length of lessons, and presentation modes (Rosenshine, 1971). In other words, maintaining student attention and interest is largely a matter of using humour, enthusiasm and variety. In one sense, teaching is performing, and it appears that some of the qualities we would seek in a performer are also those that increase the effectiveness of teachers. (Timpson and Tobin, 1982).

To tackle aggressive, immature, withdrawn and maladjusted behaviour the suggestions made by Catherine Morsink (1984) can be made use of by the teachers in such a way as to promote emotional development also. When any of the above trait is found in slow learner the teacher can make use of any relevant suggestion or suggestions in a possible mode of combination. This will ensure emotional development in course of time. Expecting emotional development in a short period is nothing short of a miracle and it is not possible also. But if Catherine's suggestions are scrupulously carried out by the teacher, the goal of emotional development can be achieved in course of time. Some important suggestions made by catherine are listed below.

- Think about the behaviours that really annoy you and establish to minimise their occurrence.
- State expectations for behaviour clearly and directly.
- Give students positive feed back on which behaviours are appropriate, and make specific corrections for inappropriate behaviour.
- Model your acceptance of individual differences and model courtesy and caring, respond to inappropriate behavioural differences consistently.
- Don't tolerate cruelty, but expect from other students a normal amount of teasing and help students cope with reality that students tease one another.
- Make your classroom a pleasant yet business like place in which students can learn.
- Set up a point or contingency system to reinforce students when their behaviour is appropriate.
- Ignore students with inappropriate behaviour if it is not dangerous or disruptive to other students; praise those with appropriate behaviour.
- Give "time out" to students who have tantrums or exhibit other behaviour disruptive to others.
- "Desensitise" students to stressful situations by taking them through series of progressively more demanding steps (for example, participating in group activity).
- Let disturbed students know you will help them when they are unable to control themselves; then do it in such a way that it demonstrates care and concern rather than a wish to dominate or punish.

All the above suggestions made for teachers can help them tackle the emotional problems of the students if carried out properly. Above all, the teacher should maintain a cordial relationship with the students, especially slow learners. The teacher should prove to be a better substitute for parents; and he should serve as a model father away from home. This unique approach of the teacher will enable him to tackle the students with emotional problems and he will ultimately be able to set the stage for onset of emotional development.

Summary

Emotions play an important role in determining whether our relations with other people are pleasant and joyful or sad and painful. These emotions affect not only our personal and social adjustment but also our physical health. It would be improper to assume that just because the slow learners are limited in intelligence, their emotional life is also similarly limited.

To ameliorate the emotional development of slow learners a psychological insight into the basic emotional needs and the factors influencing emotional development is a must for a teacher entrusted with the task of teaching slow learners. Need for security, need for giving and receiving affection, need for acceptance by other children, recognition and self esteem, need for independence and responsibility and need for new experience and activity are some of basic emotional needs. Adequate fulfillment of these basic emotional needs is important for emotional development.

The causes of emotional problems has been attributed to four major factors. They are biological disorders and diseases, pathological family relationship, negative cultural influences and undesirable experiences at school. Although in the vast majority of the cases there is no conclusive empirical evidence that any of these factors is directly responsible for disordered behaviour, it is apparent that some may give a child a predisposition to exhibit problem behaviour, and others may precipitate or trigger it.

Assessment and Measurement of emotional problems can be done in certain systematic ways such as maintaining weekly diaries, holding case conference applying the Vineland Social Maturity Scale, Stott's Bristol Social Adjustment Guides and Primer of Sociometry.

Most of the slow learners evince some certain frequent patterns of behaviour in the school as well as at home. It is these patterns of behaviour which make them markedly different from normal children. Laziness inattention, aggressiveness, immature and withdrawn and maladjustment are some of the frequent patterns of behaviour evinced by the slow learners with emotional problems.

Emotional development of slow learners is a joint responsibility of both the parents and teacher. If either of them is negligent or indifferent, the slow learners can not have a proper emotional development. The parents should ensure that the basic emotional needs of the child are adequately fulfilled. It is their primary duty to provide the child with pleasant experiences at home so that their emotional development can be influenced to a great extent. The teacher should analyse the underlying cause for each pattern of behaviour and he should launch a special attack on the cause. In promoting emotional development of slow learners suggestions made by Morsink will be very helpful to teachers.

REFERENCES

Abrami et al (1982) 'Educational Seduction'. *Review of Education Research,* 52, 446 - 462.

Bandura, A.(1973). 'Aggression: A Social Learning Analysis'. Englewood Cliffs, Prentice Hall, New Jersey.

Chivian et al (1985). 'Soviet Children and the Threat of Nuclear War'. *American Journal of Orthopsychiatry,* 55, 484 - 502.

Coats, W.D. and Smidchens, U(1966). 'Audience Recall as a Function of Speaker Dynamism'. *Journal Educational Psychology,* 57, 189 - 191.

Crocker, R.K. and Brooker, G.M. (1986). 'Classroom Control and Students Outcomes in Grades 2 and 5'. *American Educational Research Journal,* 23, 1-11.

Doll, E.A. (1935) 'The Vineland Social Maturity Scale'. Vineland Training School.

Forness, S.R. (1988) 'School Characteristics of Children and Adolescents with Depression'. In R.B. Ruthorford, C.M. Nelson and S.R. Forness(Eds) *Bases of Severe Behavioural Disorders of Children and Youth.* Little, Brown, Boston.

Goldstein, A.P. (1983). 'United States: Causes, Controls and Alternatives to Aggression'. In A.P. Goldstein and M.H. Segall (Eds) *Aggression in Global Perspective.* Pergamon Press, New York.

Guerin, G. and Maier, A.(1983). 'Informal Assessment in Education'. Mayfield, Palo Alto, C.A.

Hallahan, D.P. and Kauffman, J.M. (1991). 'Exceptional Children'. Prentice Hall, Inc, Englewood Cliffs, New Jersey.

Hawton, K. (1986). 'Suicide and Attempted Suicide Among Children and Adolescents'. Sage Publications, Newbury Park, C.A.

Kaplan, R.M. and Pascoe, G.e. (1977). 'Humorous Lectures and Humorous Examples : Some Effects upon Comprehension and Retention'. *Journal of Educational Psychology,* 69, 61-65.

Kauffman, J.M. (1989). 'Characterisations of Children's Behaviour Disorders'. (r thEd) Chas.E. Merrill, Columbus, O.H.

Kazdin, A.E. (1989). 'Developmental Psychopathology : Current Research, Issues, and Directions'. *American Psychologist,* 44, 180-187.

Klien, R.G., and Last, C.G. (1989). 'Anxiety Disorders in Children'. Sage Publications, Newbury Park, CA.

Kneedler, R. (1984). 'Special Education For Today'. Prentice Hall, Englewood Cliffs, New Jersey.

Kovacs, M. (1989) 'Affective Disorders in Children and Adolescents'. *American Psychologist,* 44, 209 - 215.

Morsink, C.D. (1984) 'Teaching Special Needs Children in Regular Classrooms'. Little, Brown and Company, Buston.

Newcomb, M.D. and Bentler, B.M.(1989). 'Substance Use and Abuse among Children and Teenagers'. *American Psychologist* 44, 242-248.

Northway, M.C. (1952) 'Prime of Sociometry'. University of Toronto Press.

Patterson, G.R. Debaryshe, H.D., and Ramsey, E.(1989). 'A Developmental Perspective on Antisocial Behaviour'. *American Psychologist,* 44, 329-335.

Plomin, R. (1989). "Environment and Genes: Determinants of Behaviour'. *Amercian Psychologist,* 44, 105 - 111.

Prior, M. and Werry, J.S. (1986) 'Autism, Schizophrenia and Allied Disorders'. In H.C. Quay and J.S. Werry (Eds) *Psychopathological Disorders of Childhood* (3rd ed), John Wiley, New York.

Quay, M. (1979) 'Classification'. In H. Quay and J. Werry (eds) *Psychopathological Disorders of Childhood* (2nd ed), Wiley, New York.

Rogoff, B., and Morelte, G.(1989). 'Perspectives on Children's Development From Cultural Psychology'. *American Psychologist,* 44, 343 - 348.

Rosenshine, B. (1971). 'Objectively Measured Behavioural

Predictors of Effectiveness in Explaining'. In I.D. Westbury and A.A.

Bellack (Eds), *Research in Classroom Processes,* Teachers College Press, New York.

Slavin, R.E. (1986). 'Educational Psychology. Theory into Practice'. Prentice Hall of India, New Delhi.

Sprafkin, J., Gadown, K.D., and Dursault, M.(1986). 'Reality Perceptions of Television: A Preliminary Comparison of Emotionally Disturbed and Nonhandicapped Children'. *American Journal of Orthopsychiatry,* 56, 147 - 152.

Stott, D.H. (1958). 'The Social Adjustment of Children'. Manual to the Bristol Social Adjustment Guides, U.L.P.

Tansley, A.E., and Gullifor, R.(1962). 'The Education of Slow Learning Children'. Routhledge Kegan Paul Ltd, London.

Taylor, R. (1984) 'Assessment of Exceptional Children: Educational and Psychological Procedures'. Prentice-Hall, Englewood Cliffs, N.J.

Thomas, A., and Chess, S.(1984). 'Genesis and Evolution of Behavioural Disorders: From Infancy to Early Adult Life'. *American Journal of Psychiatry,* 141, 1 - 9.

Timpson, W.M., and Tolin, D.N.(1982). 'Teaching as Performing'. A Guide to Energising Your Public Presentation, Prentice-Hall, Englewood Cliff, N.J.

Wychoff, W.L. (1973). 'The Effect of Stimulus Variation on Learning From Lecture'. *Journal of Experimental Education,* 41, 85-90.

5 Educational Programmes for Slow Learners

Chapter Outline

Chapter Objectives

This chapter expounds special educational programmes for slow learners. After reading this chapter you
should be able to:

- Provide special education programme for slow learners.
- Modify your instruction so as to provide appropriate level of instruction.
- Employ special methods of teaching
- Arrange for Various modes of tutoring to enhance the performance of slow learners.

Teaching effectively is the most important of all the competencies required of a successful teacher. Since effective teaching deals with the needs, interests and abilities of pupils as individuals, it requires knowledge of the environment in which the pupil lives, the development problem he or she faces and his/her mental abilities. It is more true so when the teacher is dealing with the slow learners. It also calls for an understanding of the learning processes essential for creating an environment where learning can take place and for making instruction so stimulating that every pupil will be motivated to learn. Stimulating pupils to think critically, independently and creatively is essential for effective teaching.

Further, human resource development should be at the focus of any educator for a developing country like India which has abundant human resources. In the Indian system of education, it is observed that the human resources-teachers and learners - are underdeveloped and perform less than their capabilities. The learners are under developed in the sense that they are not achieving in tune with their capabilities. Even some of the most efficient teachers are not adequately equipped to identify and guide the backward students like slow learners to reach their optimum levels. As a result, the institutions in turn are not able to send their products into the society as fully developed learners. To ensure this we need special educational programmes for backward children like slow learners.

Although much has been achieved in this field of education, there are many opportunities for experiment and research. Throughout we have been constantly aware of the need for further investigation of the learning, thinking and adjustment of slow learning children so that teaching method can be precisely planned to suit their needs (Tansley and Gulliford 1962).

Eventhough the slow learners are unable to cope satisfactorily with the usual educational standards of the ordinary schools, with proper guidance and care they are capable of being educated. In adulthood, they become self supporting, independent and socially adjusted. One defect, however, which is worth noting is that most of the slow learners are not identified at appropriate time and stage. Psychologists and educationists specify that the remedy for slow learners lies mainly in their nature and the extent of the causes which produce it. Of course, each case is unique and requires specific remedial measures. Psychologists and educationists have laid down the following remedial measures which may prove effective and conducive to slow learners. An insight into the remedial measures will be very beneficial for the teachers to provide appropriate level of instruction and appropriate educational programmes for the slow learners.

Educational Programmes for Slow Learners

Psychologists and educationists have recommended various educational programmes to surmount the problem of slow learners in the mainstreaming. Most of the measures are within the purview of the teachers. Effectiveness of certain measures have already been established by the researchers. A clear perception of the educational programmes meant for slow learners will enable the teacher to combat slow learning in an effective manner. The following are the remedial measures which constitute the educational programmes for slow learners.

- i. Motivation
- ii. Individual Attention
- iii. Restoration and Development of Self-confidence
- iv. Development of Good Work Habits
- v. Elastic Curriculum
- vi. Remedial Instruction1
- vii. Healthy Environment
- viii. Periodical Medical Check-up
- ix. Special Methods of Teaching
- x. Learning Contracts and Peer Tutoring.

i. Motivation

The Word "motivation" is used to describe a drive, need, or desire to do something. Motivation can be applied to behaviour in a wide variety of situations. One use of the concept of motivation is to describe a general tendency to strive towards certain types of goals. Success of a teacher largely depends on how effectively he motivates the students to learn.

Experience has shown us that learning failure is very often largely due to poor motivation. Children taught by a teacher using motives in a sensible, individualised way will always learn more quickly and better, even if the method used is faulty. Slow learners usually evince an attitude of avoidance resulting from previous experience of failure or dislike of a subject. They often glance at words rather than scrutinize them carefully, with the result that their errors in recall are the result of guessing from slight clues such as initial letters or superficial similarities. Fear of failure and disinterest are evident in their daily school activities. It emphasises the need to take adequate and appropriate measures to improve their academic status. When a slight improvement is noticed, the teacher should not fail to employ some effective motivational techniques to stimulate the slow learners. But in day-to-day classroom practice, most of the teachers go about their work in a routine manner without caring for the children in general and backward children in particular and apathetically carry on the classroom work, accomplishing very little. This leads to large scale wastage of human resource in terms of human potentiality.

The key to avert this state of affairs lies in motivations. That is why motivation is rightly said to be the royal road to success. An encouraging smile from the teacher can do better than his verbal instruction. When the teacher succeeds in motivating the students, his instruction will be effective and the educational objectives can be achieved. The teacher should be wary not to discourage the slow learners who usually feel frustrated. The teacher should let them understand that they are not the ignored students and they are as dear to him as others are. When the teacher evinces this type of positive attitude, all his motivational techniques will work out successfully. Moreover, motivation not only instigates the behaviour of slow learners but also reinforces the ongoing behaviour. In the classroom situation motivation is that which drives the slow learners to learn. It makes the slow learners desirous of learning to apply himself to the task. In addition to encouraging smile and kind verbal motivation, the teacher can make use of appropriate illustration, example and aids for creating motivational atmosphere inside the class.

ii. Individual Attention

"Individual attention" refers to the attention given by the teacher to a particular student. Of all the students it is the slow learners who need individual attention from the teachers. The individual differences of the children should be properly recognised and the individuality of the child must be respected. The teacher should take positive effort to ascertain the specific disability of the slow learners and accordingly he should devise his remedial instructional strategy which should cater to the needs of each slow learner. It is necessary that the handling teachers should be very kind and sympathetic towards slow learners.

Bloom (1976) advocates mastery learning strategy for backward students wherein he allows time to vary for mastery. As we have official special coaching classes for the scheduled caste and scheduled Tribes students studying in the schools for which the expenditure is borne by the state, we can have similar type of special classes for the slow learners in the evening after school hours so that they can be given more time as well as better individual attention. Some incentives may be provided to those teachers who may be entrusted with the task of instructing the slow learners in the way the government gives incentives for those teachers who take special coaching classes for the SC/ST students. If this remedial measure is enforced, better individual attention can be given to the slow learners in the special classes which will, ultimately, promote better human resource development.

iii. Restoration and Development of Self-Confidence

Slow learners are the backward children who have, even before admission to the school, experienced years of failure and frustration as a result of which their self-esteem is seriously undermined. Constant lack of academic success, rejection by other children, faulty instruction and mismanagement by parents lead to emotional disturbance, feelings of inadequacy and personality and conduct disorders. These slow learners ultimately find themselves in a vicious circle. The interplay between the causes and symptoms becomes more and more complicated and difficult to disentangle. The breaking of this vicious circle becomes one of the most important objectives of remedial treatment. This cannot be broken unless the school establishes a special educational programme for the slow learners.

The teacher should instil self confidence in the minds of slow learners. For that he should avoid magnifying the mistakes committed by the slow learners. He should also avert all sorts of sarcastic censure. He should manifest a sympathetic attitude towards slow learners. When the slow learners find themselves in some difficulties, the teacher should guide them properly. When they are right or when they give a right response, the teacher should effectively make use of that opportunity to praise the concerned slow learner for his correct response. This type of praise, as well as encouragement, will imbibe self confidence in slow learners and they can make remarkable progress and increase their learning capacity in course of time. So the teacher should take all possible effort and make use of all possible opportunities to restore and develop self-confidence in slow learners which will ultimately goad them into manifesting better attainment. Nothing succeeds like success and success leads to success.

iv. Development of Good Work Habits

Backwardness of slow learning children is often the result of development of poor attitude towards work. Work that is too difficult or beyond the entering behaviour of the slow learners usually results in boredom and poor attention. Frequent failures and frustration may cause behaviour difficulties and reluctance to try or to take initiative. If careful attention is given to individualisation of treatment, curriculum content and balance and to suitable organisation, the slow learners can develop the feeling of power to overcome difficulties and improve in self-directed application to work. Moreover, the slow learners lack the knack to assess the relative importance of work. They not only do not know how to do a work but also when to do a work and which to do first. They may be doing a work at wrong time which will eventually retard learning.

So it becomes an essential duty of the teacher to develop good work habits in slow learners. How to study each subject, how to tackle the problems related to the subject and how to make responses for the questions and how to carry out the project or enrichment activities should be well explained to slow learners and a strict vigil also should be kept to make sure that they follow the guidelines given by the teacher in learning the subject. It should be made known to them how approach and instructional strategy differ from subject to subject and how they should tackle each subject should also be made clear to them. They should be trained up to make analytical and synthesised study. They should be instructed to adapt systematic study habits at home also. If the work habits of the slow learners are developed as stated above, they will be able to attain a moderate degree of success within a considerable period of time.

v. Elastic Curriculum

Poratt (1980) identifies two basic assumptions that underlie all curricula: (1) that knowledge should be pursued for its own sake and (2) that curricula should be designed to meet the immediate and long-term needs of students. The knowledge centred curriculum focusses on the content of subject areas, whereas the needs centred curriculum assumes that human needs serve as the foundation for curriculum. In the most extreme instance the subject centred curriculum demands that the students learn content regardless of learner characteristics. The other extreme is the curriculum that attends only to the wants of the students and sacrifices content for "relevancy".

Utmost care should be taken in preparing the curriculum for the slow learners which should be as flexible as possible to suit the requirement and need of the individual slow learner who are generally interested in concrete perceptual experiences. So greater attention must be paid towards concrete aspects of work. The teachers should not lay much stress on abstract and theoretical study because the slow learners cannot understand the abstract concepts very easily. Wherever there are abstract concepts the teacher should try to establish possible relationship or point out possible associations so that the slow learners can have a grasp of the abstract concepts. There must be scope for profuse use of audio-visual aids and for concrete presentation of subject content. When there is concrete presentation of instructional content, the slow learners are able to understand in a better way and it enhances their learning capacity and learning rate to a considerable extent.

Practical work should be given due importance in the curriculum of the slow learners. In the mainstreaming also we have crafts, arts etc which provide for practical work and work experience. The four purposes of education i.e. self realisation, human relationship, economic efficiency and civic responsibility can be developed in slow learners by incorporating proper practical work and work experience in the curriculum. Practical work is one of the several fields in which the slow learners can often most easily achieve success or have it engineered for them. The work done must therefore be suited to the capacity of individual children; it should be something which produces evidence of success by looking good or being useful. In the early stages at least, slow learners need quick success; they can not be expected to persist for too long without tangible results. It is to be remembered here that learning builds on learning in the way success builds on success.

The practical works which are found to be conducive to slow learners include metal work, wood work, leather work, cane work, knitting, tailoring and other subjects of household economy. There is, too, a great deal of useful knowledge that comes through practical work, the names and uses of different woods, materials, tools and processes. There is the learning about how things are made; where materials come from; how much materials and tools cost; measurement and the appreciation of size and quantity. Wherever possible, opportunities should be taken to use interest in the craft as a starting point for the incidental discovery of more knowledge and understanding of the world around.

Physical education must not be solely concerned with the development of strength and physical skills, or indeed with physical development alone. It should be viewed as an integral part of the whole programme for personality development. It should include, at all levels, training in personal hygiene and general fitness, and the development of co-operation, courage and confidence, perseverance and independence. It should provide opportunities for exploration and experiment in the use of physical activity and the use of skill and strength in work and play. Because of their poor home environments, or as a result of rejection, slow learners have missed the opportunities for skill learning which arise naturally in play. It should be noted that the adverse effects of these missed opportunities are cumulative. Primary skills are not developed and consequently more mature ones are harder to learn. This may lead to further rejection and isolation. Physical education should take into account and help to minimise those physical limitations which occur most frequently in slow learners - poor posture and muscular incoordination, lack of stamina, specific physical defects. Finally, physical education should take advantage of the many opportunities it will have to compensate for other limitation and to ensure feelings of accomplishment and success. So the subject teachers should refrain from engaging the physical education periods for their own subjects.

vi. Remedial Instruction

Rastogi (1978) and Narayana Rao (1987) have suggested that the remedial teaching classes or special classes should be conducted systematically based on laid down guidelines. Studies have proved the effectiveness of remedial classes in case of specific slowness in a specific subject area. First, the deficiencies are determined and confirmed by experts administering some diagnostic tests to slow learners. Then the expertise of specialists may be utilised to deal with specific slowness. The following are the guidelines for the smooth working of a remedial programme.

(a) The instructional content must be very carefully graded keeping in mind the capacity, requirement, educational and experience levels of the students. In the gradation of teaching materials the principles of proceeding from easy to difficult and simple to complex must be scrupulously followed.

(b) Short frequent lessons should be introduced instead of long lessons every week. This will cater to the short span of attention of slow learners. Further, it will avert fatigue and boredom, to which the slow learners are easily susceptible.

(c) The slow learners are able to grasp concrete ideas rather than abstract ideas. Therefore there must be ample use of audio visual aids in the instructional process which can provide unique experience to the slow learners in the presentation of the content. Concrete presentation of instructional content can be made by making use of appropriate media application in the instructional process.

(d) The teacher should be aware of the fact that a friendly approach in remedial teaching is highly conducive. Friendly smile, a few encouraging words, praise at appropriate time will have a far reaching influence on the learning capacity of slow learners. The cumulative effects of these procedures will make better impact on the achievement of slow learners than even an effective instruction.

(e) To generate interest, social skills and confidence in slow learners, stress may be laid on effective use of art, music and drama. These are certain areas where they can have a moderate success which imbibes in them self confidence. Moreover, nothing succeeds like success; and success builds on success.

(f) The teachers dealing with the slow learners should give due importance to practice, drill and review which all facilitate the comprehension and retention of slow learners. Repetition and direction should also be emphasised. For this computer assisted instruction and modular instruction can be made use of since these teaching strategies effectively incorporate practice, drill review, revision and repetition in the instructional process.

(g) With a view to ensure optimum human resource development special remedial classes should be arranged for slow learners. In 1968 Bloom proposed that rather than providing all students with the same amount of instructional time and allowing learning to differ, perhaps we should require that all or almost all students reach a certain level of achievement by allowing time to differ. That is, Bloom suggests that we give students as much time and instruction as necessary to bring them all to a reasonable level of learning. If some students appear to be in danger of not learning, then they should be given additional instruction until they do learn. Bloom (1976) hypothesizes that given additional instructional time, students who do not master their lessons in the time usually allowed should be able to reach achievement - levels typically attained by only the most able students.

But the problem inherent in any mastery learning strategies is how to provide the additional instructional time to students who need it. In much of the research on mastery learning, this additional instruction is given outside of regular class time, such as after school or during recess. Those students who failed to meet a pre-establised mastery criterion (such as 90 percent correct on a quiz) following a lesson were given this extra "corrective instruction" until they could earn a 90 percent score on a similar quiz. Research on mastery learning programmes that provide corrective instruction in addition to regular class time has generally found achievement gains, particularly for low achievers (Block and Burns, 1976; Bloom, 1976, 1984).

Similarly when we provide extra time for slow learners for corrective instruction, they also can achieve the mastery level. As we have special coaching classes for the SC/ST students in the evening hours, we can have special remedial classes for the slow learners also. In case of SC/ST special coaching classes, four teachers for tackling the boys of Stds VIII to X and eight teachers handling students of Stds XI and XII are paid by the state. In similar manner, the teachers entrusted with the task of remedial coaching for slow learners also can be paid by the state with a view to optimise human resource development.

vii. Healthy Environment

Providing a healthy environment is an important aspect of remedial measures for slow learners. The school environment should be healthy and reasonably free for slow learners. Many a time poor environmental factors contribute a lot towards the slowness. Poor environmental factors should be adequately tackled or removed at the earliest so that congenial atmosphere can be created for the effective learning of slow learners. Again, the teachers should ensure a variety of approaches in the instructional presentation to teach various subjects. Most often slow learners suffer from emotional problems. So utmost care must be taken to place them in protected environment. To ensure this, the teacher himself should not criticise the slow learners nor should he allow the other students either to look down upon the slow learners or to tease them. When they have no emotional problems, their learning will be optimum.

viii. Periodical Medical Check-up

Physical anomalies sometimes serve as vital contributory factors for slow learning. Poor health and other malfunctions also have adverse effect on the learning of slow learners. If a particular anomaly is detected and correctly diagnosed, then a slow learner can become a normal learner after remedial treatment. In absence of periodical medical check-up, there will be no opportunity for the teacher to diagnose the cause of slow learning and to ensure the possible medical remedy. Moreover, for every physical malady there is a medical remedy which can remedy not only the malady but also the slow learning. So special medical check-up should be arranged periodically for every slow learner.

ix. Special Methods of Teaching

Educationists and psychologists have conducted many experiments to evolve special method of teaching for slow learners George Grapper and Lumsdaine (1961) established the effectiveness of instructional television on the achievement of low ability students. Leitner (1992) has proved that video instruction is very effective to low ability students. Block and Burns (1976) and Bloom (1976) studied the effectiveness of mastery learning strategy and found it to be more effective for low achievers. Rajaguru (1994) has proved the effectiveness of video instruction with special reference to slow learners. Ramar (1994), Reddy and Ramar (1994, 1995, 1996) have highlighted the impact of multimedia based modular approach on the achievement of low achievers. Clark (1985) points out that CAI seems to have greatest positive effect for elementary students, moderate effect for high school students, and lowest effect for college students. Effects of CAI are often strongest for low achievers. A common feature underlying all the aforesaid strategies is individualisation of instruction. The research evidences reveal that the following special methods will be very effective for slow learners.

a. Audio and Video Instructions

b. Mastery Learning Strategy with Extra Corrective Instruction.

c. Modular Instruction

d. Computer Assisted Instruction

It is not necessary here to delve into the details of each of the above instructional strategies. But it is very necessary to know how each of the above strategies is effective to slow learners and how far they help the slow learners to overcome their problems. Teachers teaching slow learners can use any single method or a combination of methods in any mode to ensure attainment of mastery level or predeterminded behavioural objectives.

a) Audio and Video Instruction

Slow learners need extra time for remedial and enrichment activities. In the audio instruction the expert's service not ordinarily available in the school is made available. They can listen to the audio instruction based on their subject units in the evening hours. They can take them home and make use of according to their convenience. Here the acquisition of informations takes place without any sort of inhibition. Also, they can listen to relevant educational radio programme which also has positive effect on the slow learner's learning.

Video instruction provides for considerable visualisation of objects and processes which is very essential for better perception of concept. What impact a visual presentation can do, any amount of verbal exposition can not do. Moreover, in a fast developing world where knowledge explosion is taking place in every sphere, it is unreasonable, to expect that written or spoken words alone could convey the volume of relevant information to the learner. Further, the video instruction provides unique experience to the slow learners in the presentation of instructional content. It penetrates more deeply into human character with an immediate excitement than any other single medium. Concrete presentation of instructional content ensured in Video instruction is very conducive for the slow learner for making a better perception of the concept. The dual effect of audio and video strengthens and enriches the understanding and expedites the mastery of the concept.

Video instructional strategy very much caters to the individual differences of slow learners. In the traditional classroom setting, the slow learners are too inhibited to ask the teacher to clarify a concept or to get a doubt cleared. But, in the video instructional strategy, even if they don't understand the concept at the first attempt, they can understand the concept thoroughly by making use of the provisions such as 'pause', 'still', and 'play back'. Not only that, but also they can take the video cassettes to their houses and view the instructional programme according to their convenience. This enables the slow learners to learn better at their own rate. Effectiveness of video instruction as a special method of teaching for slow learners has been substantiated by various research evidences (George Gropper and Lumsdaine, 1961; Leitner, 1992; Rajaguru, 1995)

b) Mastery Learning Strategy

One widely used means of adapting instruction to the needs of diverse students is called mastery learning (Block and Anderson, 1975; Block and Burno, 1976, Bloom, 1976). Mastery learning is a system of instruction that emphasises the achievement of instructional objectives by all students by allowing learning time to vary. The basic idea behind mastery learning is to make sure that all or almost all the students have learned a particular skill to a pre-established level of mastery before moving on to the next skill.

Bloom (1976) proposes that 80 percent of the students should be able to achieve at a level usually attained by only 20 percent of students when they are given additional time and that under these circumstances aptitude or ability should be nearly unrelated to achievement. Mastery learning emphasises corrective instructions in the form of remedial special classes in the evening hours. Given some extra coaching and corrective instruction, slow learners are able to make a better achievement. Corrective instruction refers to educational activities given to students who initially fail to master an objective designed to increase the number of students who master educational objectives.

This mastery learning strategy does not involve any expenditure. All that we need is an understanding dedicated teacher who can devotedly tackle the slow learners. Corrective instruction can be imparted in the remedial special classes in the evening hours. The teacher should give them some freedom and at the same time the progress of the slow learners should be monitored and guided. Peer tutoring can also be effectively made use of wherever possible. Services of aides, special education teachers, parent volunteers can also be used in remedial special classes of slow learners. For mastery learning media application, and individualised instruction also will be very conducive for slow learners. Once the slow learners have the experience of mastery learning and attain a pre-determined mastery level, the learning will build on learning leading them to a remarkable success or achievement.

c) Modular Instruction

Module is a self contained auto instructional package dealing with a single conceptual unit or subject matter. Instruction through modules has been found very effective for all levels of students and it is found more effective with regard to low achievers and slow learners. Various research evidences confirm this (Dhamija 1985; Hopper, 1982; Sahajahan, 1980, Ramar (1994); Reddy and Ramar 1994, 1995, 1996; Natarajan, 1996). This modular instruction as a special method of teaching can be very effective to slow learners since it enables the slow learners to adequately overcome their problems in learning. A detailed account of how each of the problems of slow learners is overcome in the modular instruction can be systematically listed out.

The slow learners lack concentration. So they can not concentrate on the instructional presentation for more than 45 minutes. In modular instruction a single unit is divided into three to four conceptual sub units. Each sub unit constitutes the subject content for development of one module. The duration of each module is 20 to 25 minutes only. So the slow learners will be able to concentrate on the concept. Also, it caters to the short span of attention of the slow learners.

A learning module is a self contained and self instructional package dealing with a single conceptual unit or subject matter. It can be used in any setting, convenient to the learner and the learner can complete the module at his own pace. It may be used individually or in small learning groups. In this way modular instruction accommodates instruction to individual differences. Here, what matters most is the mastery of the subject, not the time. So, the modules are very suitable to the students and they are more effective for slow learners.

One of the most frequent complaints about slow learners is the weakness of their memory. Of all the problems that hamper educational progress, the most frequent is a weakness in what may be termed long-term memory. Slow learners need to go over the material more times before it is fixed in their mind, and more frequent revision is required to prevent forgetting. The efficiency of the initial learning is important as well as actual retention and recall. Modular instruction takes care of these problems by providing frequent revision and repetition in each module.

The slow learners are very poor in abstract thinking. It is because they are unable to understand the relationship between things. They are slower to perceive and use possible association. Meaningful associations are of great importance not only for comprehension but also for prolonged retention. The learning materials presented in the module for each objective, the project work and and the practicum incorporated in the learning module enable the slow learners to surmount the problem of abstract thinking and to understand the possible association which will, ultimately, tell upon their retention.

It is a fallacy to think that just because slow learners are limited in intelligence, they can only learn by rote memorisation. They also can make meaningful learning where there is concrete presentation of subject matter. Slow learners must understand as much as they can of what they are learning; and then they need more repetition, revision and practice to ensure retention. Modular instruction takes care of concrete presentation of subject matter by incorporating necessary diagrams, sketches, pictures, worksheets, examples, dimensional drawings etc. with the learning material at appropriate places. Also, modular instruction provides for the required review, repetition, and revision by highlighting the main points in learning materials, various tests and in recapitulation and summary. It provides for practice in project work and practicum. Thus, in many ways, the modular instruction proves to be suitable for slow learners.

d) Computer Assisted Instruction

Computer assisted instruction is a kind of individualised instruction administered by a computer. The computers that are programmed to guide students through lessons at a student's own pace can help in accomodating student differences. Computer assisted instruction has its roots in programmed instruction and in the behavioural theories of learning. According to these theories, learning is accelerated by the use of controlled presentation of stimuli, followed by reinforcement based upon the learner's responses. Many CAI programmes stress drill and practice exercises, others teach students facts and concepts. CAI programmes have the following advantages.

1. Use of a structured curriculum
2. Letting students work at their own pace.
3. Giving students controlled, frequent feed-back and reinforcement.
4. Measuring performance quickly and giving students information on their performance.

Therefore, for the slow learners, who remain in the lowest rung of the ladder, CAI is reckoned as one of the most suitable strategies which can motivate them to manifest their best. Why and how far the CAI is conducive to slow learners can be listed as below.

CAI provides unique experience to the learners in respect of the presentation of the content. It ensures easy and effective transmission of instruction to the learner. It gives instant knowledge of results and provides immediate feed back which are very essential for slow learners to ameliorate their learning process.

It effectively caters to individual differences. Every student can learn at his own rate. Students will have no pinch of inhibition when they learn through CAI. The feeling that they are not preyed upon by the supervisors and the free and relaxed readiness to learn by themselves at their own rates, give the slow learners an impetus to learn better and to manifest their best.

In case of teaching science through CAI programme, important diagrams can be magnified even part by part also, so that the slow learners can understand in a better way. Moreover, the simulation technique which is possible in a CAI programme will also facilitate learning of slow learners.

Research studies (O'Donnal, 1982; Billings, 1983; Chambers and Sprecher, 1983; Atkinson, 1984; Kulik et al, 1984; Niemiec and Walberg, 1985) generally agree that CAI can be very effective in increasing student achievement, but not always. CAI is consistently effective when it is used in addition to regular classroom instruction, but has smaller and less consistent achievement effects when it entirely replaces classroom instruction. Clark (1985) points out that the positive effects of CAI seem to be greatest for elementary students, moderate for high school students, and lowest for college students. Effects of CAI are the strongest for low achievers. Delon (1970) found that CAI programme significantly increased the mathematics achievement of disadvantaged first graders. Ragosta (1983) in his major study of CAI in mathematics, reading and language found positive effects on the achievement of disadvantaged elementary students who had received ten minutes of computer time per day each. Purushotham and Stella (1990) and Stella (1993) have established the effectiveness of CAI in Indian setting with special reference to under achievers. Hence, the effectiveness of CAI will be immense for slow learners if it can be used in the remedial instruction.

It is not that the aforesaid special methods are the only methods to improve the learning capacity of the slow learners. The teacher can use any other method also according to situation and feasibility to teach the slow learners. Since the effectiveness of the above methods with reference to backward students has been confirmed by research evidences, they have been highlighted here. But the teacher has every right to choose any method of teaching that he deems fit and proper for improving the learning capacity of the slow learners. Here what matters much is development in the learning rate of slow learners, not the method that is employed. Methods are only means to achieve our preestablished behavioural objectives.

x. Learning Contracts and Peer Tutoring

a) Learning contracts

A Learning contract is an agreement between the teacher and the student to study and share information about a specific topic. It helps the classroom teacher organise the instructional programme for some exceptional students. Dunn and Dunn (1974) describe the contracting process in some detail. They discuss the importance of joint (student teacher) planning of the elements of the contract, and indicate that the contract's behavioural objectives should be personalised. They also suggest that the contract include a list of media or resources and activities the student will use, as well as any methods the student will use to report what has been learned. Finally, they suggest that the contract indicate how the student's performance will be evaluated and, if appropriate, what the schedule will be for completing the project. Contracting may be effective for gifted students or for backward students like under achievers, slow learners etc who are motivated when allowed to participate in designing their instructional activities.

b) Peer Tutoring

Long ago educators realised that students could help one another learn. When one student teaches another, this is called peer tutoring. There are two principal types of peer tutoring: cross-age tutoring where the tutor is several years older than the student being taught, and same-age peer tutoring, where one student tutors a classmate. Cross-age tutoring is more often recommended by researchers than same age tutoring (Devin - Sheehan et al, 1976), partly because of the obvious fact that older students are more likely to know the material, and partly because students may accept an old student as a tutor but resent having a classmate appointed to tutor them.

When implementing peer tutoring, it is important that the rules for tutors be quite explicit; that is, tutors show or tell their students what to do, then watch as the students perform, they repeat the demonstration or instructions if the student makes an error, and then praise the student when the response is correct. Teacher monitoring of the tutors is an integral part of the system. It is not time consuming , but it is extremely important: Each student must demonstrate mastery of the skill before teaching it, and each should use methods and materials with which the tutor and the teacher have worked previously. Learning tasks to be presented by the tutor should be structured. In every case the tutor should be briefed exactly what the learner should learn and provided with all the necessary materials. Sometimes these materials include task cards with step-by-step instruction, plus concrete materials for completion of the task. At other times the materials may be worksheets or book pages, and the task for the learner is to complete the page.

Research on Peer Tutoring

Dale (1979) suggests that peer tutoring can help mainstreamed exceptional students to "accomplish specific goals and in the process it can help the tutor to "become more accepting of differences and likenesses in individuals". Several studies provide evidence that peer or cross-age tutoring is effective with mildly handicapped students. Ehly and Larsen (1980) have summarised much of this research, indicating that cross-age tutoring studies are reported much more frequently than studies of classroom tutoring. Some of the studies reviewed by these authors suggest that the learner, being more relaxed when working with a peer than with a teacher, is better able to concentrate on learning. The Ehly and Larsen summary indicates that the learner's achievement gains may transfer to the regular classroom, and that tutoring seems to facilitate improvement in self-concept. That is one reason why it is specifically recommended for slow learners.

Research evaluating the effects of peer tutoring on student achievement has generally found that this strategy increases the achievement of both tutees and tutors (Devin - Sheehan et al, 1976). In fact, many studies have found greater achievement gains for tutors than for tutees (Cloward, 1967), and peer tutoring is often used as much to improve the achievement of low-achieving older students as to improve that of the students being tutored. As many teachers have admitted, the best way to learn something thoroughly is to have to teach it to someone else. Training of tutors seems to be critical for the effectiveness of peer tutoring (Ellson, 1976), and some of the most successful tutoring programmes have been highly structured "programmed tutoring" models (Ellson, et al, 1968). In these models peer tutors are given explicit instructions on how to introduce material.

Details of an interesting cross-age tutoring programme have been provided by Morsink, Tringo, and Janseen (1973). The tutors in these programmes were twelve to fourteen year old students with reading disabilities. They received a remedial instruction from a special education teacher whose programme was housed in a book mobile. Then they applied what they had learned by teaching it to second graders with reading disabilities, in a mainstream classroom under the supervision of the classroom teacher. They were motivated to continue by the appreciation that the teacher and the school principal showed them, and by the admiration they received from the younger children. These older students gained an average of two months in reading achievement for every month they spent in the programme (Morsink, Triango, and Janssen, 1973).

One caution about the research on peer tutoring: Almost all student of peer tutoring use tutoring in addition to regular instruction, and compare results to those for regular instruction alone. For this reason, at least part of the effectiveness of peer tutoring could be attributed to the extra instructional time rather than to the value of peer tutoring itself. However, viewed as an addition to regular classroom instruction, peer tutoring does seem to be an effective way to provide appropriate levels of instruction to students (Slavin, R.E., 1986). This makes it more relevant to slow learners who are in dire need of additional instructional time.

REFERENCES

Atkinson, M.L. (1984). 'Computer-Assisted Instruction: Current State of the Art'. *Computers in the Schools*, 1, 91 - 99

Billings, K. (1983). 'Research on School Computing'. In M.T. Grady and J.D. Gawronski (Eds), *Computers in Curriculum and Instruction* (pp 12 - 18).

Block, J.H., and Burns, R.B. (1976) 'Mastery Learning'. In L.S. Shulman (Ed)., *Review of Research in Education*, Vol. 4, F.E. Peacock, Itasca 911.

Bloom, B.S. (1976). 'Human Characteristics and School Learning'. McGraw-Hill, New York.

Chambers, J.A., and Sprecher, J.W. (1983). 'Computer-Assisted Instruction'. Prentice Hall, Englewood Cliffs, New Jersey.

Chaub, S.P. (1983). 'Educational Psychology'. Lakshmi Narain Agarwal, Agra.

Chintamani Kar (1992). 'Exceptional Children'. Their Psychology and Education'. Sterling Publishers Private Ltd, New Delhi.

Clark, R.E. (1985). 'Evidence For Confounding in Computer-based Instruction Studies: Analysing the Meta-analyses'. *Educational Communication and Technology Journal*, 33, 249 - 262.

Cloward, R.D. (1967). 'Studies in Tutoring'. *Journal of Experimental Education*, 36, 14 -25.

Dale, M. (1979) 'Peer Tutoring : Children Helping Children'. *The Exceptional Parent*, 9, 26-27.

Devin - Sheehan et al (1976). "Research on Children Tutoring Children: A Critical Review'. *Review of Educational Research*, 46, 355 - 385.

Dhamija, N. (1985). 'Effectiveness of Three Approaches of Instruction - Conventional Radio-vision and Modular Approach on Achievement of Students in Social Studies'. in M.D. Buch (Ed) *Fourth Survey of Research in Education*, NCERT, New Delhi.

Dunn, R., and Dunn, K. (1974). 'Practical Approaches to Individualising Instruction'. Parker, West Nyack, New York.

Ellson, D.G. (1976) 'Tutoring'. In N.C. Cage (Ed) *The Psychology of Teaching Methods* (pp-130-165). University of Chicago Press, Chicago.

Hallatian, D.P., and Kauffman, J.M.(1991) 'Exceptional Children'. Prentice Hall, Inc, Englewood Cliffs, New Jersey.

Hopper, W.A.P. (1982). 'An Experimental Study in the Use of Modular Approach For Teaching Biology in Std XI'. in M.B. Buch (Ed) *Third Survey of Research in Education*, NCERT, New Delhi.

Kulick, C., and Kulink, J., and Bangert-Drowns, R.L.(1984). 'Effects of Computer-Based Education of Elementary School Pupils'. Paper presented at the Annual Convention of the American Educational Research Association, San Francisco.

Leitner, R.K. (1992). 'Comparing the Effects on Reading Comprehension of Educational Video, Direct Experience and Print'. in Dissertation Abstracts International, Vol. 53, No.3, September 1992.

Morsink, C.V. (1984). 'Teaching Special Needs Children in Regular Classrooms'. Little, Brown and Company, Boston.

Morsink, C.V., Triango, J., and Janssen, D.(1973)'. A supplementary Resource Room For Inner City Children'. *Bureau of School Services Bulletin,* 45, 63-72.

Narayana Rao, S., (1987). 'Educational Psychology'. Wiley Eastern Limited, New Delhi.

Niemiec, R.P., and Walberg, H.J. (1985) 'Computers and Achievement in the Elementary Schools'. *Journal of Educational Computing Research,* 1, 435 - 440.

O'Donnel, H.(1982) 'Computer Literacy. Classroom Applications'. *Reading Teacher,* 35, 614 - 617.

Pralt, D. (1980) 'Curriculum Design and Development'. Harcourt Brace Jovanovich, New York.

Rastogi, K.G. (1978). 'Educational Psychology'. Rastogi Publications, Meerut.

Reddy and Ramar (1994). 'Effectiveness of Multimedia Based Modular Approach in Teaching Social Science to Low Achievers'. *Media and Technology For Human Resource Development,* Vol. 6, No.3, April - June 1994.

Reddy and Ramar (1995). 'Effectiveness of Multimedia Based Modular Approach in Teaching Science to Low Achievers'. *Journal of Research in Educational Media,* Vol.2, No.2, January 1995.

Reddy and Ramar (1995). 'Effectiveness of Multimedia Based Modular Approach in Teaching Maths to Low Achievers'. *Journal of Higher Education.* U.G.C, Vol.18, No.2, Summer 1995.

Reddy and Ramar (1996). 'Relative Effectiveness of Video Instruction in Teaching Science and Social Science to Slow Learners'. Paper Presented in the IIIrd National Conference on Development of Educational Technology, Bharathidasan University, December 27, 1996.

Sahajahan (1980). 'An Experimental Study of Teaching Science in Stds VI and VII Through Modular'. in M.B. Buch (Ed) *Third Survey of Research in Education,* NCERT, New Delhi.

Soundararaja Rao and Rajaguru (1995). ' Effectiveness of Video Assisted Instruction on the Achievement of Slow Learners'. *Journal of Educational Research and Extension*, Vol.32, No.2, Oct. 1995.

Stella. A. (1993). 'Effectiveness of Computer Assisted Instruction with Special Reference to Under Achievers'. Media and Technology For Human Resource Developments, Vol.5, No.3, April 1993.

Tansley, A.E., and Gulliford, R.(1962). 'The Education of Slow Learning Children'. Routledge Kegan Paul Ltd, London.

Teaching Language to Slow Learners

Chapter Outline

Chapter Objectives

After reading this chapter you should
be able to:

- List out the causes of poor language development of slow learners
- Understand the basic principles of teaching reading.
- Describe various methods of teaching reading.
- Analyse the difficulties experienced by the slow learners in spelling
- Describe the methods of teaching spelling.
- Describe the reading problems of slow learners.
- Use various techniques to remediate oral language problems.
- Device remedial programme for written language difficulties.

Teachers give considerable thought to the ways of achieving good standards in reading and writing. Reading and writing are, of course, important but it must not be forgotten that they are only subsidiary skills in language. Children's ability to express themselves orally and to comprehend what is said to them is more important. After they leave the school, the slow learners may make little use of their reading and writing but will certainly make daily use of language to communicate with others. In school itself, language is fundamental to much that we do. This is most obvious in basic subjects. Children need a varied vocabulary and an ability to talk in sentences for developing readiness for reading. Both remembering words in reading and spelling and good comprehension in reading are promoted by understanding the words used and being able to relate them to meaningful experiences (Tansley and Gulliford, 1962). Written English is very much dependent on oral English because children, and even many adults for that matter, write as they talk. Finally, we have to note the inherent link between thinking and language. A greater ability in using words is a means to more effective thinking and an increasing understanding of experience is reflected in a widening vocabulary. In short, language is of primary importance since it is so much a vital part of mental growth.

Language Development of Slow Learners

Children with normal intelligence and from good home background usually arrive at school age with language sufficiently mature for them. Such children are able to use speech as a means of getting on with other children and to make progress in pre-reading and pre-number work. But slow learners do not have sufficient language development at school age. Their primary difficulty is delayed development or disability in the comprehension and use of language (Iskson and Miller, 1976; Vogel 1975; Wiig and Semel, 1976). Some of them have severe defects of articulation. Others use a small vocabulary and brief sentences. They have difficulty in finding and combining words. They often have recourse to gestures or to action rather than words. They need a great deal of speech stimulation through play, through listening to adults and talking with them. With older slow learners, the difficulties are in knowing what to say, or if they know what to say in finding ways of saying it. A limited vocabulary is one of the chief weaknesses. The lack of a word, or their inability to call it up when it is needed, results in hesitations, new starts and roundabout ways of saying things.

They are not able to express their ideas logically. Their expression lacks orders, sequence and selectivity. The difficulty in knowing what to select to say is a common weakness found in the expression of slow learners. The slow learners make less use of different parts of speech. Sentences are mostly stung together with 'and' or 'then'. They do not make much use of conjunctions, adjectives and adverbs. They get confused in the use of words such as prepositions and pronouns. Errors in usage are, of course, frequent. Many of these are indeed the common and accepted forms in the child's environment. It makes the remedy difficult because what the child hears out of school is in continual opposition to what he hears in school. Finally, it is to be remembered that language is concerned with communication and this involves listening as well as talking. Slow learners are poor at remembering messages, and listening to instructions, stories and other forms of the spoken word. So the teachers have to give special attention to promote listening and reproducing what has been said.

The Causes of Poor Language Development

There are four vital factors which cause poor language development. A proper understanding of these factors will enable the teacher to decide what factors to be taken into account in providing the conditions in school for improvement. The four vital causative factors are:

i) Poor background of speech and language at home.
ii) A limited background of experience.
iii) Emotional and social factors.
iv) The limitations of slow learner's thinking.

i) Poor Background of Speech and Language

Children learn mother tongue and English even before they come to school and continue to be influenced all their lives by the mother tongue and English they hear out of school. Slow learners start talking rather late and most of them have less encouragement and stimulation to talk at home. Limited vocabulary and poor expression of the parents do not give the children proper models for emulation. Moreover, most of the students do not converse with children, telling them stories, answering questions and giving them the experiences of listening and talking that many average children have in their homes. Language is acquired not just by imitation but in this interchange of talk which stimulates thinking and creates the need to find and practise techniques of expression. Verbal abilities develop very early, and by age three, children are already skilful talkers. By the end of the pre-school years, children can use and understand an almost infinite number of sentences, can hold conversations and know about written language (Gleason, 1981; Menyuk, 1982; Schickedanz, et al 1982). So it is more important to provide the children with proper background for speech and language development at home itself. The difference that a better verbal background makes is sometimes demonstrated by sub-normal children who come from good homes (such cases are, of course, rare). Their vocabulary is surprisingly extensive even though their low intelligence still limits their use of it. This deficiency should be made up in schools by giving children as many opportunites as possible to talk with others.

ii) Background of Experience

An interesting environment favours the acquisition of nouns, interesting activities favour the acquisition of verbs and that the other parts of speech are relatively more dependent on the quality of the child's thinking. Learning to read is a process of learning how language works rather than acquiring a series of independent reading skills (Mckenzie, 1977; Schickedanz, 1982). Even before entering school, children begin to build an understanding of written language. Many researchers suggest that this knowledge follows a course of development similar to that of spoken language. From seeing print, children make guesses about how it works. This process works best when children have many books, magazines and other printed materials available. (Mckenzie, 1977; Schickedanz, 1982) If they are read to frequently, children between three and five years of age dramatically increase their understanding of reading (Taylor, 1983). Children who are taken on holidays or for day trips, or who have plenty of toys and activities at home, are more likely to acquire a better vocabulary than children who live a very restricted life as so many slow learners do. Teachers who have taken children out on many trips can understand how much children gain in vocabulary from seeing new places, as well as in spontaneity of expression about the things that excite them. But it is not only the experience itself that matters. What is important is the use to which experience is put. Experiences must be worked over in talk, question and answer as they are in good families, if children are to get the maximum benefit from them.

iii) Emotional and Social Factors

In infancy, speech develops in the encouraging, approving atmosphere of a home, the close relationship with mother being particularly important. Any disturbance in this relationship or in the normal family pattern is likely to be reflected in the poorer language development, as it is in the case of deprived children. Later in childhood, insecurity or emotional disturbance may result in the child who is timid and silent, or in more serious cases, in the child who will not talk. The language programme should include attempts to help these children to a better adjustment so that they can gradually become able to participate in classroom talk. Some verbal expression is so easily influenced by emotional conditions, it is important for all children that the atmosphere of the class should be encouraging so that children feel able to ask questions, seek help, and make suggestions without fear of disapproval or criticism. Social relationships within a class are also important. Children who are unsociable, or who are not accepted by others, miss the interchange of ideas and chatter on the way to school, in the playground or in play generally. Play ensures emotional stability and makes children sociable. Play also involves interactions with peers, which can encourage social problem solving. While thinking up make believe roles for each other, children can co-ordinate their actions in cooperative manner, making prosocial behaviours possible (Damson, 1983, 1984). Reading and writing can be viewed as sophisticated forms of representational thought that are built on the early experiences with symbolism that children have during play (Wolfgang and Sanders, 1981). Play also gives children safe situations in which to express ideas and feelings. Missing this, they miss the practice in talking with others that the normally outgoing child has, and miss also the extension of general knowledge and interest that come from sharing experiences with others.

iv) Limitations of Thinking

As we have noted in the first chapter, slow learners are limited in their ability to think and reason about their experiences. They have a poor capacity to generalise from experience and so develop the concepts which are summed up in words. This is especially to when they are dealing with words for abstractions rather than for things. Hence their attention to words which stand for a "family" or class of words e.g. fruits, tools, vegetables, seasons, instruments should be drawn. They should be given practice in using words to describe the uses and compare the appearance of things. Because of limited intelligence there is a reduced awareness of significant relationships in their experience such as those involving the use of prepositions, adverbs and comparatives.

Relationships of cause, result, time and place which would find expression in the appropriate adverbial clauses are slow to appear in the speech of slow learners and are less frequently used. It is not just that they do not have the words for ideas which they perceive in an undefined, non-verbal way. They do not connect things in their experience in a way that calls for the use of these parts of speech. The practical implication is that incidental opportunities should be made use of to help children pattern their experience and to find words to talk about it. Intelligent children do this for themselves with a minimum of adult guidance in their ceaseless exploration and discovery of their environment, whereas slow learners need help. Just as the development of number concepts and processes can not be left merely to chance, so in the field of language concepts and relationships need to be more consciously defined and verbalised. Language skills are acquired and practised as children find a need to talk about their activities. Opportunities for this exist in every part of school work. Although the method is informal, it is very fruitful, for the teacher will be able to lead children on to greater fluency of expression partly by example, partly by practice, partly by definite guidance.

Some Basic Principles of Teaching Reading

This is not the place to dwell upon the psychology and teaching of reading in greater detail. There are many books available for further study in this regard. The following points, however, are of special importance in relation to the teaching of slow learners and other backward children. An insight into there basic principles will ensure a better preparedness on the part of the teacher to teach reading to slow learners. The important basic principles are:

i) The importance of reading readiness

ii) Importance of good teacher - child relationship.

iii) Importance of motivation.

i) The Importance of Reading Readiness

Slow learners do not become ready to respond to the formal and systematic teaching of reading until very much later than ordinary children. Research into readiness for learning has shown that children's success in reading at later stages is often delayed by introducing them to instruction before they are able to benefit from it. Yet even to-day children are introduced to formal reading lessons before they are ready with the result that they become frustrated, bored, puzzled and lacking in confidence. Then it becomes all the more difficult to teach them when they do become ready to learn. It is therefore essential that teachers of young children and of slow learners should be aware of what readiness for reading entails and how readiness can be promoted. The teacher has to assess certain vital factors which influence reading readiness before he decides upon any relevant strategy to teach reading to slow learners. The main factors which should be assessed by the teacher are:

a) Mental Maturity

b) Background of Experience

c) Specific Abilities

d) Personal Characteristics

e) Health.

a) Mental Maturity

Learning to read requires the association of meanings with the correct printed symbols to understand the meanings of words and ideas in his reading. The child must have an adequate background of experience language and mental maturity. When he is mentally mature he will be able to make necessary discrimination between letters, sounds and word shapes. A mental age of six or six and a half is an adequate stage of mental maturity at which children can succeed on the beginning stages of formal, systematic reading. This is, of course only a rough guide because much depends on other factors in the child. Sometimes children with mental ages of six or more are backward verbally or they are still too immature in personal and social development to make any marked progress. At the same time we have children who make progress with apparently lower mental ages. To make an assessment of mental maturity the teacher should take note of the child's response to verbal instructions, his understanding of stories, his language development generally, and his ability to use instructional materials and to plan activities purposefully. The teacher should bear in mind that intellectual development can not be thought of as isolated from such things as memory, attention, concentration emotional development and social background and experience.

b) Background of Experience

Experience provides interest and knowledge upon which the teaching of reading can be based. It influences the child's language growth and the extent to which stories and books are likely to appeal to him. Most of the slow learners come from unstimulating homes and they lack adequate background of experience. It is therefore very essential to devise a pre reading programme which should attempt, in every possible way, to make up for this limitation.

c) Specific Abilities

Before the teacher starts teaching reading to children he should ensure that they have adequate visual readiness, auditory readiness and motor readiness. Serious defects, if any, in visual acuity should be discovered and referred for treatment. Even if the child shows signs of eye strain, e.g. frequent blinking, watering, inflamed eyes, head held to one side when looking at pictures, an early investigation must be arranged to ensure remediation. The child should develop visual perception and discrimination. He should have ability to interpret pictures, to match and compare shapes and patterns. It is important to ensure that these skills are sufficiently developed and the child can see likeness and differences in shapes, letters and words. Otherwise, the beginning of reading may need to be delayed.

The teacher has to assess the auditory readiness also. It is sad to note that hearing deficiencies are more easily overlooked. Even when the child has some degree of hearing impairment, his speech suggests inaccurate hearing of sounds. Such child is inattentive or does not respond to or frequently misunderstands directions, or assumes a peculiar position when spoken to. Sometimes hearing may be adequate but the child may still be poor at discriminating sounds, (Wepmen, 1960). He may not be able to distinguish between three and tree, stop and staff, bay and pay, etc, Before introducing reading and phonic work it is important to recognise these deficiencies and appropriate remediation must be made in order to ensure auditory readiness for reading. It will be meaningless to attempt teaching reading without ensuring auditory readiness on the part of learners.

Motor readiness is essential to develop adequate reading readiness. Some children have greater difficulty in acquiring habits of moving the eyes from left to right along the line, to fixate at certain points to look at the words, and then to move to the beginning of the next line.

These children need additional practice in achieving controlled left to right movements. They evince general clumsiness and lack of hand - eye co-ordination. These affect his reading readiness. So it is the primary duty of the teacher to ensure hand-eye coordination before taking any effort to teach reading.

e) Health

A good health is a prerequisite condition to participate fully in school activities. Recurrent illness, tiredness and listlessness very much affect the child's span of attention, his interest and the amount of effort he makes. Since poor physical condition is a common feature found among most of the slow learners it is essential to watch this aspect carefully. A good health is indispensable to develop reading skill in slow learners. Otherwise fatigue and inattention will set in soon. The teacher may suggest to the parents to take some steps to improve the health of the child so that the child becomes able to participate fully in school activities.

Readiness is thus a complex matter involving the interaction of many factors. Auditory perception, discrimination and intelligence are important if we emphasis phonic methods at an early stage. For writing motor co-ordination is essential. Whatever is our aim, each child's weakness must be noted so that he can be given experiences which may help him to overcome the weakness. Regular records of each child's progress should be kept, these records will bring to light any irregularities in maturation and development and demonstrate individual differences. There should be no time limit for this programme. It should be rather looked upon as a period of becoming more and more ready for higher levels of activity - a period of growing into reading.

Importance of Good Teacher-Child Relationship

Experiences of earlier failures very much hamper the progress of slow learners. This gives rise to feelings of personal inadequacy, frustration and antagonism towards school in general and reading in particular. In some children these feelings manifest themselves as aggressiveness or stubbornness while in others as withdrawal, apathy and hopelessness. So it becomes the primary task of the teacher to replace these feelings by ones of co-operation, mutual trust, optimism and enthusiasm because no permanent learning can take place in the presence of emotional stress. The teacher should make all possible efforts to understand the needs of the slow learners and he should take remedial measure to overcome the inadequacy. Though this is difficult in many cases, a dedicated teacher can rise to the occasion. Moreover, it is not easy to determine the causes of the child's backwardness. It is difficult to differentiate between symptoms and causes. The child's emotional disturbance may be caused by reading failure or be the cause of it. It is also possible that these two may be symptoms of other causes like parental pressure, ill-health, irregular attendance and so on. It is therefore very important for the teacher to concern himself with building up good relationship with the child, with making his learning procedures appropriate, and with the development of good motivation. Developing reading readiness largely depends on the quality of the relationship that the teacher has with the child. A cordial relation will go a long way in drawing the best of the child.

The Importance of Good Motivation

Learning failure is very often the resultant product of poor motivation. Many disabled learners have poor attitudes and motivation partly because they have experienced repeated failure. Fernald (1943) described the negative attitude of non reader as a major problem requiring that the teacher develop entirely new strategies. Researchers who compared disabled readers and normal learners in their ability to attach auditory meanings to visual abstract symbols found that the performance of the disabled readers was significantly poorer (Birch and Belmont, 1964; Guthrie, 1974). Steinhauser and Guthrie (1974) reporting on a task requiring subjects to indicate whether letter patterns in words looked the same and had the same sound; concluded that disabled readers would match symbols that were visually alike, but that they had trouble matching sounds with visual symbols. Later research supports the assumption that auditory visual interpretation is related to reading ability (Deverensky, 1977; Ward 1977), but indicates that the variables are related in a complex manner, depending on the students development, IQ and economic background. This difficulty like poor attention calls for greater motivation from the teacher. Children taught by a teacher who is adept at motivating children in a sensible and individualised way will always learn more quickly and better, even if the method used by him is faulty. Dolch (1957) has suggested five types of motives which can be employed in teaching reading. They are the play motive, the story motive, the ultility motive; the mastery motive, and please the teacher motive.

The Play Motive

The play motive is used when we devise apparatus and games by means of which words phrases and other aspects of reading can be practised in a way that draws upon the enjoyment of play. By playing snap with words and by playing Deminoes or Lotto with words and phrases instead of numbers a basic sight vocabulary or the words coming in a new look can be practised. 'Spell-right' 'scribble' and many games like this are now in use. Special softwares for reading are also available. This makes learning reading possible through computer games also. There are devised gadgets with lights which flash when words are correctly matched. This play motive has been found to be of immense value in learning to read, especially in the early stages of acquiring a basic vocabulary, or with an older child whose previous experience of reading has produced an antipathy to reading books and for whom reading has to be motivated in an enjoyable way to ensure subsequent success. This play motive also serves as a means of providing activities which lead to a point where other motives such as the story motive and the utility motive or the mastery motive can begin to take effect.

b) The Story Motive

The Story motive can be powerful one at all stages of reading. It is better to get children on reading to simple stories sooner. We have to look at the simplest reading materials to see whether they have sacrificed the story element in order to achieve a scientific vocabulary control. Both are important when the reading age reaches seven, the story motive can be extremely useful. It is always better to read for or with the child the first two or three pages of a story about adventures, smugglers or pirates. Once we arouse their interest in reading, children will be eager to read on independently. Simple books with good stories are very useful for this purpose. The story aspect arouses and also sustains their interest. It ignites the spark of their imagination. Once they become interested, they get absorbed in reading which ultimately becomes a habit formation. This habit formation leads to more or voracious reading which results in enrichment of active as well as passive vocabulary. English versions of Amar Chitra Katha series are very useful for this purpose.

c) The Utility Motive

Utility Motive can be used at all stages of reading at varying degrees. Even in the pre-reading period, reading should be related to the activities of the children. When they realise the usefulness of reading in their daily life it gives them an impetus for reading. Children always see the usefulness of reading if it can be related to their interests and hobbies. This is very effective with older children. It is surprising what difficult passages can be read when the children want to read instructions about how to make model, to read a letter that has been written to him, or to find information about games of his choice or pets or aircrafts etc. At the later stages of school, the utility motive can work through the need to read instructions or follow directions in connection with practical work or real life situations. Thus the utility motive expedites reading readiness when the children realise the usefulness of reading.

d) The Mastery Motive

It is the mastery motive that has the greatest importance is teaching of slow learners. Most children want to learn despite their failure developing in them an attitude of indifference and hostility. Once they taste success the materials should be graded to ensure its continuation the desire to master reading is the chief motive for progress. Children seldom need encouragement to note that they are going on to a new book, or to make a record of the number of supplementary readers they have read. They may not do it at older age. But at early stage they are very particular about it. Harnessing this motive satisfactorily is not an easy task. If the teacher lays too much emphasis on achievement it can lead to anxiety both in teacher and children. This can be averted to some extent by preparing the pupils adequately for the next stage. A thorough knowledge of the stages in the learning process is very much essential for the teacher and he should be able to anticipate or decide which part will be difficult for slow learners, e.g. phonic readiness, blending and sylla bification, reading for comprehension. When success is in the air and children are keen to get continued sign of progress, the teacher should have the knack to hold them back. Children often want to go on to the next book before they have. adequately consolidated at the previous stage. This poses a very real problem. To achieve adequate consolidation of previous learning and at the same time maintain the child's feelings of mastery and success calls for great skill and understanding on the teacher's part. It all depends on how judiciously the teacher makes use of appropriate supplementary or the materials made by him i.e. books, cards and written exercises.

e) The Please-the-Teacher Motive

When there is a very good teacher. Child relationship the please-the-teacher motive will be in operation. It is in direct proportion to the degree to which the teacher is prepared not to let the child down. The teachers earnest concern for the child instills equal degree of earnest effort in the child. This motive needs to be supplemented by the other motives we have mentioned above. Besides, as the child begins to experience success in his reading he should become personally involved, setting and accepting his own standards.

Reading As a Part of Language Development

Reading should be looked upon as one aspect of an integrated programme of language development, which also includes speaking, writing and spelling. In the development of reading skills, the child's speaking and meaning vocabulary, i.e. active and passive vocabulary should always be well ahead of what he is reading. The words and the ideas that the child is reading should always be well based on the experiences and language which he understands and uses. If it is beyond his experience level he can not get optimum benefit out of it. Moreover, children should deem reading as a skill which is useful for 'getting information and for giving him enjoyment. Reading holds the key to the storehouse of information and it lays before us new pastures for browsing. Also reading extends the boundaries of knowledge. It is a part of language refinement and development and it should not be thought of as an isolated skill.

Reading Method

Reading is a means of fixing still more firmly what the child has already learnt by listening and speaking. It involves three processes ie. interpreting the symbols making the correct sound and understanding the sense. So the act of reading may also be defined as a process of sight, sound and sense. There are a few methods of teaching reading and it is important for the teacher, to have a thorough knowledge of these methods. Also, they should know how far each method is applicable to slow learner and which method works well with slow learners.

The following are the chief methods of reading:

i) Alphabet Method

ii) Look and say Method

iii) Sentence Method

iv) Phonic Method

v) Story Method

vi) Compromise Method

i) Alphabet Method

According to this method, the letters of English alphabet are taught first in regular order. Once the child masters the letters, simple syllables are taught and then combinations of syllables are taught. Then come the smaller words and finally the longer words and sentences. This was the method most widely used in the past. This method is essential for all the learners whether they are normal or backward. It is the method which is widely used to start with. This method helps to fix the English letters firmly in the minds of the pupils. It facilitates learning of spelling. Above all, it seems to be a logical method. But this method has some disadvantages also. It causes monotony. It is tiresome. The children take a long time to learn all the letters of the alphabet. This method is psychologically unsound. Generally the children see the whole word or sentences and not the individual letter. This method is not very effective for slow learners who appear to be visually ready for reading before they are auditorily ready. Hence a visual method will be more appropriate for the slow learners at early stages. If possible, this method should be supplemented with simultaneous visual projection of the letter and words.

ii) Look and Say Method

It is a very simple method which makes use of visual effect which is very much essential for slow learners. The teacher holds up to the class a card with a word (ie. cat, rat, mat etc.) First the teacher spells the word and makes a correct pronunciation of the word. The children look at the card and say the concerned word in chorus just as the teacher pronounces it. This is repeated several times. This repetition is useful for slow learners who need frequent repetition and revision. Several such cards are used to teach reading. Also, it should be remembered that print medium is the affordable technology in a developing country like India. Here, the word becomes the basic unit, not the letter. This method, also known as word method, is better than alphabet method in teaching reading to slow learners. The children are active in this method and they learn by doing. Moreover; the visual effect facilitates retention of words. This is an analytical method. It promotes word recognition and facilitates retention of words. It is more meaningful than alphabet method.

But this method is not without disadvantages. It concentrates on the individual word rather than the whole sentence. Sentence is the unit of thought, not the words. It is, therefore, desirable to teach groups of words or short sentences. But to teach the slow learners at early stage this method is very useful.

iii) Sentence Method

This method makes use of the principle that sentence is the unit of thought. So, whole sentences are taught to teach reading. This is therefore look and say method with sentence as the unit instead of the word. The procedure adopted is exactly the same as in the look and say method. Cards with simple sentences written on them are held up before the pupils.

e.g. This is an apple This is a book

The teacher holds up the card and pronounces each word clearly. Then the teacher says, "This is an apple", and the children repeat after him. The sentence is repeated several times with correct pronunciation. This repetitions and drill are very essential for the slow learners to make faster learning. Again this method makes use of visual effect and so retention aspect is properly taken care of. The children learn the sentences orally. After thorough drilling, the teacher takes up the individual words. The teacher points out each word individually and teaches the children to read the words. The children repeat and learn the individual words. In this way a large number of short sentences are used and the children are taught to read them orally. The children are kept active and interested in the learning process. Teaching reading by this method is natural and it is more effective for slow learners since it makes use of visual effect, repetition and drill which are very essential for slow learner to learn anything for that matter, not to speak of learning to read. It is psychologically sound since sentence is the unit of thought. In this method children experience difficulty in recognition of new words. This defect may be rectified by making use of the phonic method properly.

iv) Phonic Method

In this method, the children utter the sounds of the letters and join the sounds together to pronounce the word (e.g. /k/ /A/ /T/ : (KAT) for the word CAT and so on). The phonic method is also a word method. Here the same sounding words are selected and grouped together as shown below. The words are chosen from the text book. Meaningless words should not be coined merely for the purpose of teaching reading.

cat	way	ring	bell	can	mill	fall
rat	say	sing	tell	pen	hill	hall
sat	may	ding	fell	man	till	ball
mat	day	king	sell	ran	fill	tall

Correct pronunciation is aimed at right from the beginning in this method. But there are some disadvantages inherent in this method. Perfection in correct pronunciation is not always possible with all the teachers. Several words in English language are unphonetic. This method should be cautiously used for slow learners. We have already stressed that readiness is very important at all levels of learning. Readiness for learning word recognition techniques is no exception. Research evidences show that children are unable to profit adequately from phonic training until they have a mental age of seven. Teaching of phonics to children with a mental age of five and a half years is largely a waste of time; and a mental age of seven is needed for the best results (Arthur Smith, 1957; Dolch, E.W. and Bloomster, M. 1937; Tinker, 1952).

Assessing Phonic Readiness

There appears to be a high correlation between phonic readiness and a mechanical reading age of seven. However, the teachers may not know a child's mental age or reading age and will need some practical way of assessing the phonic readiness in classroom. The following abilities which can be observed or tested informally in the classroom will give the teacher the required insight into the phonic readiness of the learners.

i) Is the child able to give the more usual sounds for the common letters?

ii) Can the child discriminate between sounds?

iii) Can the child select the non-rhyming word in a set of rhyming words or can he give a word either spontaneously or from a given choice of words, which rhymes with another word or group of words?

iv) Can the child blend sounds, i.e. letters, phonograms orsyllables? The child who is unable to put the sounds of a simple word together can not make satisfactory phonic progress. Very often slow learners are able to hear individual sounds but they are unable to remember them in sequence and synthesise them into words. Where there is marked deficiency in auditory memory and blending, it is better to ensure that the children learn to blend sounds before they are presented with visual symbols.

Techniques to Teach Phonics to Slow learners

The development and use of phonic knowledge is a vital part of the reading programme and requires good systematic teaching. The followings are some useful techniques to teach phonic to slow learners. When the teacher employs these techniques he can be well assured that his teaching of phonics is reasonably sound and takes its proper place in the reading programme.

(a) New sounds should be introduced in words which are known by sight, or in words included in simple sentences, which help the child to make intelligent guesses from context clues. From these words the child should be encouraged to make a generalisation about the phonogram's sound, e.g. from *man, cat, has,* infer the sound made by the middle letter. He can then be asked to apply this generalisation to words which he can not read but which can reasonably be expected to occur in his spoken vocabulary. References to vocabulary studies is useful in this context. This application should then be consolidated by a variety of interesting written exercises and oral practice.

(b) New learning should be integrated immediately into reading for meaning by using it in passages to be read and understood. In this way the usefulness of the new knowledge and skill is demonstrated to the child.

(c) The teacher should teach only those phonic elements which are likely to be most useful in maintaining reading progress and language development.

(d) Any new words containing phonic elements which the child has not studied earlier should normally be treated as sight words. Throughout, a balance should be maintained between a visual and auditory approach. Phonically irregular words should be introduced gradually.

(e) The teacher should avoid class teaching and cater to individual differences. Every child should be allowed to go ahead at his own rate, the more efficient the teacher is, the bigger will be the spread of attainment.

(f) The teacher should not make use of too many rules.

(g) The teacher should pay keen attention to proper articulation and correct pronunciation, but without over-emphasising individual sounds to the detriment of good blending.

(h) The teacher should not over emphasise the teaching of phonics at the expense of other word recognition techniques, and of reading for meaning.

v) Story Method

This method advocates the reading of a connected passage involving a few sentences in a meaningful way. This is simply an extension of sentence method. In this method great emphasis is laid on the meaning. But this method is more suitable to the children whose mother tongue is English than to the children who study English as a foreign language. This method is not suitable for slow learners at early stage. But at a later stage when they have developed some reading skill his method can be introduced. The story part of this method has a motivational quality of its own. Children are fond of reading stories whether they are normal readers or not. They have their own preferences. When they read a story book of their choice they are prompted to read for a reasonable long time which the slow learners can not do otherwise. The teacher also has to develop basic reading skill in them so that the slow learners become ready to read story book which facilitates rapid reading. If the story book is well illustrated it will be an added quality since it will attract and sustain the interest of the slow learners in reading for a longer time. When we take the slow learners to the library we can observe how with enthusiasm they look for profusely illustrated story books. By giving very small story books to the slow learners for reading at home, the teacher can promote supplementary reading.

vi) Compromise Method

Compromise method makes use of more than one method in a judicious mode of combination. A combination of look and say method and sentence method is desirable and practicable. Phonic method may also be used wherever possible. This method is more suitable for all categories of learners, whether they are normal or backward. When the teacher follows this compromise method he can be sure that his instruction reaches all the students and he can achieve pre-determined behavioural objectives. Moreover, it gives room for variety which can sustain the interest of the students for a reasonable time.

Applying any single method, however best it may be, may become monotonus and the children, especially slow learners, may experience boredom and fatique soon. Further, this compromise method is suitable to develop formal reading in the classroom as well as supplementary reading at home. Even in the classroom during a single period the teacher can make use of all the methods i.e. alphabet method, look and say method, sentence method and phonic method to teach reading to children. At the end of the period he may supply the children with interesting story books of their choice so that they can attempt supplementary reading at home. If not every day, the teacher may try to provide for supplementary reading at every week end. Thus rapid reading can be developed in children at early stage itself.

The Development of Rapid Reading for Comprehension

It is for the sake of convenience only that this topic is dealt with separately. But it should be remembered that reading for comprehension is an integral part of developmental reading at all stages. During the preliminary stage of building a sight vocabulary, the content must be restricted but ideas built around this content should be expanded and enriched by discussion, direct experience and pictorial illustration. During this stage, when skill in word recognition promotes growth in reading power, a wide variety of interesting, easy, attractively illustrated books is essential. The choice of books should cater to individual interests and reading levels of children. Backward children like slow learners evince particular preference for adventure, mystery, detective and travel stories. Backward girl students seem to prefer adventure stories which centre round family situations, bible stories, fairy tales, and books about domestic animals. Children can often manage books which are a little hard for them if they are really interested. Generally speaking, the range of difficulty should be such that each child has a choice of books which are just below his point of difficulty for word recognition.

One of the objectives of reading programme is to ensure that word recognition, reading for comprehension and spoken vocabularies should develop eventually more or less at the same rate. With slow learners, particular attention should be paid to word meaning, comprehension and development of ideas. Comprehension must be emphasised throughout. This can be done by judicious testing of understanding through oral and written exercises, discussing for content and richness of concept formation, paying particular attention to dictionary exercises and the giving of definitions, and encouraging children to ask question and use suitably graded reference books. The following exercises will be very useful in this regard; choosing antonyms and synonyms, following or completing directions, selecting phrases or sentences in answers to questions, rewriting a given passage in other words, selecting single words for given definitions and vice versa, changing tense, gender, number, comparative and superlative, classifying words according to the qualities, uses or actions they represent, sentence completion and story writing when certain significant words are furnished.

Writing play an important part throughout reading programme. It assists visual discrimination and memory, and the association between visual and auditory patterns. Also, it encourages the child to realise the relationship between reading and writing in communication. It is also of much use in expanding vocabulary and inculcating habits of clear and concise expression.

Spelling

A knowledge of correct spelling is required for easy reading and writing. Wrong spelling often leads to confusion and misunderstanding. This results, sometimes, in serious consequences. A person's entire education itself is judged by his ability to spell correctly. Hence teaching of spelling warrants greater attention from the beginning itself. English spelling has its own peculiarities, difficulties and illogicalities. These confuse slow learners to a great extent. Even Englishmen themselves are dissatisfied with their spelling. Max Muller the great German linguist remarked that "English spelling is a national misfortune to England and an international misfortune to the rest of the word." Many Spelling Reformation Associations were formed and they all strived for the reformation of English spelling. Even G.B. Shaw, the great English playwright of this century left a large sum of money in his will to help the schemes for reformation in English. All these efforts have not yielded fruitful results. The Americans who were dissatisfied with the spelling have taken some liberties and have effected some changes in spelling e.g. color for colour, program for programme etc. But in India we follow the English traditions. So there is a greater need for us to make the best of a bad business and learn the surest and the quickest methods of teaching spelling to our children, as it exists at present.

Difficulties Experienced by Slow Learners in Spelling

Slow learners experience many difficulties in spelling. Some of them are listed below.

(i) Some words with different spelling have same or similar pronunciation. These words confuse the slow learners when they read, listen to and write down in dictation. Some such words are:

here, hear, ear	price, praise, prize,	right, rite, write,	
rain, reign	sun, son	prey, pray	were, wear,
our, hour	vain, vein	ice, eyes	ware, where
meat, meet	soul, sole	week, weak	rise, rice
sea, see	weight, wait	lack, lake	roll, role
stationery, stationary		no, know	

(ii) There are some words with two pronunciation. Due to stress shift or change in tense the pronunciation of these words differs. It poses problem for children in reading. Instead of reading conduct he may read it as 'conduct since he is more familiar with that pronunciation. The following are some words with two pronunciations.

conduct, lead, wind, bow, convict, contest, read

(iii) There are some words in which some letters are silent.

So the slow learners experience difficulty in spelling of these words. Often they get confused. In dictation they miss the silent letter and in reading they often pronounce the silent letter also. It is more true so at early stage. Some such words are listed below.

bomb, balm, realm, honour, condemn, psalm, bird, island, know

(iv) There are some words which have illogical pronunciations. Slow learners find it very difficult to read these words and they get confused in spelling while writing these words. e.g.

colonel, Lieutenant, mischievous, wright

(v) There are some words which have same ending sound but different spellings. So the slow learners get confused whether they should use 'sion' or 'tion', 'cian' in writing. Some such words are:

mission, station, omission, commission, comparison, musician.

Methods of Teaching Spelling

Spelling can be taught quite easily if the teachers are careful and resourceful from the beginning of the course in English. The incidental method and the drill method are the widely used methods in teaching spelling at early stage.

i) Incidental Method

In this method spelling is taught only incidentally. No separate time is set apart for teaching spelling. It does not involve drill of any kind. In the classroom teaching the difficult words are brought to the notice of the children as and when they occur. The peculiarities of spelling are explained and the children are instructed to make a note of them and learn them well. Spelling associations are also made. The words with regular spelling are also incidentally dealt with and correlated with similar words already learnt. But this method is suitable for only bright children. This will not be effective for slow learners. The English spelling is difficult and slow learners can not absorb the spelling correctly. So conscious and formal teaching of spelling becomes necessary.

ii) Drill Methods

There are three kinds of drill methods. They are the oral drill, the motor drill and the visual drill. In this method, the need for teaching spelling of the words directly and providing regular practice also is realised and so regular drill is provided.

a) Oral Drill Method

In the past, this was the method widely followed. In this method each letter is pronounced clearly and then the whole word is pronounced. It is repeated several times to fix the spelling in the minds of the children. Suppose we teach spelling of the words Book, Bags etc, the children will be asked to chant as follows:

bee oh oh kay Book.

be aye gee ess bags.

The children will have to repeat the sound several times to fix the spelling in their minds. There may be an occasional dictation but most of the skill will be carried out only orally. In this method, attempt is made to establish aural oral associations of the letters and their pronunciations. It is suitable for slow learners for they need drill to learn anything for that matter. But this is not a sound method. Spelling is more a matter of eyes than that of the ears. Spelling is more a matter of sight than of sound. So it is very important to make the appeal to the eyes than to the ears. In this method there is no scope for visualisation which is very essential for learning spelling. So we can not deem it a very sound method.

b) Motor Drill Method

In this method, a word is written on the blackboard or a flash card is shown. The children are asked to write the spelling of the word several times on paper. Thereby muscular associations are established. Writing is a slow and thoughtful process. The muscles of the hand help the ear, eye and the muscles and nerves of throat and fix spelling firmly in the minds of children. This is a better method but to write down every word is tedious. To ensure motor drill, exercises such as copy writing, transcribing from the black board or the text book, dictation etc can be effectively made use of.

c) Visual Drill Method

It is also known as look-say-write method. In the early stages, look-say-write method is the best method to teach spelling. It is very suitable for slow learners since they need visual effect in their learning process for better learning. It involves a very simple procedure. A word or a short sentence is written on the black board or a flash card is shown to the children. The children look at the sentence they say the word or the sentence orally. Then they write in their note books. There is multi-appeal to the eye, ear and hand in this method. So the triple bond helps to fix the spelling easily and firmly in their minds. In the higher stages also this method is the best. As mentioned earlier, copy writing, transcription, dictation and composition exercises can be effectively made use of for acquiring correct spelling. Visual drill can be practised by using flash cards, or by using teacher's model handwriting on the blackboard or by using spelling games. The MELT programme suggests a regular daily practice for two minutes to teach spelling on these lines. Six words are taken at a time and they are fixed scientifically.

It is important to begin systematic teaching of spelling with the teaching of word recognition skills i.e. phonic and structural analysis. There is no doubt that spelling weakness is a common complaint with slow learners. There may be many causes for this weakness but the principal one is inefficient teaching, e.g. too many words to be learnt at a time, too much attention to rules; insufficient attention to individualisation or group work, which results in a failure to provide for the wide range of attainments and abilities in a class, not enough revision, particularly of words of persistent difficulty; lack of understanding on the teacher's part of what spellings involves and failure to give the child a definite technique for learning words.

Measures to Teach Spelling to Slow Learners

The learning should make use of several modes of perceiving the word-visual, auditory and kinaesthetic and should utilise the association with meaning. With children who have special difficulty, tracing the word with finger contact should also be used. Tansley and Gulliford have laid down the following measures to teach spelling to slow learners.

(a) The teacher prepares a set of graded assignments, each of not more than 15 words. The words of the set are selected because of their frequency in written usage and are arranged so as to coincide with the words used in word recognition, and to maintain a balance between phonically regular and irregular words. There should be adequate provision for revisions in these assignments.

(b) The class is given a spelling test and from the results the children are grouped in pairs according to spelling attainment. Each pairs is then given the most appropriate assignment for their level of attainment.

(c) Each child copies out the assignment ready for words study with his partner. The teacher ensures that the assignment has been copied correctly and that each child knows the words and pronounces them as correctly and distinctly as speech development will allow. Each word is then studied. The child looks at the word, says it and tries to memorise its visual form. Without looking again at the word, he tries to write it and then checks his efforts against the correct version. He repeats this procedure until his spelling is correct. When he and his partner have completed the assignment in this way, they test each other by writing the words when asked. Oral recall is not encouraged since spelling is needed principally for writing, and oral production adds an unnecessary difficulty. Moreover, writing the word and saying it at the same time assists visual, auditory and kinaesthetic memory. When the pair are satisfied with their results they are tested by the teacher. When the teacher is also satisfied he can ask the children to write sentences which illustrate the meaning of the words, or to give orally such sentences, or to answer comprehension exercises based on the word meanings. When this is completed, the whole process is repeated with the next assignment.

Reading Problems of Slow Learners

As in the case of mildly disabled readers, the most common

problems of slow learners also involve (1) a slower rate of progress (2) poor comprehension (3) poor sight recognition (4) too rapid careless reading, and (5) poor phonic skills. A brief account of the pattern of each problem and remedial suggestions are listed below. An insight into these problems and remedial measures will give the teacher a better expertise to teach slow learners.

1. An Even (slower) Rate of Progress

Instructional Level	Comprehension	Rate	Word Recognition

This chart shows the problem pattern of some slow learners. These children's instructional and listening comprehension levels are similar. This means that their understanding is the same for material that is read to them as for that which they read to themselves. Word recognition on the list of graded words at instructional level is about 80 percent accurate, and ability to read words in context is slightly higher.

These children seem to be making an even rate of progress across the skills and should profit from a continuation of the developmental programme in a basal series at instructional level. A high interest, low vocabulary series might increase their enjoyment of reading.

2. Poor Comprehension

Instructional Level	Comprehension	Rate	Word Recognition

Some children may evince pattern of problem as shown in the chart. Such children's instructional level is the same as their ability to comprehend material read out loud to them. Their oral and silent reading rates are adequate, but comprehension is poor. Silent comprehension may be lower than oral reading comprehension at the same book level. Word recognition on a list and in context may remain high, but these children are unable to retell the story they have read or to answer questions about it.

Word recognition is a major strength. They read fluently and with average speed. Their remedial needs include group instruction at the instructional level with emphasis on comprehension. Reinforcement should be given for formal reading, beginning with reading to find factual answers. If oral reading results in better comprehension than silent reading it would be appropriate to use records, tapes or other audio materials. It is important to check these children's vocabulary to see if poor understanding of words interferes with comprehension. Besides, the teacher should check the specific kind of comprehension that is causing the difficulty (understanding main ideas, reading for details and so on) and then plan remedial programme appropriately. The teacher should define new words, use concrete materials, and aviod asking children complex comprehension questions at this time. Services of a remedial instructor may also be used to help these children to comprehend ideas in print or to develop vocabulary and oral language skill.

3. Poor Sight Recognition

Instructional Level	Comprehension	Rate	Word Recognition

Some of the slow learners exhibit pattern of problem as shown in the chart. These children read slowly at instructional level, by using phonics and context to attack words. They can comprehend well, but they fail to recognise one of every five words they see. They attempt to sound out every unknown word phonetically and this shows oral reading to a halting, laborious effort. Silent reading seems to be done in the same manner, since rate and comprehension are equal to oral levels and they are observed pointing their fingers and moving their lips as they read. Ability to comprehend material read out to them is at least two years higher than their ability to read to themselves with equal comprehension. When presented with a list of isolated words at instructional level, they may know only about thirty percent of the words by sight. They try to sound out words, and they are sometimes successful with those words which are phonetically regular, but they miss all others.

These students have knowledge of letter sounds for consonants and short vowels as a major strength. Ability to use context clues may also be good, as is comprehension. The major remedy that they need at this time is development of rapid word recognition skill to increase sight vocabulary. These children should be given much practice with reinforcement for increase in speed of recognition. The teacher can include Dolch words and common patterns for long vowels in words for rapid recognition. The teacher should encourage them to reread selections rapidly trying to increase their fluency. The teacher should not encourage them to sound out words at this time.

4. Too Rapid Careless Reading

Instructional Level	Comprehension	Rate	Word Recognition

Some slow learners disclose problem pattern as shown in the chart. These students instructional level is slightly lower than their listening comprehension level. Oral reading is rapid and smooth but it may be marked by many substitutions. Their reading rate is far above average. Their style of oral paragraph reading is one of hurrifying, calling, words anything that resembles them in beginning sound or in general configuration and failing to correct themselves when these words do not make sense in the context of the sentence. They appear more interested in finishing the task than in getting meaning from printed words. Their word recognition from a list of isolated words is also hurried with inattention to details. However, they can recognise words. They may read only 50 percent of the graded words correctly by sight, but they will be able to read another 40 percent correctly when instructed to look at them more carefully.

For these children reading rate and listening comprehension are strengths. Word recognition and word analysis abilities are also present but are not being used properly. The major remedial need for them is to develop ability to read carefully and accurately. Instruction in the use of context clues, using material that give them an immediate check on their answers might also be helpful. Reinforcement for slower, more careful reading for meaning is very much needed. A more thorough study of classroom conditions that are reinforcing rapid, as opposed to careful, reading might also be used. If the reinforcement programme fails, a more complete analysis of their ability to comprehend oral language might also be suggested. These children can receive their reading instruction in the classroom at grade level. The teacher should make every possible effort to slow those children down, and should develop a reinforcement programme to encourage careful reading. If this programme is effective after a month or so, these students should not require any help from the remedial instructor.

5. Poor Phonic Skills

Instructional Level	Comprehension	Rate	Word Recognition

This pattern of problem shown in the chart is found in some slow learners. These children's instructional level is lower than their ability to comprehend material that is read aloud to them. They read at the same rate both silently and orally, and their rate is average for this instructional level Word recognition is their major problem. Word recognition in oral paragraph is marked by hesitations, substitutions, and self-corrections. They often read a word incorrectly, then correct it when the context of the sentence provides clue to them. Most of their substitutions make sense in the sentence, and all of them are real words. They make many more errors on the isolated word list than on the paragraphs. If they do not know a word by sight, they are unable to read it correctly even when given unlimited time. Their errors on the list are frequently substitutions of words that begin with the same consonant, but have different vowel sounds and / or word endings. These children's strengths are their comprehension of language and their ability to use context in reading.

Remedial programme for these children should focus on giving them the ability to use structural and phonetic clues for attacking unknown words. The teacher should take effort to pinpoint exactly which sounds and symbols are unknown to them. These students require daily focussed skill based instruction in reading.

Speech and Language Problem

The acquisition of speech and language in normal children follows a general developmental sequence (Bloom and Lahey, 1978). Many exceptional students, however, exhibit speech problems and language difficulties concurrently with other handicapping conditions. The speech and language problems are usually not severe enough to warrant labelling the student aphasic, but they do have a great effect on the student's social acceptance and academic success (Traver and Ellsworth, 1981).

The process of language and its interrelationship with speech can be illustrated by the analysing of three types of language. Receptive language is the process of receiving and understanding a spoken message. Inner language is the integration of the spoken message with past experiences and the meaningful association of the idea with other bits of information. Expressive language is the process of recalling words or sounds previously mastered and using them to transmit a message (Culatta, Page and Culatta, 1981; Glass, Christiansen and Christiansen, 1982). Speech is the mechanism by which expressive language is conveyed.

Patterns of Speech or Language Problem

The regular classroom teacher is usually the first person to detect speech and language problems. By virtue of his position, observation and frequent interaction the class teacher can easily detect the problems and he can guess the probable causes also. Receptive language problems are most commonly indicated by difficulty in following directions or understanding verbal explanations. If a receptive language deficit is inherent in a slow learner he will manifest the following signs.

i) He will understand verbal statements only when they are accompanied by gestures and repetitions of the message.

ii) He does not change facial expressions during conversation or maintain eye contact for the duration of a message.

iii) He begins to respond to a direction before it is completed or waits an unusually long time to respond.

iv) He refuses to comply to a request and does not appear to have understood what was asked.

v) He does not demonstrate the ability to follow new directions that differ from previous actions.

vi) He has difficulty in completing worksheets or tasks when the directions are verbally presented (adapted from Culatta, Page and Culatta, 1981).

An expressive language deficit is evidenced by a student who has trouble in verbally expressing thoughts. When the slow learner has expressive language deficit, he evinces the following problem patterns.

i) He quickly becomes frustrated when he is not able to find the desired words to express an idea.

ii) He uses gestures instead of words.

iii) He experiences difficulty in incorporating several ideas into one sentence.

iv) He uses a small vocabulary instead of varying words, and makes grammatical errors in an inconsistent pattern.

v) He often pauses to try to recall words or makes associations such as "The thing that looks like a . . . ." instead of using particular words (adapted from Culatta, Page and Culatta, 1981).

Problems with content of oral language are demonstrated by the in appropriate use of words. Students with form difficulties use incorrect word order in their communication. Usage deficits are evidenced by frequently making statements that are not appropriate for the particular context.

Remediating Oral Language Problems

The speech and language assessment will yield information on the type of problem the slow learner has e.g. articulation difficulties, receptive language deficits, semantic problems etc. Before developing a oral language programme for the slow learners the teacher should first ensure that a positive and conducive classroom climate is present. The atmosphere of the classroom should be such that it should encourage slow learners to share ideas about their experiences and what they are learning. The teacher should be supportive of verbal expressions and he should encourage the children to communicate. The teacher should not correct the grammatical mistakes continually. If he does so, the slow learners will become reluctant to express their ideas. When the students commit mistakes, the teacher should model correct grammar by just rephrasing what the students say.

A second step is to set aside time in the day for oral language activities. Many teachers feel that school time should be spent on academics such as reading and mathematics and not on talking. Most of the slow learners do not get many opportunities for oral expression nor do they have any good models in their home environments. If any progress is to be made it must be programmed into school setting. Brief time blocks during the day can be set aside for thought sharing sessions, in order to get the slow learners comfortable with communicating their ideas verbally. These sessions can be structured around a particular topic such as a school event, or they can be open for student input. Certain ground rules should be established to guide the sessions so that they do not get out of control or become dominated by one or two students. The following are such rules that the teacher should observe in his remediation.

i) One student can talk for three minutes.

ii) When someone is talking, there should be no interruptions.

iii) Questions may be asked after the student completes his talking.

iv) No student should be allowed to criticise another student.

Two other elements which are important in designing a remediation programme are teacher behaviours and classroom organisational patterns that can facilitate oral expression. Cohen and Plaskon (1980) cited the following questions a teacher should ask about the classroom.

i) How can I adapt the classroom environment to promote oral language?

ii) How sensitive am I to my own "teacher talk", both the verbal and non verbal characteristics of my actions?

iii) How able am I to cope with disabilities and to improve the speech of the students?

iv) What kind of opportunities and stimuli do I provide

that encourage communication encounters among children in the class?

There are five general principles which the teacher should keep in mind in developing a classroom programme for expressive language.

1. The teacher should model appropriate speech and language.
2. Oral language activities should be regular part of the school day. Oral expression should be taught system-atically instead of only as a by-product of another subject area (e.g. social studies discussion) or left completely unstructured.
3. The teacher and peers should reinforce the progress in the quantity and quality of a slow learner's verbal attempts at communication and interaction.
4. Students should be encouraged to realise the value of oral communication through role playing sample social interactions (e.g.requesting information on an upcoming event, exchanging a defective product)
5. Whenever possible, individual needs and goals should be recognised and programmed for in the classroom.

Remedial Techniques

The quality (Content, form and use) and quantity of oral expression can be targeted separately or in combination. Quality elements such as vocabulary and syntax can be programmed in a sequential skill based approach (Nelson, 1979). This approach is very useful for slow learners. The teacher should design an activity to demonstrate a particular function of language. Oral language includes providing for interaction, reporting an event, giving directions, conveying an evaluation, giving or receiving information, and facilitating dramatisation of a story. These functions are similar to those discussed by Halliday (1973) and Bereiter and Englemann (1966). Some activities that can be designed to exemplify these functions are given below and such many additional ones can be developed by the teacher.

i) Technique to Promote Interaction

Interactive oral expression involves communicating ideas between two or more persons as in discussion on a particular topic, a debate, a panel discussion on an issue, or a general conversation in person or on the telephone. To promote this oral skill, the teacher should divide the students into two groups and have theme present the pros and cons of a proposal or programme related to school or society. The theme of the topic should be within the experience level of the students.

Technique to Promote Reporting

Reporting involves transmitting a message or theme, as in making an announcement about a specific event or describing something that has taken place. Reporting is done by one individual to another and does not involve interaction between the speaker and listener exemplified by the interactive function. To promote reporting skill, the teacher should allow students to select jobs within the school, such as writer, book keeper, games secretary, scout master, gardener, lab assistant etc. The teacher should arrange for students to observe the persons in these jobs for ten minutes or so. Then they should report back to their classmates on what they observed and what they believe to be the major responsibilities of those persons. Whenever there is function in the school, such as school day, sports day, an organised debate or guest lecture or cultural show the students may be instructed to make a reporting on these events.

ii) Technique to Exemplify Directional Functions

Directional functions include providing verbal instructions to another person on how to complete a task or reach a goal. Directional activities should focus on providing explanations, demonstrating how to do a certain assignment, or setting up a particular structure such as a meeting. To promote skill in directional functions the teacher should have the student select a favourite task such as making an ice cream sundae on preparing butter milk. The teacher may ask one student to explain to another student how to obtain community certificate or income certificate from the local revenue officer. The teacher may ask yet another student to direct other student how to pay electricity bill or how to lodge complaint in EB office.

iv) Technique to Promote Evaluative Function

Evaluating functions comprise those in which some type of qualitative judgement is conveyed to the listener. The speaker must be able not only to describe what is being evaluated, but also to point out the good and bad aspects. Evaluative activities can include such typical classroom assignments as reviews of books and critiques of special programmes. To promote skill in evaluative functions the teacher can bring in magazines that contain advertisements for a variety of products. The teacher can instruct each of the students to select an advertisement, describe it and tell why it would or would not be effective in convincing them to try a particular product. The teacher may also ask the students to comment on the quality of additional learning materials supplied to them or to comment on the effectiveness of the AV aids used in the classroom.

Technique to Amplify Informational Activities

Informational activities include too-way communications such as interview and those in which one person is responsible for providing relevant data to another person as in interactions. The main resposes of informational activities are to gather data by asking questions and then transmit the information to someone else. To promote this skill in students the teacher can ask the students to interview someone in another class to find out that person's favourite hobby or sport. The teacher should instruct the students to prepare an introduction of that person to present to their classmates.

Techniques to Develop Skill in Dramatisation

Dramatisation involves acting out of an event or interchange that has been written (e.g., a play or a story) or observed (e.g., a television programme). The students need not develop their own ways of expressing themselves; instead, they can interpret a character's emotions or imitate what they have seen.

To boost up their skill in dramatisation, the teacher can ask the students to act out a scene from a favourite movie, story or television programme. This will not only develop their oral language skill but also it will bring to light the latent artistic skill, if any. Desire to manifest their latent artistic talent may sometimes serve as an impetus to develop oral language skill.

These activities should be adapted to meet age and grade levels of students. These activities further illustrate how oral expression lessons can be designed around communication functions. As mentioned earlier, specific skills can be still targeted within the activities. In all structured oral language activities the students should be directed to use correct grammar and speak in standard English in order to gain experience, especially if they speak a different language or dialect. Students also should be required to monitor their language so that they can evaluate their performance in general and against targeted goals Students in the mainstreaming require supplementary practice on the self evaluation procedure. This can be provided by tape recording oral expression activities and having the students review the tape later. The teacher or a peer can help the students in discussing performance and identifying areas that need additional work. These are just a few ways and means of developing oral language skill. Now we shall pass on to the development of written language skill.

Written Language

Written language is a curriculum area that poses great difficulty for slow learners. Without direct intervention, most of the slow learners may not be able to develop writing skills that are necessary to communicate effectively through written language. Meticulous planning and execution of written language programmes is essential to improve slow learner's writing skills. Written language is far more complex than oral language. Oral language allows the speakers to repeat statements and words without loss of communication power, but written language does not allow for such redundancy. Writers must communicate their thoughts succinctly without undue repetition of ideas and words. Much of what occurs to facilitate effective communication in oral language-intonations, gestures, and continuous audience feed back to monitor the listener's comprehension-is not available in the written mode (Bruce, Collins, Rubin, and Genter, 1977). Written language also requires the learner to be more aware of the specific organisational schemes underlying the composition of sentences, stories, descriptions, comparison-contrast passages, and expository prose (Meyer, 1979). All of these factors combine to make written language a skill that is not only complex, but that must be directly taught if it is to be acquired by the slow learners.

Remedial Programme for Written Language Difficulties

Organisational patterns in written expression need to be elucidated to the slow learners so that they can use these structures to improve their written language performance. Assessment and remediation procedures are very much required for improving students motivation, teaching the mechanics of writing, increasing written productivity, and improving student composition of specific text structures (e.g. stories, description, comparison-contrast, and expository prose). These have been well illustrated by Morsink (1984) as follows.

i) Improving Students Motivation for Written Expression

One of the first considerations in setting up a writing programme is students motivation and attitudes towards writing (Alley and Deshler, 1979; Polloway, Paton and Cohen, 1981). Positive attitude is very essential to writing improvement. Slow learners have serious difficulties in handwriting language, and spelling that obstruct the writing process. For these children writing is an agonising process in which they ponder the spelling of words and struggle with the correct formation of letters. When these frustrating experiences recur year after year, many slow learners try to avoid writing and lose sight of the function of writing as a communicative process. To promote students interest in writing and to allow them to develop creativity and writing fluency, ample opportunities for expressive writing should be provided, and the writing activities should be carefully chosen. Assignments should stimulate the generation of ideas by calling on students prior experiences or personal interests, or by providing motivating topics. Story starters are a useful instructional tool for stimulating students writing efforts. Students with minimal writing skills can dictate stories to teachers, peers, or tape recorders and this will remove the drudgery of writing while contributing much to students' understanding of the writing process

(Hennings and Grant, 1981). Teachers can guide the writing process by providing questions that help students to decide what information to include. A student properly motivated will apply himself with all his mind and with all his strength to the task assigned or undertaken. That is why improving students' motivations occupies the foremost place in the remedial programme for writing skills.

ii) Improving General Writing Mechanics

Deficit in language skills related to the mechanics of writing are among the most common problems of slow learners. These skills include use of specific word classes (nouns, verbs etc), capitalisation, and punctuation conventions. To develop writing mechanics in slow learner, teacher can develop individualised programmes to allow students to progress at their own pace. The programmes might centre on teacher constructed packets, grouped by ability levels rather than taken from a specific text book. (Toye and Phelps, 1981). The packets can be arranged in groups of correlated skills related to particular concepts such as capitalisation, punctuation, suffixes nouns, verbs. The instructional packets designed for these sets of correlated skills can include old workbook pages from grade levels 1 through 8. The packets can also include information pages, which introduce each skill. The information pages should be in primary type, with reading levels of second and third grade. They should feature simple examples and repeated statements of grammatical rules, capitalisation, punctuation, etc., so that they can be used as references as students work through the packets.

The students work should be evaluated once a week, then concepts needed by the students should be reviewed. All mistakes must be corrected, since packets are sequential. After the students have completed a packet there will be an oral one-to-one conference in which the teacher asks questions to ascertain the students' mastery of concepts. If the conference indicates a need for more instruction, the students can be recycled through the packet or alternate activities. The packets can be used to teach any of the specific organisational schemes mentioned earlier. For sample and specimen Morsink (1984) may be perused.

iii) Increasing Written Productivity

Another problem that teachers face in developing programme for reluctant writers is their low level of written output. Slow learners often write the minimum amount necessary to complete assignments. In such cases, writing productivity is the major objective of the writing programme. To measure students productivity the teacher must collect several written samples. These samples should be analysed to determine students' level of productivity. Production deficiencies constitute perhaps the easiest written language subskill area to remediate. One basic intervention strategy is to tell students to increase their use of deficient target structure (Kraetsch 1981). Although telling students to increase the number of sentences they write in their stories is a simple strategy, it will not work if students lack a basic understanding of the target structure. Whenever teachers target specific subskill areas for instruction, scope and sequence charts should be consulted to ensure that a thorough instructional sequence is adhered to.

iv) Improving Compositions

Although the quantity of students' writing may affect students' writing performance, another major source of writing difficulty involves the construction of compositions based on organisational patterns. To improve skill in composition the teacher has to use many patterns such as story structure, comparison-contrast, and expository text. In the story writing stage students are expected to use story structure in their written compositions. To develop this skill the teacher must provide a story guide(hints) to develop into a story. As Yatvin (1981) and Gratiam (1982) have suggested, such outlines give shape to ideas, determine what information to include, and transform loosely related ideas into an organised net work of information. When this type of exercises are frequently given to slow learners they are able to compose story on the basis of the story guide (hints) provided which in course of time develops in him composition skill and creative thinking. After giving story guide or hints the teacher should provide direct instruction on transforming ideas into well written stories. Finally, teachers need to show students how to improve story writing through revision and editing. In the long run the teacher should reduce students' reliance on story guides so that the composition and revision processes become internalised.

Although story structure is one type of organisation schemes, other writing schemes are available for different writing purposes. These schemes include description, comparison-contrast, and expository text.

Description involves an object's event's or person's attributes, sensory characteristics, function, or location. Since description underlies all forms of writing, mastery of its structure is essential. Students description skills can be assessed by giving students stimulus pictures and asking them to describe the events or objects in the pictures. A critical scrutiny of students' description of stimulus pictures will enable the teacher to assess how much skill they possess and whether they need instructional intervention. Hennings and Grant (1981) recommend attributes guides as one technique to make the writer aware of the relevant dimensions of some article or event. As with story guides, these frameworks provide the basis of an outline that can subsequently guide students' writing. Attribute guides can be changed by providing different attribute categories and articles to be described. For added transfer of writing in specific subject areas, attribute guides can be made specific to such content as science or history.

Comparison - contrast passages have much in common with description. However, it is more difficult than description because writers must consider the essential features of several objects or events in parallel. Two or more things are compared and contrasted in terms of their respective colours, sizes, shapes, textures, sounds, tastes, smells, or affective characteristics. To teach and develop comparison-contrast schemes the teacher should build on students' already developed understanding of the description schemes. The attribute guide can be slightly modified to illustralte the importance of specific attributes in the planning and composition stages. Even if the students are able to use such guides successfully in the planning stage, the teacher should see whether they will be able to transform them into acceptable compositions. Often direct instruction and modelling are necessary to complete the composition process. With comparison-contrast structures two alternative formats may be demonstrated compositions in which two or more things to be compared or contrasted are presented in separate and sequential paragraphs, and compositions in which the specific attributes of two or more things are presented and contrasted point by point. These formats can be modelled through a group composition process or through teacher modelling of the desired features. Public posting of comparison-contrast passages also can help students by providing permanent model of the desired finished product.

A final type of written structure involves expository writing. Expository writing is writing for the purpose of providing information. It requires a lot of planning and organisation since expository paragraphs must not only present the reader with a topic, but then substantiate it with supporting details. One helpful way of introducing expository structures to students is known as statement-pie (Englert and Lichter, 1982; Hanau, 1974).

Proof

Information

Examples.

Statement-pie teaches students to start paragraphs in an organised way beginning with the statement or main idea. Research supports the notion that written passages appear better organised and more comprehensible to readers if they start with a main idea or topic statement. Statement-pie reinforces that notion in clearly understandable language. Discrimination and categorisation of statements and pies can also improve students' acquisition of statement-pie concepts. Expository text also can provide practice in differentiating statement pie information in the context of expository prose. Once students are skilled in recognising statements and pies, they are ready to begin constructing written compositions using the statement-pie techniques. To transform the statement-pie outline into a composition, teachers should inform students that each individual statement with its set of related pies comprises a separate paragraph. Pies are transformed into complete sentences using part of the statement as a stem for the sentence (Englert and Lichter, 1982).

Summary

Children's ability to express themselves orally and to comprehend what is said to them is very important. In school itself, language is fundamental to much that we do. But slow learners do not have sufficient language development at school stage. Their primary difficulty is delayed development or disability in the comprehension and use of language. There are four vital factors such as poor background of speech and language at home, a limited background of experience, emotional and social factors and the limitations of slow learner's thinking which cause poor language development in slow learners. A proper understanding of these factors will enable the teacher to decide what factors to be taken into account in providing the conditions in school for improvement.

The importance of reading readiness, importance of good teacher child relationship and importance of motivation are the basic principles of teaching reading to slow learners. The teacher has to assess certain vital factors such as mental maturity, background of experience, specific abilities, personal characteristics, and health which influence reading before he decides upon any relevant strategy to teach reading to slow learners. Developing reading readiness largely depends on the quality of the relationship that the teacher has with the child. Learning failure is very often the resultant product of poor motivation. Children taught by a teacher who is adept at motivating children in a sensible and individualised way will always learn more quickly and better, even if the method used by him is faulty.

There are various methods such as alphabet method, look and say method, sentence method, phonic method, story method and compromise method to teach reading to slow learners. Applying any single method, however best it may be, may become monotonous and the children especially slow learners may experience boredom and fatigue soon. So the teacher has to use various methods, with possible visual effects, in a judicious mode of combination to teach reading to slow learners.

A knowledge of correct spelling is required for easy reading and writing. English spelling has its own peculiarities, difficulties and illogicalities. Spelling can be taught quite easily if the teachers are careful and resourceful from the beginning of the course in English. The incidental method and the drill method are the widely used methods in teaching spelling at early stage.

The most common reading problems of slow learners include a slower rate of progress, poor comprehension, poor sight recognition, too rapid careless reading, and poor phonic skills. The teacher has to design remedial programmes to overcome each of these difficulties.

Many exceptional children exhibit speech problems and language difficulties concurrently with other handicapping conditions. ·The classroom teachers is usually the first person to detect speech and language problems. To promote speech and language development the teacher should first ensure that a positive and conducive classroom climate is present. A second step is to set aside time in the day for oral language activities.

Written language is a curriculum area that poses great difficulty for slow learners. Without direct intervention, most of the slow learners may not be able to develop writing skills that are necessary to communicate effectively through written language. Organisational patterns in written expression need to be elucidated to slow learners so that they can use these structures to improve their written language performance. Assessment and remediation procedures are very much required for improving students' motivation, teaching the mechanics of writing, increasing written productivity and improving student composition of specific text structures (e.g. stories, description, comparison-contrast, and expository prose).

REFERENCE

Alley, G., and Destiler, D. (1979) 'Teaching the Learning Disabled Adolescent : Strategies and Methods'. Love, Denver.

Arthur Smith, B.(1957) 'What Research Says About Phonic Instruction'. *J. Ed. Res.*, 51.

Bereiter, C., and Englemann, S. (1966) 'Teaching Disadvantaged Children in the Preschool'. Prentice Hall, Englewood Cliffs, N.J.

Birch, H., and Belmont, L.(1964) 'Auditory Visual Integration in Normal and Retarded Readers'. *American Journal of Orthopsychiatry*, 34, 852-861.

Bloom, L., and Latiey M(1978) 'Language Development and Language Disorders'. John Wiley and Sons, New York.

Culatta, B., Page, J., and Culatta, R. (1981) 'Improving Language Functioning: A Manual for Language Clinicians and Teachers Working in Regular Educational Settings'. Dean's Grant Project, University of Kentucky.

Deverensky, J.(1977) 'Cross Model Functioning and Reading Achievement'. *Journal of Reading Behaviour*, 9, 233-251.

Dolch, E.W. (1951) 'Psychology and Teaching of Reading'. Garrard.

Dolch, E.W., and Bloomster, M. 'Phonic Readiness'. *Elem. School Journal*, Vol. 38.

Englert, C.S., and Lichter, A. (1982) 'Using Statement-pie to Teach Reading and Writing Skills'. *Teaching Exceptional Children,* 14(5), 164-170.

Fernald, G. (1943) 'Remedial Techniques in Basic School Subjects'. World Book Co.

Glass, R.M., and Christiansen, J.L. (1982) 'Teaching Exceptional Students in the Regular Classroom'. Little, Brown and Co, Boston.

Gleason, J.B. (1981) 'Code Switching in Children's Language'. In E.M. Hetherington and R.D. Parke (Eds) *Contemporary Reading in Child Psychology,* (2nd Ed) McGraw-Hill, New York.

Gratiam, S. (1982) 'Composition Research and Practice: A Unified Approach'. *Focus on Exceptional Children,* 14(8), 1-16.

Guthrie, J. (1974) 'Identification and Instruction of Children with Reading Disability'. Second Annual Report to the Spencer Foundation, ERIC Document Reproduction Service No.098 516.

Halliday, M.A.K. (1973) 'Explorations in the Functions of Language'. Edward Arnold Publishers, London.

Hanau, L. (1974) 'The Study Game: How to Play and Win with Statement-pie'. Barnes and Noble, New York.

Hennings, D.G., and Grant., B.M. (1981) 'Written Expression in the Language Arts: Ideas and Skills'. Teachers College Press, Columbia University, NY.

Isakson, R., and Miller, J.(1976) 'Sensitivity to Syntactic and Semantic Cues in Good and Poor Comprehenders'. *Journal of Educational Psychology,* 68, 187-192.

Kraetsch., G. (1981) 'The Effects of Oral Instructions on the Expansion of Written Language'. *Learning Disability Quarterly*, 4, 82-90.

Mckenzie, G. (1979) 'Effects of Question and Testlike Events on Achievement and on - task Behaviour in a Classroom Concept Learning Presentation'. *Journal of Educational Research*, 72, 348-350.

Menyuk, P. (1982). 'Language and Development', In C & Kapp and J.B. Krakow (Eds) *The Child: Development in a Social Context*, 282-331.

Meyer, B.J.E. (1979) 'Research on Prose Comprehension : Application for Composition Teachers'. Paper Presented at the Annual Meeting of the Conference on College Composition and Communication, ERIC Document Reproduction Service.

Morsink, C.V. (1984) 'Teaching Special Needs Children in Regular Classrooms'. Little Brown and Co., Boston.

Nelson, N.W. (1979) 'Planning Individualised Speech and Language Intervention Programmes'. Tucson, ARIZ.

Polloway, E.A., Patton, J.R., and Cohen, S.B. (1981) 'Written Language for Mildly Handicapped Students'. *Focus on Exceptional Children* 14(3) 1-16.

Schickendanz, J.A. (1982) 'The Acquisition of Written Language in Young Children'. In B. Spodek (Ed) *Handbook of Research in Early Childhood Education*, pp 242-263, Free Press, New York

Schickendanz, J.A., Schickendanz, D.L., and Forsyth, P.D. (1982) 'Towards understanding Children'. Little, Brown and Co, Boston.

Slavin, R.E. (1986) 'Educational Psychology: Theory into Practice'. Prentice Hall, New Delhi.

Tansley, A.E., and Gulliford. R. (1962) 'The Education of Slow Learning Children' Routledge and Kegan Paul Ltd, London.

Tinker, M. (1952) "Teaching Elementary Reading'. Appleton-Century-Crofts.

Toye, G., and Phelps, P. (1981) 'Individualised Language'. In C. Morsink (Ed) Mainstreaming: Making It work in Your Classroom., Dean's Grant, University of Kentucky, Lexington, KUY.

Vogel, S. (1974) 'Syntactic Abilities in Normal and Dyslexic Children'. University Park Press, Baltimore.

Ward, C. (1977) 'Variables Influencing Auditory Visual Integration in Normal and Retarded Children'. *Journal of Reading Behaviours,* 9, 290-295.

Wepman, J. (1960) 'Auditory Discrimination Speech and Reading'. *Elementary School Journal,* 60, 325-333.

Wiig, G., and Semel. E. (1976) 'Language Disabilities in Children and Adolescents'. Merill, Columbus, Ohio.

Wolfgang, D.C., and Sanders, S. (1981) 'Defending Young Children's Play as the Ladder to Literacy'. *Theory into Practice,* 20, 116-120.

Yatvin, J.A. (1981) 'A Functional Writing Programme For the Middle Grades'. In S.m. Haley James ed, *Perspectives on Writing in Grades,* 1-8, National Council for Teachers of English, Urbana ill

7 Teaching Mathematics to Slow Learners

Chapter Outline

Chapter Objectives

This chapter highlights the modus oper-andi of teachings mathematics to slow learners. After going through this chapter should be able to:

- Understand the basic principles of teaching number to slow learners.
- List out causes of poor arithmetical ability of slow learners.
- Devise exercises to develop cardinal and ordinal relationships.
- Design a teaching programme to teach slow learners.
- Enumerate the factors that influence learning mathematics.
- Individualise mathematics instrucation for slow learners.

Mathematics disabilities in students with normal mental ability have been recognised since early in the twentieth century, but they have never received the degree of attention that reading disabilities have received. Various authors whose works provided suggestions relative to mathematic disabilities were primarily concerned with students considered to be brain injured. It is Johnson and Mykle Bust (1967) for the first time provided specific educational suggestions for normal students with mathematic problems without emphasing the characteristics of brain injury. Since that time, various authors have provided a section or chapter on the types of arithmetic or mathematics problems' the backward children may experience and how to teach arithmetic skills. However, despite the increased attention given to mathematics during this brief time span, Cawley (1981) noted "that information is so sparse in this area that there is not enough of a history to generate issues and controversies. The virtues and values of one intervention approach versus another are virtually unknown" (pp. 89-90).

In many respects, Cawley is right. We are in a state of infancy regarding how to most effectively teach learning disabled students whose disability is manifested in the area of mathematics but these backward students such as learning disabled, slow learners are with us now and will not wait until we have completed all required research. In this chapter the ideas and teaching suggestions of various authorities who have attempted to provide guidance are outlined. They are discussed in two parts as teaching number to younger slow learners (stds 1 to 3) and teaching mathematics to older slow learners in classes 4 to 10.

Part - A. The Teaching of Numbers to Younger Slow Learners

Most experienced teachers of slow learners feel happy about the methods of teaching reading but they are not so sure of the best way of going about the teaching of arithmetic. Recent developments in the theory and practice of number teaching, notably tne discoveries of Piaget have provided the basis for rethinking the approach to the teaching of number with slow learners. A brief discussion is made in this part of this chapter to show how these new ideas can be incorporated into a number scheme. Number is concerned with the quantitative relationships within and between groups, and the number system is designed to help us put order into the numerical situations we meet in our everyday environment. Arithmetic is a way of thinking about and using number. Arithmetic teaching is therefore concerned with the application of the number system to the arrangement, manipulation and measurement of quantities and the development of the ability to deal with number relationships symbolically and by abstraction, i.e. in the absence of concrete objects.

Principles of Teaching Number

Certain principles are fundamental to number teaching. A thorough knowledge of these principles is very essential for teacher teaching number to the slow learners to modify or design his instructional programme. Important principles are:

i) Importance of Number Readiness

ii) Importance of Number relationships

iii) Decimal Nature and Inter-relatedness.

i) Importance of Number Readiness

Cruickshank and others (1961) have noted that number concepts are rooted in accurate perception of objects in space and until the child is able to perceive form, he can not go on with arithmetic. Because of hyperactivity distractibility, and perseveration, the number experiences that normal children have in abundance lose their significance for slow learners (Kaliski, 1967). It is therefore very necessary to understand how the child's ideas of quantity develop and to study the stages in the process. A child should have developed an understanding of simple groupings such as those to ten to pass on to more complex groupings needed for an understanding of the decimal nature of the number systems. When can the teacher expect the child to have developed this understanding? An appreciation of the importance of number readiness is fundamental to sound arithmetic teaching. Piaget and his disciples have done some works of supreme importance in this regard. Implications of Piaget's findings in the slow learner's development of number concepts are to be discussed. The teacher should ensure that the child has the prerequisite number readiness before any number concept is taught to him.

ii) Importance of Number Relationships

Arithmetic teaching should be designed in such a way that it should make apparent to the child the importance of number relationships from the beginning. This requires on the part of the teacher an awareness of the importance of equipping the child with an adequate meaningful number vocabulary with which to express and encourage the development of numerical ideas. It also emphasises the close consideration which must be given to the teaching materials used. Just surrounding the child with varied attractive objects to count and arrange, with shops, post office and the like is not sufficient. It is to be noted that number relationships are not necessarily learned from number situations posed in a school setting. But appreciation of these relationships is very essential for the successful application of number to social situations. It is always desirable to provide, as soon as children have begun to acquire simple concepts, many challenging practical experiences, since these do give ample opportunities, with wise teacher direction, for the expression and use of quantitative relationships.

iii) Decimal Nature and Inter-relatedness

The teacher should understand the decimal nature of the number system and the inter-relatedness of processes. He should devise his teaching in such systematic and graded manner that it should enable the child to become more and more aware of the quantitative aspects of the environment. A proper understanding of the number system and number operations is essential for the child if meaningful learning is to be achieved.

Causes of Poor Arithmetical Ability

Slow Learners are poor in arithmetical abilities. Their learning rate is very low in arithmetic. The extent to which the slow learner is considerably less competent than his age mates or peers is a major factor in his inability to learn arithmetic. There are two chief factors which are responsible for the poor performance of slow learners in arithmetic. They are:

i) Cognitive Factor

ii) Home Environment

i) Cognitive Factor

Slow learners have limited cognitive abilities. They are slow to see relationships, particularly when they are expressed in symbolic rather than concrete ways. Moreover they have additional difficulty in making the transfer of knowledge to practical situations in money, time and measurement. Due to this difficulty, they have a tendency to use fingers and counters as props for a long time and lack the confidence, even when they are ready, to dispense with them. Reisman and Kauffman (1980) remark that generic factors influence the learning of mathematics. Their text is addressed to teaching all exceptional students and the major content is applicable to slow learners. Generic factors include cognitive factor. Awareness of these cognitive factors is essential if the teacher is to plan meaningful instruction.

ii) Home Environment

Most of the slow learners are from such environments that do not provide them with opportunities of assimilating the elementary ideas of the number which much younger children from better homes acquire even in their pre school years. Children coming from better class homes have a much larger store of number ideas and experiences than the children from poorer homes. It indicates that the children coming from poor homes are devoid of stimulation and they start school with considerable disadvantages. Their school experiences in number will not be interesting and exciting if the school does not provide remedial treatment from the outset. This is rarely found in schools, since the schools are often quite unaware of the basic principles of number readiness and are therefore too prone to start normal teaching too early. The backwardness of slow learners coming from poor home environment which is further handicapped by limited intellectual capacity ultimately becomes cumulative. Such slow learners lag increasingly behind their peers. Their learning difficulty increases as time goes on. Their attitudes to number lessons become antagonistic orapathetic their work habits deteriorate and in many cases emotional 'blocking' occurs. They become conditioned to the fact that they cannot keep up with their agemates and teachers start regarding such student as a case. At this stage the slow learners become neglected because the teacher is not able to find time to help them.

Salient Features of Teaching Number to Slow Learners

Any instructional strategy devised to circumvent the learning difficulties of slow learners in arithmetic must take into consideration the preceding generalisations. This also should for the basis form planning the arithmetic curriculum and for selecting appropriate teaching method. A teacher teaching slow learners should bear in mind to incorporate the following salient features in his instructional approaches.

1. The substance and method of our teaching must be related to the child's individual psychological, educational and social needs. Methods should be selected in such a way that it should enable the teacher to capitalise on abilities and minimise (or) correct weaknesses.
2. What he teaches the slow learners must be meaningful and purposeful to them. Only then can the child develop interest for the concept. A good arithmetic teaching does not require any extraneous tricks to make it vital. On the other hand, it must be self motivating.
3. Our methods must be concerned with developing insights into the nature of number system and how it is used in the study of the organisation and arrangement of number groups i.e. quantitative relationships. Most of the slow learners are capable of understanding and applying sufficient of the simpler of these relationships to deal eventually with the necessary arithmetical situations they are likely to meet in the post-school life.
4. Informal diagnosis followed by appropriate treatment is very essential for good arithmetic teaching. This is particularly important in the emotional field since progress will be impossible until earlier bad attitudes and lack of confidence have been replaced by feelings of success, interest and enthusiasm.

What to Teach?

Slow Learners are to be equipped with sufficient mathematical knowledge in order to enable them to cope with the arithmetic they may require after leaving the school. Research evidences show that the arithmetic needed in adult life is not extensive and that nearly all the numerical problems which adults have to tackle are concerned with money and time. Our curriculum for slow learners must therefore concentrate on these aspects and it should be strictly utilitarian. It should not be a watered down version of curriculum used with normal children. The curriculum should be specially designed both in content and arrangement in such a way that it should meet the children's needs. Our teaching methods should also be so designed that the curriculum can be taught with understanding and continuing success. Reisman and Kauffman (1980) advocate differential instruction and emphasise selecting methods and materials that are relevant to the individual learners. The curriculum designed for slow learners should encompass the following activities.

A. Essential Minimum

Level - I
1. Notation and recognition of numbers to 20
2. Number facts to 12 (+, -, x)
3. Money to 1/- making up the amount with 10p and 20p coins.
4. Telling time to hours.

Level - II
1. Notation and recognition to 100
2. Number facts to 20 (+, -, x)
3. Money more than Re1. making up an amount from various coins.
4. Telling time to nearest five minutes.

Level - III
1. Money to 100/-
2. Telling time to minutes.

B. Additional Desirable Content

Level - IV
1. Number facts to 100 - mechanical and problem

2. Money to 1000/- Wages, deductions, personal and family budgeting.
3. Time in social situations, e.g. at work, in travel and leisure, estimation of time.
4. Linear measure - metre centimetre, feet and inches to be applied to home, garden,etc.
5. Weight - Kilograms and grams related to shopping, cooking etc.
6. Capacity - Litres and gallons related to day-to-day life.

Level - V

1. Number facts to 1000 and above excluding compound multiplication and long division.
2. Weight - Tons and Quintals - firewood supply or food grains.
3. Linear measure to l.m.m.
4. Simple banking, hire purchase and use of postal order, money order etc.
5. Simple graphs and their interpretations.

The Importance of Number Readiness

It is a well acknowledged fact that formal teaching of the basic subjects should not be attempted until the child is phychologically ready. Educational literature contains many references to reading readiness but little has been said about readiness for number. The work of Piaget (1952) on the way a child's concept of number develops has important implications for the beginnings of number work. He demonstrated by developmental studies that each child passes through a series of stages in acquiring number ideas. The sequence of each stage is always the same although the length of time taken for each stage differs from child to child. Those who take more time are slow learners. Piaget postulated three stages which he described as pre-operational, intuitive and operational. In the first stage the child is unable to understand the simplest of quantitative relationships and uses crude perceptual approximation in making judgements. He has no idea of what Piaget calls 'Conservation' or the invariability of quantity. At this stage, the child can count by rote in correct sequence but he is unable to appreciate that, say, six balls close together are equal to six balls spaced out, although by simple comparison, he has previously realised that the groups are identical. He is not able to see that six balls remain six balls irrespective of their arrangement. He is perceptually deceived and he is not yet able to analyse logically his numerical experiences. He has little idea of number.

In the second stage, the child is able to appreciate conservation but he is still unable to rationalise what he thinks is right with what he naturally sees. He is still grouping to equate what he suspects is intellectually acceptable with the apparent inconsistency of his perceptions. For example, now the child is able to say that six balls are six balls whether they are close together or separated in groups but he still tends to believe that six balls spaced out are more than six balls close together. When questioned, he will give the correct answers, or answers which suggest correct assumptions, but he will be unable to give acceptable explanations. Piaget calls this the 'intuitive stage'.

In the third stage the child is able to assume constancy however the material is arranged and he can give satisfactory explanations. He now understands what is meant by a quantity and its measurement in units. His thinking is now sufficiently flexible for him to appreciate different arrangements of elements within a given group and the inter-relatedness of arithmetic processes. Now he is able to understand the complementary nature of number combinations, he understands that if $3 + 2 = 5$, then $2 + 3 = 5$, $5 - 2 = 3$ and $5 - 3 = 2$, In short, he is intellectually ready to begin to study logical number with real understanding. In other words, he is said to have acquired number readiness. Piaget and his collaborators explored other areas of the child's thinking in relation to number, e.g. cardinal and ordinal aspects and the relationship between these, the ability to make a series and relate it to other series, and to classify. Teachers of backward students should study Piaget's work in greater detail so that they can devise such instructional strategies that will utilise student strengths to circumvent weak or deficient areas.

Children must be at the operational stage to learn number work. It is true that many children not at operational level are able to count with one-to-one correspondence, and to carry out simple numerical operations even in the abstract. But these are not based on real understanding. They are more the result of memorising than true learning. Or, we can say they are mental habits rather than mental operations. The child is not capable of reversible thinking, e.g. the child may know 5+4 make 9 but he will be unable to manipulate this piece of information to discover that, in consequence, 4+5 also make 9. When we study the development of younger slow learners we can find that children who are fully aware of conservation are capable of reversible thinking - the quantitative relationships within groups and the complementary nature of numerical processes are understood.

If the growth of number readiness follows the pattern so strikingly demonstrated by Piaget, a question naturally arises in our mind whether the teacher can do anything to foster it, or is it purely a matter of maturation. Though the development of number readiness is obviously related to maturation the stages of readiness can be hastened by the teacher by incorporating the following principles in his readiness programme. If the readiness programme is well based on these principles, the stage of readiness can be hastened.

These principles suggested by Tansley and Gulliford are:

i) The teacher must understand how number concepts are developed and, by observing the child's reactions, appreciate how to prepare him for the next stage.

ii) The teacher must provide experiences which will help the child at his level of development to develop ideas of quantity and to appreciate relationships by experiment, estimation and checking.

iii) The teacher must equip the child with the vocabulary of number so that he can express his ideas and use language to fix, integrate and expand them.

The slow learners must be taught the meanings of more same and less, long and short, heavy and light, fast and slow, high and low, first and last beginning, middle and end, before, after and next. This can be done by experiment and discussion and this should be a part of number lessons for several years. It is also important to develop flexible thinking in the use of comparative terms such as longer, shorter, lighter, heavier etc. Whenever the teacher gets an opportunity to point out the use of language in defining relationships in groups, mass length, space or time, he should not fail to make use of it. Children should be encouraged to talk about and discuss their developing number ideas as they arise. Opportunities for this will occur frequently in free play and craft lessons. If the teacher chooses simple materials for use in a readiness programme, he can manipulate this so as to encourage the type of thinking that is necessary for the development of number concepts. It is wrong to assume that surrounding the child with things to count, measure and weigh or providing a wide variety of presentations of number in social situations will entail correct patterns of thought. What is needed is a definite programme of exercises and experiences, posed in play situations when possible, which is so designed and presented that it predisposes the child to make judgements at his levels of development. There are certain exercises which are of great value in the development of number readiness. An insight into these exercises is essential for a teacher to develop number readiness of slow learners.

Exercises Emphasising Constancy or Conservation of Quantities

To programme exercises to emphasise constancy or conservation of quantities materials such as wet sand, clay, plasticine, containers of various sizes, wooden rods and blocks, cardboard strips, home-made weights and scale are required. Then the exercises can be activated as follows.

i) The teacher should make two identical mounds of sand (e.g. sand pies) in order to get a rough indication of the children's level of development. If the children agree that the mounds are the same, the teacher should change the shape of one and ask if the two quantities of sand are still the same. Whatever answers they give, the teacher should ask individual children to tell him the reasons for their answers. The teacher should vary the way in which the shape is changed in order to increase or decrease the difficulty of the exercise, e.g. the mound can be knocked out, spread out evenly, re-formed into one shape or a number of shapes.

ii) The children should be allowed to work in pairs. One of the pair may take a handful of any rough measure of sand. The second child is then asked to take the same amount of sand. The two children then check as follows.

a) By weighing on opposite sides of scales.

b) By weighing both amounts separately using unit weights and pairing the two lines of pies of sand.

c) By making paired lines of sand pies using a plastic cup.

The teacher should remind the children of the purpose of the activity since they tend to forget the purpose in the excitement of the play situations. It is often desirable to engage two children to do these exercises and the remaining children can just watch their performance. In this case the spectators also derive considerable benefit from the mental activity stimulated by the physical activity of the two children doing the exercise. Sometimes the spectators develop a better awareness of the purpose of the exercise than the performers.

The children can use a plastic cup to make sand pies on a play wood board or, on the floor itself. This exercise will be very useful for pairing exercises.

o o o o o o o sand pies	o o o o o o o o o o sand pies
o o o o o o o sand pies	o o o o o o o sand pies

The children can assume "sameness" when two lines are identical. Where inequality exists slow learners should be asked which of the pair has more sand. The term 'less' should be introduced later. When there are equal lines of sand pies one line may be altered and a test for constancy can be made.

Exercises Designed to Develop Cardinal Relationships

These exercises can be designed by using counters, shells, or beads. The same procedure followed in the previous exercise is applicable here also. The child is instructed to take what he considers to be, by rough estimation, the same number as his partner. The children then check by pairing. The child who has more is then asked to make his group the same as his partner's. Again test for the assumption of constancy should be made, e.g. one group can be spread out more than the other and the child is asked to say whether the two groups are still the same.

Using cards with dots placed in a random fashion, three or more for each number from 3 to 9, the children can play the following games.

a) Finding 'pairs' from jumbled cards.
b) Starting with a hand of five cards children complete to find five matching cards from the pack.
c) Teacher makes a pattern with counters, etc., and children seek cards with the same pattern.

Variations in these games are possible. The teacher should encourage children to acquire the ability to estimate since estimation will be important throughout number work. These exercises will ultimately lead to counting with one-to-one correspondence. When counting with one-to-one correspondence becomes operational, cardinal exercises in classroom exercises can be used; for instance, such exercises as: 'Bring enough chocolates so that each boy and girl in your class can have one or two'. 'How many more benches do we need?'

Exercises Designed to Develop Ordinal Relationships

Exercises can be designed to develop ordinal relationships, i.e. the ability to put things in order according to size. These exercises include the following activities.

1. Picking out smallest and largest, or shortest and longest, or lightest or heaviest from groups, beginning with examples where the discrimination is easy. In the classroom situation, the teacher can select the tallest boy and the shortest boy in the class and then he can ask the remaining children who is the tallest

and who is the shortest. The teacher can then select two children of almost same size and thus several children can be put in order of size. The same exercise can be repeated using other materials such as books, trees, rods etc.

2. Placing cards in sequence according to length of lines and size of shapes drawn on them.
3. Placing rods, blocks, cards, balls etc. in order of size or to complete a series.
4. making double series such as dolls with sticks, footballs and players, cars and garages and so on.
5. Making stains with blocks of different sizes.

Other Useful Exercises

The teacher should use graded exercises to ask children to classify objects. Graded exercises are very useful since classification plays an important part in number, e.g. putting all the counters of one type or colour together, all the rods of the same length. For this the teacher can use apparatus which includes sets of cards containing common elements in their patterns, e.g. find the cards with squares or circles, straight or warry lines, dots or crosses. Classification exercises are also included in the language development programme. The teacher can include those exercises which require the children to make or complete from a range of alternatives a given pattern when only a part of it is given. For example, the teacher can give the child a length of cardboard or wood and ask him to select from other lengths two which will make the same length. Alternatively, the teacher can supply one part and ask the child to find the other. In the readiness programme the child can thus use arithmetical processes - putting together and taking apart - and see their inter - relatedness without having the ability to use arithmetical terms, symbols or signs. When these are introduced the child can understand that they are conventions and a form of shorthand which he can use to help him express and manipulate number situations or operations simply, quickly and accurately.

The teacher should arrange these pre-number lessons so that each child gets the opportunity to move with reasonable freedom from one aspect of the programme to the others since the various sections are not mutually exclusive but part of an integrated plan. The teacher should keep suitable records of each child's progress bearing in mind the three stages of development mentioned earlier. The teacher should provide the child with opportunities to experiment and discover, to estimate and check, and eventually to liberate himself from irrational thinking. Throughout the number readiness programme the teacher should encourage discussion and the asking questions. When this number readiness programme is successfully completed the child will be ready to begin a systematic study of number system. His study will now be based on real understanding as on his ability to apply rational thinking to quantitative situations because the child can assume constancy now. He realises that symbols represent quantities which are invariable. He is now able to appreciate the inter relatedness and complementary nature of processes and has elementary ideas of part-whole relationships. Thus after successful completion of number readiness programme, the stage is set for teaching number.

How to Teach?

The teacher has to first ascertain whether the child is ready to start systematic number work. If the child is found ready, the teacher can go ahead with his teaching task. The slow learners take usually long time to develop number readiness. The teacher teaching number to slow learners should bear in mind the following important principles. They are:

1. Utilitarian approach
2. Teaching relationships
3. Facilitating application
4. Introduction of symbols and signs
5. Getting ready
6. Emphasis on mental and oral work
7. Revision and drill
8. Appropriate use of vocabulary

1. *Utilitarian Approach*

The teacher should understand the number system as a logical system. It is for the teacher to decide from the system which parts are going to be uselul as a basis for the development of those certain attainments which the slow learners will be in need of in the affairs of his daily life. In the younger slow learner the teacher should develop ability to deal relationally with groups of up to 20. This will suffice to begin with. The success that he experiences at this stage will influence his further learning in future. It will serve an impetus for learning arithmetic and then mathematics. If the slow learner is taught each number from 1 to 20 and he knows all the additions, subtraction, and multiplication facts within 20 and can apply them to social situations, he is well prepared for the future. He will be able to manage most of his number requirements in future life. Moreover, if the child's number thinking is truly relational at this level of 20, he can certainly make further advancements if time and circumstances permit.

2. *Teaching Relationships*

When a particular number is taught, all facts except division which need not be stressed at this stage and the relationships between them should be taught. The child should be enabled to appreciate the complementary nature of addition and subtraction. He should also understand how a new group is related to those he has already learned. This will give him an understanding of the relationship between cardinal and ordinal number, e.g. when a group has a tenth element it is bigger than a group of five of the same element.

3. *Facilitating Application*

The teacher should provide opportunities to use the number concept learnt in practical, everyday situations. The child must be able to apply the number concepts to practical situations, It serves two purposes. It enables the child to become socially competent and it fixes the particular number concept permanently in his mind. Or, we can say it is stored in his meta memory. For example, when the child has learnt the meaning of six, he should use this knowledge to deal with six rupees, six metres, six hours, six books six of anything for that matter. This is a very important and essential principle. The teacher should provide counters, pencils cubes, or rods and the like to slow learner with which he can study his groups. The teacher should guide his thinking to discover the quantitative relationships. Once the concept is thoroughly learnt by the slow learner, he can apply it to practical situations.

4. Introduction of Symbols and Signs

Number symbols and signs should be introduced only when the child understands the quantities and processes for which they stand. For example, when the child is able to understand that the addition process is simply the putting together of two groups to make another groups equal to the two groups together, then the + sign can be introduced as a shorthand sign for 'putting together'. When he appreciates that if a group is separated into two groups and one group is taken away he is subtracting, the - sign can be introduced. Likewise multiplication should be understood as the putting together of equal parts and when the child understands this the x sign can be introduced. To introduce ÷ sign the child must be able to understand division as the separating out into equal parts.

5. Getting Ready

It is important to note that the development of number readiness does not end when the child is ready to begin formal number work. The child is always getting ready for the next stage in understanding. This is how learning leads to further learning. This 'getting ready' is essentially a process of integrating previous learning to a level that anticipates the new learning that logically follows. For example, in the addition process, a slow learning child needs much practice in the simpler stages. He must have a thorough understanding of the importance of ten and of the use of zero as a place holder before he starts using carrying figures. Similarly, dealing with money also requires similar understanding. This integration takes a long time with slow learners whose understandings develop slowly. So the teacher has to pay a very careful attention to the grading of new situations because it is the quality rather than quantity of the child's thinking that is of real importance. It is the primary duty of the teacher to ensure that the child gets ready for the new learning.

6. *Emphasis on Mental and Oral Work*

Mental and oral work should be emphasised at early stages. The child should be encouraged to check his answers with whatever apparatus the teacher decides to use. When the child is provided with opportunities to check his answer, he has to handle the apparatus given by the teacher and this facilitates concrete learning. Many low-cost aids like counters, dice, beads etc can be used for this purpose. The child's checking his own answer is a kind of self evaluation which enables the child to understand where he is and it facilitates faster and concrete learning.

7. *Revision and Drill*

Slow learner's retention power is poor. They need more revision to fix the concept in their minds. That is why even though due attention has been given to the gradual building of understanding frequent revision is necessary. Drill is an exercise which facilitates the retention of the slow learners. Drill is very essential for slow learners to ensure longer retention. But mechanical drill without proper understanding is not desirable. Drill must always follow understanding and its purpose must be made obvious to the child. In the early stages for teaching the tables revisions and drill can be effectively made use of by the teacher since it will form the base for all future learning.

8. *Appropriate Level of Vocabulary*

It is important that the vocabulary used by the teacher should be appropriate to the reading level of the slow learner. When the teacher introduces the problems, he must ensure that the vocabulary used is at the child's reading level. In the reading programme the basic sight vocabulary of 200 words does not include such words as how, many, altogether, cost, long, what time, away, etc. These must be made clear to the child if the child is to develop independence in understanding number problems.

'B' Teaching Mathematics to Slow Learners

Older slow learners experience difficulty in learning mathematics. There is no provision for detention at primary level. As a result, without adequately developing number readiness and without learning arithmetic properly most of the slow learners proceed to middle school level where such slow learners invariably experience difficulty in learning mathematics.

Mathematics has its roots deep in the soil of everyday life and is basic in our highest technological achievements. We use mathematics when we count the lumps of sugar for our breakfast cup of coffee, build our houses, erect lofty skyscrapers, construct imposing bridges, assemble radios or put together super sonic airplanes. Even though almost every thing of a concrete character is mathematics it is reputed to be and actually is, the most abstract and the most hypothetical of the sciences. Hence, it is but natural that students encounter varied problems in learning mathematics. The worst sufferers in this respect are the slow learners who lack the capability and the skills for abstract thinking and problem solving skill required for learning mathematics. Moreover, the very fact that mathematics is the mother of all sciences emphasises the need to probe into the causes of learning difficulties in methematics and to evolve a special instructional strategy for the slow learners so that they can circumvent their weak or deficient areas and make an adequate learning of mathematics.

Factors Influencing Learning Mathematics

Reisman and Kauffman (1980) in the text *Teaching Mathematics to Children With Special Needs,* speak of 'generic factors' that influence the learning of mathematics. Their text is addressed to teaching all exceptional students and the major content of their text is applicable to slow learners. They group generic factors into four areas. The four areas are:

1. Cognitive factors
2. Psychomotor factors
3. Physical and sensory factors
4. Social and emotional factors

The first second and fourth of these areas apply directly

to students with learning problems and they deserve detailed discussion. In all cases, it is a matter of the degree to which a student who has difficulty in learning mathematics is different or less able than normal students that affects his ability to learn mathematics. A clear perception of how each factor influences learning mathematics is very essential for the teacher to tackle the learning problems of slow learners.

i) Cognitive Factors

Cognitive factor's that influence the learning of mathematics, are manifold. We shall analyse these factors with special reference to slow learners. Rate and amount of learning compared to age peers plays an important role in learning mathematics. Slow learners very much lag behind in learning rate as well as in amount of learning when compared with their age mates. So they are unable to cope with age peers. Their speed of learning related to specific content is also slow. They take much longer time to learn a concept than normal children. Their ability to retain information in memory is also poor. • Mathematics is a subject which requires the learners to keep many things in their memory. But slow learners are very poor in this respect. They need more repetition which is seldom provided in the classroom. When it is rarely done so, other normal children become impatient and it amounts to regardless wasting of their time. Since they don't have adequate verbal skill that also affects their learning mathematics. Their ability to learn arbitrary associations and symbol systems is also poor. Also, they dont have the required ability to form relationships, concepts and generalisations. They are not able to attend to details and differentiate the essential from the non-essential. They find it very difficult to use problem solving strategies. They are very poor in their ability to make meaningful data-based decisions and judgements. They don't have the ability to infer, hypothesise, abstract and cope with complexity. All these cognitive factors affect the slow learners' learning of mathematics.

It is therefore very essential for the teacher to devise such instructional strategy that will utilise student strengths so that weak or deficient areas can be circumvented and more normal learning will be possible. Reisman and Kauffman (1980) advocate differential instruction and emphasise selecting methods and materials that are relevant to the individual learners. Awareness of these factors is essential if the teacher is to plan meaningful instruction.

ii) Psychomotor Factors

Generic factors that affect mathematics learning include inefficiency in the use of psychomotor abilities, including those abilities needed in searching as well as in producing spoken or written responses (Reisman and Kauffman, 1980) The psychomotor factors include visual perceptual disorders, auditory perceptual disorders and rules of general language as applied to mathematics. Poor visual discrimination, figure-ground disorders, form-constancy problem, visual-sequential memory difficulties and spatial relationships problems are some visual perceptual disorders that affect slow learners learning of mathematics. Auditory perceptual disorders that affect slow learners' learning of mathematics include poor auditory discriminations, figure-ground disorders, sound blending difficulty and auditory sequential memory difficulties. Similarly inadequate knowledge of phonologic rules, morphologic rules, syntactic rules and semantic rules also affect the learning of slow learners. As with the cognitive factors, the teacher's role is to determine the extent to which any given student is deficient in these factors and to adjust instructional strategies accordingly.

iii) Social and Emotional Factors

The third general category of factors that affects learning in mathematics and applies directly to students with learning problems like slow learners is that of social and emotional factors. The most important of these factors are hyperactivity, distractibility, impulsivity, aggressiveness withdrawal, immaturity inadequacy and deficiencies in moral development. Since these factors have been dealt with in detail in earlier chapter, no elaboration is made here. A teacher teaching slow learners has to devise such instructional strategies which will be useful to reduce the negative effect of these factors on the slow learners' learning of mathematics to a considerable extent.

Awareness of these three categories of factors that influence learning in mathematics and careful observation and analysis of how students approach mathematics learning can be of assistance in developing practical ideas as to how to modify curriculum and specific instructional strategies to attempt to meet individual needs. Reisman and Kauffman(1980) recognise the need for verified research on teaching mathematics to exceptional children. They state that research dealing with teaching mathematics differently to different types of learners is unresolved for 'normal' and is sparse and unsupported for exceptional children.

Basic Principles of Mathematics Instruction to Slow Learners

Like most other curriculum content area investigations, the research in mathematics education has laid great emphasis on looking for the elusive best method. This research has paved the way for formulation of certain basic principles for the teaching of mathematics, but the work has not led to any statement of the best method, or the characteristics of the best teachers. Two of the basic principles that serve as guides for teaching both normal and backward students are the need for a logically constructed sequence of mathematical content, and the benefits of making use of concrete manipulatives in order to facilitate retention and transfer of concepts and skills learned. In addition to these two, individualisation of instruction is also very effective to slow learners.

i) Content Sequence

Researches have discovered two things about the curricular sequence of mathematics. First, the mathematics to be learned should be logically sequenced, presenting lower-order skills and concepts before proceeding to higher-order, or more complex, skills and concepts. Second, for most math topics, more than one sequence can provide the hierarchy from lower-to higher-order concepts and skills. A learning hierarchy should be developed by considering mathematical structure of the skill to be learned and analysing the sub concepts and skills necessary for reaching this goal. Phillips and Kane (1973) point out that learning mathematics depends on the presentation of such a logically sequenced curriculum. Their work also points out that the sequence from lower to higher order concepts and skills is not unique. They found that of seven sequence they tested, best retention resulted from the sequence that included hierarchical analysis. So the teacher entrusted with the task of teaching slow learners should follow this principle in their mathematics instruction for optimum effectiveness.

ii) Use of Concrete Manipulatives

New strategies on mathematics instruction focus on the student being able to acquire, or see meanings in the mathematics learned. It is a fight against learning by rote. Bruner (1966) provided the principal research base for this approach. Bruner suggested three steps for presentation of mathematical content. First of all, concrete manipulatives that show the students underlying concepts should be used to develop intuitive understanding. Second, the pictures of these manipulatives should be used. to extend the understanding. Last, purely symbolic notation and the accompanying rules should be presented in a way that shows the relationship between the manipulatives and the pictures used and the abstract concept or skill to be learned. Suydam and Higgins (1977) found that in nearly half of the investigations reviewed, students who had learned with the aid of concrete manipulatives had higher achievement than students having no such aids in the development of the mathematical ideas and skills under investigation. The remaining studies typically showed no significant differences between groups using aids and groups not using aids. But rarely did the results of a study favour the group not using manipulatives. The consistency of these findings, over all grade levels, for students of varying ability levels, and for many mathematical concepts and skills, suggests the necessity of concrete manipulatives.

The review of research by Suydam and Higgins further indicated in support of Bruner's suggested sequence that pictorial representations typically lead to greater achievement than does purely symbolic treatment. But instruction employing pictorial representations alone was rarely superior to instruction employing concrete experiences. The basic premise of proponents of the use of manipulatives is that the manipulatives enable children to see the abstractions of mathematics. Recent research evidences confirm that visual perceptions strongly influence a child's ability to conceptualise mathematics. (Grayson, Wheatley, Frankland, Mitchell, and Karaft, 1978). This may be why the research has found strength in the use of concrete manipulatives. It may also explain why greater retention and transfer (application of concepts and skills) occurs when concrete experiences form the basis of mathematics learning (Suydam and Higgins, 1977).

The ability to 'see' mathematics may also be applied to the learning of mathematical content typically considered to be strictly a function of memorisation of the basic facts. Several researches have found particular success in the use of "remembering strategies" for the basic facts (Cifarelli and Grayson, 1979; Davis, 1978; Folsom, 1975; Thornton, 1978). Drill and practice play a vital role in learning mathematics. Drill is very important for slow learners to master mathematical skills. But the drill should come only after a conceptual, or meaningful, level of development has taken place (Davis, 1978; Folsom, 1975; Hazekamp, 1978; Rathmell, 1978). Shuster and Pigge (1965) have established through their research that there are intimate relationships among the time, meaning, and relation in the learning of mathematics. This work suggests that drill and practice should constitute less than half of the time spent in instruction. At least half of the time should be spent on providing meaningful development through concrete manipulatives and pictures.

Several investigators have found that spaced repetition also applies to drill (Davis, 1978; Good and Grouws, 1979; Mathematics Resource Project, 1970). They suggest that frequent short periods of drill spread out over several days are better than longer, concentrated periods of practice. Work by Horowitz (1975) suggests further that practice should begin several days after the skill has been presented meaningfully. Therefore, whether it is a conceptual knowledge or skill acquisition, the research evidences stack up in favour of using manipulatives for providing a foundation for abstract, symbolic mathematical learning.

Individualising Mathematics Instruction For Slow Learners

Individualised approaches for the slow learners focus on two aspects pacing of content coverage, and modality of presentation.

More emphasis is placed on the former than latter. The main reason for the emphasis on pacing is the availability of materials. A critical review of commercially produced individualised materials reveals that most of them individualise with regard to pacing. That is, all the students are supposed to learn the same content, in the same sequence, presented in the same way, but at their own speed.

i) Pacing of Content Coverage

Schoen (1976) reviewed individualised mathematics programme and related research data and found that generally the self-paced programme led to no better mathematical achievement than traditional programmes. Students given self paced materials obviously will be less involved in interaction with their teacher and peers. Self paced work also places greater responsibility on the student for self motivation. A student who is not self motivated may put forth less effort, which leads to less engaged time. It is common sense to say that students learn more if they spend more time on task. This consideration is crucial in the case of slow learners who tend to be easily distracted. This is not to say that pacing is not important. Content pacing is very essential for the slow learners. Content pacing refers to how much mathematics is presented in one day, and how many exercises are assigned. Pacing in terms of when certain concepts and materials should be presented - not how fast a student completes a series of assignments - is very important. For facilitating slow learners' mathematics learning small steps should be taken towards building mathematical concepts. Assignments, too will have to be shortened in order to achieve greater success.

ii) Modes of Presentation

Another aspect of individualisation in mathematics, which is particularly appropriate for slow learners is using different modes of instruction. Researchers stress that rote memorisation of mathematics is not particularly effective for students with mathematics learning problems. Very often the "show and do" method described by Strauss and Letitinen (1947) is the exact method used in self paced materials. Instruction should include the use of concrete manipulative materials as a basis for the abstract (Horowitz, 1975; Johnson and Myklebust, 1967; Schefflin and Seltzer, 1974). Games may be used to motivate the development of abstract number concepts (Orlands, 1969; Ross, 1967). Inductive methods, in which students discover the rules for mathematical operations, can also be helpful (Armstrong, 1969). All these are applicable to normal students as well. Adjustments for the affective dimension take the form of providing greater success. For slow learners higher success levels lead not only to immediate achievement, but to retention and better attitudes as well. This may be one quality of concrete manipulatives that leads to their effectiveness; with the help of concrete manipulatives, students can usually get correct responses.

Procedure For the Classroom Teacher

The classroom teacher can assist the slow learners in mathematics learning in at least three ways:

i) By establishing a whole class routine that allows for individualisation.

ii) By ensuring that the slow learner is placed at the appropriate level within the scope and sequence of skills.

iii) By effectuating minor adaptations in the way instruction is presented.

i) A Routine For Individualisation

It is very important for the teacher to use a routine in order to attend to both the mathematical and psycho-educational strengths and weaknesses of the slow learners. The routine establishes portions of the math instructional time for work on new material, mental skills and remediation, and provides a sense of predictability for the mathematically handicapped students. The portion of this routine which is most critical is the development of new materials. The routine encompasses a text book presentation, a game and a ditto. These three elements serve as the basis for a grouping model which provides various forms of individualisation. When the teacher uses the routine properly he can individualise within the group.

ii) Placing Slow Learners at Appropriate Level in Skill Sequence

It is important to provide students with mathematics instruction for which they have the prerequisite skills to perform at a reasonable level of success. There are several sources where from informations regarding scope and sequence of skills and their prerequisites can be obtained. Continuous Pupil Progress Profile (Fayetle County, 1980) and Developing Mathematical Processes (1979) are such sources. To make certain that the student is placed at the appropriate instructional level within the skill sequence, the teacher can design a probe (mini test) measuring mastery of the skill the student has been just taught. The probe's title pin-points the skill it measures. For example:

Add fractions with like denominators, no reducing

$$\begin{array}{cccc} \frac{1}{5} & \frac{4}{6} & \frac{3}{9} & \frac{2}{7} \\ \\ +\frac{1}{5} & +\frac{2}{6} & +\frac{2}{9} & +\frac{5}{7} \end{array} \quad \text{etc.,}$$

A typical probe would have about twenty stimulus items, and an ideal one would present some of the items more than once. Any probe should be administered three to five days in a row to document mastery. Probes may be timed, and more rapid (correct) responses will also indicate progress. The teachers first decision, then should be to determine whether the student having math difficulty is placed at the appropriate instructional level within the skill sequence as indicated by the mastery of the probe. If a student fails in the probe, the teacher will have to reteach the skill. This is where the additional instructional time advocated by Bloom for backward students becomes useful.

Adaptations in Presentation of Instruction

If a student is in need of reteaching on a skill, the teacher should carefully observe the student's written work and oral responses to instruction, since these deservations may indicate what types of adaptations are necessary. Analysis of the problem should begin at a simple, most obvious level and proceed to the more complex. Adaptations in presentation of instruction can be made by the teacher in three ways. They are:

i) Providing additional Practice

ii) Providing performance cues, and

iii) Using interactive unit.

i) Additional Practice

A slow learner's performance in a computational skill may be inconsistent (sometimes right, sometimes wrong). Such student needs more practice on the skill. Practice should follow understanding of the concept, as indicated by the student's ability to demonstrate it using concrete materials. Practice should be varied and interesting. Whenever possible, practice activities should be self correcting so that the monitoring of practice does not consume the time of the teacher. Additional Practice enhances the understanding and mastery of the concept. At the same time it is important to ensure that the additional practice does not end up in fatigue or boredom.

ii) Performance Cues

Sometimes slow learners know how to perform each of the steps in a mathematical process, but they are unable to remember the order in which to do them. In this case, the teacher can help the students by adding performance cues, such a green dot showing where to start and a red one indicating where to stop.

iii) Using Intractive Unit

The slow learners may have difficulty in math because either the teacher's presentation or the required learner's response is wrong. These two are the parts of interactive unit. Interactive unit describes what the teacher and the learner do in math activities. The teacher may construct or manipulate concrete materials. The teacher may present or show or display. He may explain verbally or graphically symbolise. The learners response may be to construct or manipulate concrete materials. He may identify or point to or show response. He may state verbally or graphically symbolise. For every subskill or instructional objective, it is possible to have sixteen different interactive units. A student who is unable to grasp the concept when the teacher gives a verbal explanation and requires a written response may be able to perform quite well when the interactive unit is construct - construct, or construct-identify. All these three types of adaptations are relatively easy for the teacher to make the provision of more practice, the addition of performance cues, and a modification in the presentation or response format of the interactive unit.

Summary

We are in a state of infancy regarding how to most effectively teach mathematics to backward children like learning disabled, slow learners etc. Despite the increased attention given to mathematics during this century, information is so sparse in this area that there is not enough of a history to generate issues and controversies. The virtues and values of one intervention approach versus another are virtually unknown. Arithmetic is a way of thinking about and using number. Arithmatic teaching is therefore concerned with application of number system to the arrangement, manipulation and measurement of quantities and the development of the ability to deal with number relationships symbolically and by abstraction.

Importance of number readiness, importance of number relationships and decimal nature of the number system and the inter-relatedness of processes are the three principles of teaching number to slow learners. Cognitive factors, and home environment are the chief causes of arithmetic disability.

There are certain exercises which are of great value in the development of number readiness. An insight into these exercises is essential for a teacher to develop number readiness of slow learners. Exercises emphasising constancy or conservation of quantities, exercises designed to develop cordinal relationships, and exercises designed to develop ordinal relationships are some vital exercises which promote number readiness of slow learners.

The teacher teaching number to slow learners should bear in mind the important principles such as ulititarian approach, teaching relationships, facilitating application, introduction of symbols and signs, getting ready, emphasis on mental and oral work, revision and drill, and appropriate use of vocabulary, in teaching number to slow learners.

Older slow learners experience difficulty in learning mathematics. Cognitive factors, psychomotor factors, physical and sensory factors and social and emotional factors are the vital factors that influence learning mathematics. Basic principle of teaching mathematics to slow learners include content sequence, use of concrete manipulatives and individualising mathematics instruction for slow learners.

The classroom teacher can assist the slow learners in mathematics learning by establishing a whole class routine that allows for individualisation, by ensuring that slow learner is placed at the appropriate level within the scope and sequence of skills and by effectuating minor adaptations in the way instruction is presented.

REFERENCE

Armstrong, J.R. (1969) 'The Mathematically Handicapped: A Critical Review of the Related Literature'. The University of Wisconsin, Madison, WIS.

Cawley, J. (1981) 'Commentary: Topics in Learning and Learning Disabilities'. Aspen, Rockville, M.D.

Cifarelli, V.V., and Wheatley, G.H. (1979) 'Formal Thinking Strategies: A Pre-requisite for Learning Basic Concepts'. *Jounal of Research in Mathematics Education,* 10(5), 368 - 370.

Cruickshank, W. and others (1961) 'A Teaching Method For Brain Injured and Hyperactive Children'. Syracuse University Press, Syarcuse, NY.

Davis, E.J. (1978) 'Suggestions for Teaching the Basic Facts of Arithmetic'. In M.N. Suydam and R.E. Reys, eds, *Developing Computational Skills* NCTM Year Book, Reston, Va.

Fayette County (1980) 'Continuous Pupil Progress Profile in Mathematics'. Fayette County Public School, Lexington, KY.

Folsom, M. (1975) 'Operations on Whole Numbers'. In J.N. Payne, ed., *Mathematics Learning in Early Childhood,* 37th NCTM Year book, Reston, Va.

Gearheart, B.R. (1985) 'Learning Disabilities: Educational Strategies'. Times Mirror / Mosby College Publishing, Toronto.

Good, T.L. and Grouws, D.A. (1979) 'The Missouri Mathematics Effectivenss Project: An Experimental Study in Fourth Grade Classrooms' *Journal of Educational Psychology,* 71, 355 - 362

Hazekamp, D.W. (1978) 'Teaching Multiplication and Division Algorithms'. M. Suydam and R. Reys, eds, *Developing Computational Skills*, NCTM Yearbook, Reston, Va.

Horowitz, S. (1975) 'Effects of Amount of Immediate and of Delayed Practice on Retention of Mathematics Rules'. Paper Presented at the Annual Meeting of the American Educational Research Association, Wastington, D.C.

Johnson, D.J., and Mykelbust, H.R. (1967) 'Learning Disabilities: Educational Principles and Practices'. Grune and Stratton, New York.

Kaliski, L.(1967) 'Arithmetic and the Brain Injured Child'. In E. Fierson and W. Brabe (Eds) *Educating Children With Learning Disabilities,* Appleton, Century - Crofts, New York.

Morsink, C.V. (1984) 'Teaching Special Needs Children in Regular Classrooms'. Little, Brown and Co, Boston.

Orlando, C. (1969) 'Remedial Techiniques For use with Educable Mentally Retarded Children with Specific Learning Disabilities'. In J.F. Cawley, (Ed) Brief *Inquiries Concerning Learning Disabilities and Intellectual Variability Among Disadvantaged Children,* University of Connecticut, Storrs Conn.

Phillips, E.R., and Kane, R. (1973) 'Validating Learning Hierarchies For Sequencing Mathematical Tasks in Elementary School Mathematics. *Journal of Research in Mathematics Education,* 4, 141-145.

Piaget, J. (1952) 'The Child's Conception of Number'. Routledge and Kegan Paul, London.

Rathmell, E.C. (1978) 'Using Teaching Strategies to Teach Basic Facts'. In M. Suydam and R. Reys (Eds) *Developing Computational Skills,* NCTM Year book, Reston, Va.

Reisman, F. and Kauffman, S. (1980) 'Teaching Mathematics to Children With Special Needs'. Charles E. Merrill, Columbus, OH.

Ross, D. (1967) 'The use of Games to Facilitate the Learning of Basic Number Concpets in Preschool Educable Mentally Retarded Children'. Office of Education, Bureau of Research, Washington. D.C.

Schefflin, M., and Seltzer, C.. (1974) 'Math Manipulatives for Learning Disabilities'. *Academic Therapy,* 9(5), 357 - 362.

Schoen, H.L. (1976) 'Self-paced Mathematics Instruction: How Effective has It Been? *Arithmetic Teacher*, 23(2) 90 - 96.

Shuster, A.H., and Piggie, F. (1965) 'Retention Efficiency of Meaningful Teaching'. *The Arithmetic Teacher,* 12, 24 - 31.

Suydam, M.N., and Higgins, J.L. (1977) 'Activity Based Learning in Elementary School Mathematics'. Recommendations From Research, NCTM, Reston, Va.

Tansley, A.E., and Gulliford, R. (1962) 'The Education of Slow Learning Children'. Routledge, Kegan Paul Ltd, London.

Thornton, C.A. (1978) 'Emphasising Thinking Strategies in Basic Fact Instruction'. *Journal for Research in Mathematics Education,* 9, 214 - 227.

Teaching of Vocational Education and Physical Education to Slow Learners

Chapter Outline

Chapter Objectives

After reading the chapter on teaching vocational education and physical education to slow learners the readers should be able to:

- Understand the purpose and importance of teaching vocational education to slow learners
- Understand how the teach vocational subjects to slow learners
- Know the role of teacher in teaching vocational education
- Understand the importance of physical education.
- Understand the aims of teaching physical education to slow learners.
- Devise physical education programme for slow learners

Teaching vocational subjects and physical education plays a vital role in the career as well as personality development of slow learners. We should not view work in vocational subjects as something separate but it shall be viewed as a continuation and extension of work done elsewhere in the school. What the child can accomplish in the vocational subjects depends partly on experiences he has had of practical work in various forms in younger age groups. Weaving and tailoring are some subjects which can provide preparatory experience for his future career. Hoyt (1975) defines career education as the totality of experience through which one learns about and prepares to engage in work as a part of his or her way of living. Career education attempts to make education's efforts more meaningful and relevant to the type of preparation individuals will need for living and working successfully in their communities (Brolin and Kakaska, 1979).

One of the major challenges of teaching slow learners is assisting them as they begin to explore career options. Most of them begin seriously to consider their future careers while in high school or higher secondary school. Since they don't experience adequate success in the academic area, it is but natural that they crave for choosing a career for themselves on completion of school education. An effective teaching of vocational subjects can ensure a smooth transition from school life to social life. Career education or vocational education is an essential component of slow learners' curriculum. To facilitate slow learners' becoming self-sustaining, contributing members of society education must provide a learning programme that reflects the competencies needed for full participation in the real word. The teacher should lay more emphasis on career education for slow learners as they explore career options and make realistic appraisals of themselves, their interests and their abilities. Realistic advice must be given by the teacher if the student is considering a career that would be impossible because of his limited capacity. Students who express interest in a particular field should be assisted in selecting potential careers that fit their abilities.

Career education concepts can be taught through the regular academic curriculum. The method makes the content more realistic and meaningful. For example, the secondary school mathematic teacher can present basic subtraction and addition computations as these skills relate to using a checking amount correctly. The realistic use of mathematics helps the student see the relationship between academic work and the real world. Besides, teaching vocational subjects can open up further avenues for future career. Backward children are always eager to engage themselves in woodworks, metal work. cane work, crafts, tailoring, weaving and the teacher who can utilise this eagerness effectively can make an important contribution to the work of the school. This plays a vital role in the education of slow learners.

Vocational subjects are the fields in which most of the slow learners can often more easily achieve success or have it engineered for them. The practical work done in the school must be suited to the capacity of the students and it should also be something which produces evidence of success by looking good or being useful. Especially in the early stages, the slow learners need quick success. They can not be expected to persist for too long without tangible results. Standards of proficiency in execution are quite essential but at the same time they should never be stressed to the point that the students sense failure and lose the pleasure and satisfaction of achievement. The teacher who is accustomed to higher standards may not be able to tolerate the poor standard of the slow learners but it should be remembered that children are more likely to raise their own standards if they first feel that what they are going to do is worthwhile and enjoyable. As they get more involved in the work, they will put in more effort and want to finish the jobs better. Hence it is very important for the teacher to provide guidance and assistance wherever necessary so that the slow learners can be geared into action.

This will also serve three purposes.

1. The students cultivate a good relationship with the teacher which has a direct bearing on the aspects of other school work.
2. It imbibes in slow learners an improved attitude towards themselves.
3. Enjoyment of practical works makes possible further

progress towards the acquisition of some real skills.

The first essentials therefore are that success should be ensured and that what is done should be valuable in the eyes of the students.

This warrants a sort of prevocational education, the training of students in job related skills. Prevocational education is another important function of secondary schools. Students, whether they go to college or for vocational training or directly into the job market, can profit from appropriate prevocational training. According to Morsink (1984) this area includes the development of such skills as:

- locating suitable employment
- completing an application form
- being able to go through an employment interview
- Dressing appropriately for work and maintaining personal hygiene
- having good work habits such as being on time and behaving honestly
- interacting appropriately with peers, subordinates and supervisors
- using public and private transportation for work purposes
- understanding and computing pay and benefits.

Purpose of Teaching Vocational Subjects

Teaching of vocational subjects to slow learners serves three important purposes. They are:

i) Development of habits of work
ii) Fosters positive attitude towards work
iii) Ensures smooth transition.

i) Development of Habits of Work

Schools can hardly provide training in the variety of operations and for many situations that the slow learners will have to face after leaving the school. In any case, if there is any training to be given, employers usually prefer to train youngsters themselves in their own way for the job. But vocational subjects can develop some of the characteristics of good worker - persistence and the habit of sticking at a job until finished; the ability to think out how to accomplish a task and to carry on without waiting for someone else to say what should be done next. Children who have not been encouraged to do things for themselves at home or even in the classroom may manifest their lack of practical sense and personal competence in the vocational subjects. That's why the teacher has to provide adequate opportunities for students to acquire these skills. The teacher teaching vocational subjects can do much to encourage independence and competence. Coaxing such children forward will give immense satisfaction to the teacher. A teacher who does not know the children intimately can not possibly judge how effective the work is.

ii) Attitude Towards Work

Teaching vocational subjects fosters positive attitude toward work. There are various vocational subjects which vary from location to location. Also vocational subjects differ from school to school. The components of vocational subjects available in the school largely depend on the requirement of the locality in which the school is embedded. Even if the acquisition of skills is not the first priority, the vocational subjects are nevertheless important. Slow learners are often poor in co-ordination and badly need opportunities for developing it, not merely for the sake of skills themselves, but because of the confidence that comes from knowing how to do things. Moreover, while they may not get opportunities to use these skills at work in school, they may find many occasions at home for application of their skills. They can use their skills in some of the simple operations involved in household jobs. This gives them self confidence and they evince a positive attitude towards work. They should learn that there are right and wrong ways of using tools and of going about a job. Once they learn the right ways of doing things it gives them a sense of achievement and they develop intrinsic interest in the work. This intrinsic interest in work will shape a positive attitude towards work which will ultimately tell upon their future performance.

iii) Smooth Transition

Preparing students for continued education, adult responsibilities, independence and employment have always been goals of secondary education. Most students complete high school and find jobs, enter a vocational training programme, or go to college without experiencing major difficulties of adjustment. We know that dropout and unemployment rates are far too high for all youths, especially in economically depressed communities, but the outlook for students with disabilities may be even worse (Hendrick, MacMillan, and Balow, 1989; Wolman, Bruininks and Thurlow, 1989). Studies of what happens to students will disabilities during and after their high school years strongly suggest, that a higher percentage of them, compared to students without disabilities, have difficulty in making the transition from adolescence to adulthood and from school to work. Many dropout of school, experience great difficulty in finding and holding a job, do not find work suited to their capabilities, do not receive further training or education, or become dependent on their families (Edgar, 1987; Neel, Meadows, Levine, and Edgar, 1988).

A smooth and successful transition to adult life is difficult for any adolescent. Individuals may find different routes to adulthood. Our goal must be to provide the special assistance needed by adolescents and young adults with disabilities that will help them achieve the most rewarding, productive, independent, and integrated adult life possible. One of education's great challenges of the 1990 is to devise an effective array of programmes that will meet the individual needs of students on the paths to adulthood. This is where the practical works perfectly fit in. There is, too, a great deal of useful knowledge that comes through practical work the names and uses of different words, materials, tools and processes. There is the learning about how things are made; where materials, come from; how much materials and tools cost, measurement and appreciation of sign and quantity. Wherever possible, opportunities should be taken to use interest in the craft as a starting point for the incidental discovery of more knowledge and understanding of the world around.

Practical work can contribute to verbal development and number knowledge which are very essential for adult life. Slow learning children do not want reading interposed between them and their favourite activities at every turn. However, practical work can contribute to verbal development when children are allowed to talk about what they are doing so that they get practice in explanations and in using the right words for tools and processes. Practical works necessitate verbal communication on the part of slow learners. Moreover, only this type of skill is required in their adult life. When the slow learners' skills are developed in vocational subjects in a desired manner it ensures a smooth transition from school work to social work and the students will not experience any difficulty when they enter into adult life or undertake a job for livelihood. There are also many occasions for the application of number knowledge in measuring and estimating costs. This kind of number knowledge is required in adult life. The slow learners need not remember algebra, trigonometry and other mathematical concepts to be a self supporting individual of the society. If they have the ability to apply number knowledge to measuring and estimating tasks in adult life that will suffice. It is therefore a matter of more importance to teach vocational subjects to slow learners effectively. The practical or work experience or the SUPW (the socially useful productive work) periods should be properly utilised for teaching practical subjects so that transition can be ensured from school to work and adult life.

Importance of Teaching Vocational Subjects in Mainstreaming

Most of the slow learners are in the mainstreaming. Their disability or learning problem is not so severe as to warrant placement in special school. Special school in a way prepare the learners there for a self supporting adult life. They don't stress development of cognitive abilities. It should be remembered here that blind and deaf are capable of cognitive development. Generally the special schools give much importance to practical work so that the inmates can find some ways and means to lead a reasonably self supporting life. But that much of focussed attention is not found in the ordinary school. In every school there will be a few periods for vocational subjects. It may be, art, craft, weaving, tailoring, agriculture etc. There are more than sixty components of vocational subjects. In addition we have period, for work experience and SUPW and community service. These are the periods which the slow learners look forward with relief. These are the fields in which they can achieve moderate success and don't feel lagging behind much. Sometimes compensation mechanism drives them to do better in practical work than normal students. Gopal and Manikandan were very poor in English and mathematics. They could not even get pass score in any subject. But in vocational subjects their performance was more than adequate. Gopal was good at weaving; Manikandan was good at tailoring. Though both of them could not pass S.S.L.C public exams in the first attempt, they subsequently passed S.S.L.C exams and now they are successful handloom supervisor and tailor respectively leading a normal life which is not markedly different from that of his elite classmates. An effective teaching of vocational subjects can thus draw out latent talent of slow learners and it provides for compensation mechanism to work in, in some cases. Moreover, in most of the school, the vocational subjects included in the curriculum reflect the trade requirement and opportunity of the locality. For example, in places like Rajapalayam, Thiruppur, Coimbatore, Erode etc, we have weaving as the main vocational subject. These are the areas where handloom and powerloom factories are located. These factories are always in need of semi-skilled persons. Therefore the slow learners who adequately develop their skill in weaving in the school itself are able to find a satisfactory job when they leave the school. It is to be remembered here that most of the slow learners do not go for higher education. They start seeking job after school education. Similarly the students who develop their skill in wood work, metal work, clay work etc are able to find satisfactory jobs in Khadi Board or in related small scale or cottage industry. Above all, tailoring is a vocational subject which enables the slow learners to stand on their own in adult life. Thus these vocational subjects provide smooth transition from school life to adult life.

It is therefore very important to deal with vocational subjects effectively in the school stage. But the state of affairs prevalent is not encouraging. Teachers are available for all the vocational subjects. Each school has one or two vocational subjects in their curriculum. But in classroom practice these vocational subjects are not given due importance. They are not taught as they should be taught. Sometimes the class size also limits the effective teaching of vocational subjects. In many school, the practical rooms are not properly maintained. They have practical subjects only for name sake and there is not worthwhile teaching learning process taking place. In such schools the slow learners do not find any opportunity to learn practical work and they don't have a smooth transition to adult life. They never get any opportunity to experience moderate success in the school subjects. As they are weak in academic subject and they don't get any other opportunity to experience a moderate degree of success in the vocational subjects, they become more frustrated which affects their further learning. It is therefore very essential to teach vocational subjects properly not only for smooth transition from school life to adult life but also for the personality development of backward children. It contributes to their personality development in the sense that the experience of success gives them self-confidence, boosts up their self-image, and in a way prepares them for social life where they don't feel left behind or lagging behind.

Teaching vocational subjects or works provides many benefits for slow learners. A few of these are:

1. Under the supervision of the teacher they learn the practical work properly. They experience a moderate degree of success which in turn fosters self-confidence in them.
2. It ensures smooth transition from sheltered school to competitive employment.
3. It provides for easier job entry on completion of school education.
4. The students get the needed work experience which is required for social or adult life.
5. It provides for an alternative to dropping out of school.

How to Teach Vocational Subjects to Slow Learners

Essentially every high school provides courses of study in vocational education. There are various components as mentioned earlier. At higher secondary level we have vocational group wherein the students study the concerned vocational subject only. National Education Commission (1966) rightly emphasised the inclusion of vocational education in the school curriculum. At high school level, 3 to 4 periods are allotted for voational subjects per week whereas at higher secondary school there are full fledged vocational courses. In practice, only slow learners and backward students are admitted to these courses even though there may be a few exceptions. All the poor scorers in S.S.L.C public exams are usually admitted to these courses This course is even referred to as a dumping ground for slow learners. The main idea behind this is that they should not suffer after leaving school and they should have - smooth transition from school life to adult life. Besides, these students usually do not go for college education. They usually start seeking job after leaving the school. So giving them admission to vocational courses is an appropriate decision and it is not a matter for criticism as it is made out often. For students, whether they are slow or normal, who choose to enter a trade or skilled job area, vocational education is a necessity, since they must learn job entry skills. Slow learners can benefit and succeed in vocational training. They often develop into very skilled craftspersons. This makes vocational education all the more important.

Adolescence is a time of significant growth that characterises the young person's transition from childhood to adulthood. Like all other periods of growth, this one can be unsettling. In order to become fully functioning adults, adolescents must assert their independence. This process is part of growing to self actualisation (Maslow, 1950); it may also be described as the development of field independence (Wilkin et al, 1977), or the development of an internal locus of control (Rotter, Seeman and Liverant, 1962). These are very much fostered by vocational education. Teachers can be especially helpful in assisting the slow learners to develop independence. Teachers are not counsellors, and they are not specialists in the use of adaptive equipment that may assist the slow learners in developing independence. But they can be facilitators, caring friends and guides. It is the quality that matters much. The teachers can ensure smooth transition through vocational education by modifying their instruction. Certain modifications of instructions and techniques are essential to facilitate better acquisition of vocational expertise and smoother transition. An effective strategy of vocational instruction should include the following.

i. Ensuring proper training environment
ii. Providing concrete step-by-step procedure and /or demonstration
iii. Planning for success.
iv. Using positive reinforcement
v. Providing rules and regulations.

i) Providing Proper Training Environment

The teacher should ensure a stable and predictable training environment. If the environment is not congenial the slow learners' learning will be considerably affected. The training programme must be stable and the outcome predictable. If these are not ensured, the slow learners may not evince required degree of enthusiasm in the vocational training. A calm manner and a structured learning situation help to provide a stable environment for the learner. The teacher should provide clear cut directions for using any machines or other equipment. Slow learners who have learning problems experience difficulty in knowing what is important and what exactly is meant when vague terms or confusing directions are given. In stead of posing like a task master the teacher should act like a guide or facilitator. He should also ensure that proper infrastructure is available adequate to the number of students to be trained up in vocational skills. Above all, the teacher should ensure a voluntary co-operation and co-ordination among the learners.

ii) Providing concrete Procedure and/or Demonstration

The teacher should provide concrete step-by-step procedures. He should provide adequate demonstration also. Vocational skills are usually sequential. Therefore a sequential method of instruction will allow the student to predict what task comes next, and to adapt easily. The teacher should give a step-by-step explanation as to how to do, and he should demonstrate by doing it himself.

Though he is an expert, he should follow the sequential order without skipping any step or stage. This type of vocational instruction will facilitate better mastery of the craft or trade. Besides providing step-by-step procedure, the teacher should also observe how they proceed and progress and extend guidance wherever necessary. The teacher should ensure that the students also follow the logical sequential order. To teach certain vocational subjects appropriate audio visual aids can be used. With the advancement of educational technology, video has become very useful to provide step by step procedures and / or demonstration for most of the vocational subjects.

iii) Planning for Success

The teacher should be pragmatic in his approach. Whatever he assigns should be feasible for slow learners. He should establish attainable goals that lead to vocational competency. The teacher teaching slow learners can easily see the capability and the limit of his students. Since the slow learners are less in number in the mainstreaming class the teacher can easily pay individual attention to them and thereby he can develop a thorough understanding of their strengths and weaknesses. This knowledge is very essential for the teacher so that he can include such skills that can be attained by the students. As these goals are accomplished, students may gradually build more self-confidence and believe that they can attain further skills. With self confidence there comes interest and when these two factors are in operation, there will be better mastery. As we know, nothing succeeds like success and success leads to success. It is therefore very important for the teacher to plan his vocational training in such a way that the students should experience success.

iv) Using Positive Reinforcement

Positive reinforcement is essential if a better learning is to take place. It is more applicable and effective to slow learners. So the teacher should ensure positive reinforcement whenever possible and necessary. As often as possible, the teacher should reinforce the students after successful completion of a task. Positive reinforcement, consistently and appropriately applied, is particularly effective for slow learners. Praise, when used, should be specific, uncontrived, and in language that builds up self-esteem rather than patronising student. Praise should primarily be used to reinforce appropriate behaviours and to give feed back to students on what they are doing right. Overall, it is a good idea to use praise frequently, especially with young children and in classrooms with many low achieving students (Brophy, 1981). However, what is more important than the amount of praise given is the way it is given (Hafpaktitis et al, 1985). O' Leary and O'Leary (1977) hold that praise is effective as a classroom motivator to the extent that it is contingent, specific and credible. Brophy (1981) observes that students who do well should not be praised for a merely average performance, but students who usually do less well should be praised when they do better. He also notes that low achieving or disruptive students should be praised adequately when the occasion arises.

Positive reinforcement will be more effective when it is subtle. A smile, a nod, a positive signal, or a written remark can make a real difference to slow learners. It motivates them to apply more effort and to do better. Skinner(1953) and other behavioural theorists argue that students who have been reinforced for studying (for example, by receiving good grades or the approval of teachers and parents) will be motivated to study, but students who have not been reinforced for studying (because they studied but did not get good grades, or because their teachers or parents did not praise their studying) will be unmotivated. It is therefore very important for the teacher teaching slow learners to encourage them for serious efforts or attempts, even if the result is not totally successful. The slow learners have experienced many failures and they often need encouragement to embark on new tasks.

v) Providing Rules and Regulations

In teaching vocational subjects it is more important to provide safety and laboratory or workshop rules. The teacher should keep a chart of these rules in clear view. The rules should be made clear to the students and they should strictly be instructed to observe the rules. The teacher should provide written directions for using any machines or other equipment.

He should stress safety regulations. Also the teacher should react calmly to inappropriate behaviour, while firmly enforcing rules and regulation. Even though the teacher is expected to be sympathetic and kind, he should not be lax in enforcement of rules and regulations. Without adherence to rules and regulations the students can not make any marked progress in vocational training.

The Role of Teacher

The teacher's role is significant and vital in teaching adolescent slow learners. Teaching slow learners can be rewarding. It is much satisfying to watch their slow progress. Vocational subjects are such fields where the slow learners can make a marked progress. By assisting the slow learners as they develop into young adults, the teachers can see the results of their own efforts. It provides immense job satisfaction to the industrious and dedicated teachers. Slow learners profit from good teaching, positive support and appropriate guidance. A good teaching without complementary positive support and appropriate guidance will not have desired effect on the learning of slow learners. Apart from teaching well, the teacher should give positive support and appropriate guidance. This will enable the slow learners to develop their skill in vocational subjects. The involvement of the teacher in the vocational programme is directly related to the improvement of slow learners. The teacher should not set higher goals for slow learners. He should set goals that may be attained by them or he should encourage students to set goals for themselves. One fundamental principle of motivation is that people work harder for goals they themselves set than for goals set for them by others. The teacher dealing with slow learners should not fail to capitalise on this principle. When we encourage the slow learners to set goals for themselves it gives them an impetus to put in more effort to achieve that goal. It motivates as well as activates the slow learners in all earnestness as it imbibes in them a sense of responsibility for their attainment. Then, within a few years, the teachers can observe these students' entries into the world of adult society. When they fare well in the society it gives a sense of satisfaction to teachers that they have prepared them well for social well being. At the same time it is important to realise that adolescents have many personal, family, and peer pressures acting on them (Schwartz, 1983). Teachers must be prepared to deal with these pressures in a reasonable, non judgemental manner. Slow learners have additional needs and also they need teachers' help and guidance more than their classmates. The teachers, whether they provide direct instructional service, or interact in less formal manner, must be prepared to recognise and deal with these needs. These needs can be met in very simple ways such as:

- Setting goals that can be attained by slow learners
- Providing written directions for using any machines or other equipment.
- Getting the slow learner's attention. This may be accomplished by seating the student close to the teacher so that eye contact can be established.
- Speaking more slowly and clearly with normal speech
- Using audio visual aids profusely. Overhead transparencies are helpful for illustrating or explaining procedures. Slide presentations and film strips are excellent aids in presenting various skills. Video is extremely useful to show clear demonstration. It ensures effective transmission of instruction from the point of origin to the point of reception with an immediate excitement.
- Using different teaching method and modifying instructional materials. In the vocational education work experience and acquisition of skill must be emphasised. More importance must be given to practical work.
- Reinforcing positive behaviour. Positive reinforcer strengthens behaviour.

In almost all ways, however, slow learners are the same as others. They generally have the same desires, needs and emotions as their peers. Teachers should try to interact with slow learners in a normal fashion. They should also expect a normal level of achievement and a normal set of behaviours. It is no use expecting a high level of achievement from slow learners whose learning rate is low. Slow learning adolescents are really adolescents-normal in almost every respect. When treated as such they will respond appropriately.

It is very important for the teachers to realise that slow learners deserve a solid foundation on which to build their futures. Teachers, whether academic, vocational, or in any other discipline, are the ones who provide the building blocks for their foundation. The teachers must realise this basic principle and they should strive for providing appropriate vocational training to slow learners, since most of them will not be going for higer education. Vocational subjects are the fields in which they can achieve moderate success and they provide adequate transition to the slow learners from school life to adult life. So we can conclude that vocational subjects serve as foundation on which the slow learners can build their futures. So the teachers, by way of effective vocational training, can provide the building blocks for their foundation. Here the teacher not only teaches but also makes him self-reliant, self-confident and a normal social being. Thus the slow learners can best be served by teachers who are their advocates in the development of independent living skills, including the knowledge of new technology. When the teachers succeed in their venture to make the slow learners a self-supportive social man it is a service not only to the concerned slow learner but also to the nation, as a whole, since it makes concrete contribution to the human resource development of the country which is the need of the hour for a developing country like India.

Physical Education

Modern thinkers in education now-a-days emphasise that the best individual is one who is physically fit, mentally sound and sharp, emotionally balanced and socially well adjusted. Education is a dynamic force in the life of every individual, influencing his physical, mental, emotional social and ethical development. Physical education is an important part of educational process. It is not a 'frill' or an 'ornament' to deck with the school programme as a means of keeping children busy. Through well directed physical education programme, children develop skills for the worthy use of leisure time, engage in activities conducive to healthy living, develop socially and contribute to their physical and mental health. A study of history reveals that other civilizations have recognised the important place of physical education in the training of their youth. In ancient Athens, for example, three main subjects were studied by every Athenian. The subjects studied were gymnastics, grammar and music. Physical education is education through physical activities in which the body is the primary tool. Its aim is the same as that of education to bring about an all round development of an individual and make him an effective member of the society. Physical education is the education of body and mind. Plato emphasised that body and mind should be driven alike; like a pair of horses hitched to a shaft.

Definitions of Physical Education

D. Oberteuffer defines physical education as the sum of changes in the individual caused by experiences centred in motor activity.

According to Jesse Peiring Williams Physical education is the sum of man's physical activities selected as to the kind and conducted as to outcomes.

In the words of Bacher physical education as an integral part of the total education process is a field of endeavour which has as its aim, the development of physically, mentally, emotionally and socially fit citizens through the medium of physical activities which have been selected with a view to realising these outcomes.

According to Edward Hitch Cock physical education is such a cultivation of powers and capabilities of students as will enable him to maintain his bodily conditions in the best working order, while providing at the same time for the greatest efficiency of his intellectual and spiritual life.

Voltmer and Essilinger define physical education as the process by which changes in the individual are brought about through his movement experiences. According to Nixon and Jewett physical education is that phase of the total process of education which is concerned with the development and utilisation of the individual's movement potential and related responses, and with the stable behaviour modification in the individual which results from these responses.

Importance Physical Education

'A sound mind in a sound body' is a tenet. Physical education plays a vital role in the intellectual as well as emotional development of a child. Hence the physical education must not be solely concerned with the development of strength and physical skills, or indeed with physical development alone. It should be viewed as an integral part of the whole programme for personality development. Nor should the physical education be looked upon as something which happens in the playground or gymnasium at a set time. It should be occurring at all sorts of time and in all kinds of situations. For example, the teacher should give proper attention to posture and general bearing whenever appropriate. It may be while the students are sitting at a desk or table, or it may be walking about the school, or it may be standing informally in a group, or when being spoken to by the teacher. Attention should be drawn to correct breathing when speaking, reading orally or singing. Also, the teacher can help in learning to skip, to catch or kick a ball when suitable opportunities arise in casual play situations. Thus there are many opportunities in classroom situations to impart physical education by the class teacher and other subject teacher. This was very much emphasised in the Indian Guru Kula system of education where the students were expected to evince a standard physical behaviour. Though no separate time was allotted for sports and games in those days, physical education was embedded in much of their activities.

Physical education should include, at all levels, training in personal hygiene and general fitness, and the development of co-operation, courage and confidence, perseverance and independence. It should provide ample opportunities for exploration and experiment in the use of physical activity and the use of skill and strength in work and play. Because of their poor home environment, or as a result of rejection by peer group, the slow learners often miss the opportunities for skill learning which arise naturally in play. Play is very important since children spend a major portion of their time playing. Play contributes to development and it involves interactions with peers, which can encourage social problem solving. While thinking up make-believe roles for each other, children can coordinate their actions in a cooperative manner, making prosocial behaviours possible (Damon, 1983, 1984). Play reveals important elements of children's ability to make sense of their environment; of their linguistic cognitive, and social skills and of their general personality development. It is associated with creativity, especially the ability to be less literal and more flexible is one's thinking (Fein, 1979; Christie, 1980; yawkey, 1980). Elkind (1986) who regards play as an essential component of early childhood education has shown its relationship to success with academic skills. Reading and writing, for example, can be viewed as sophisticated forms of representational thought that are built on the early experiences with symbolism that children have during play (Wollfgang and Sanders, 1981). So for younger slow learners, who are in the primary grades, adequate opportunities must be provided for play so that proper physical as well as personality development can be ensured. Despite the overwhelming evidence supporting the importance of play to all aspects of development, schools are providing fewer and fewer play opportunities for children. Moreover, for primary grades we don't have structured syllabus of physical education as we have for high school classes. However, a resourceful teacher can provide many opportunities for different types of play for primary grades students. It should be noted that the adverse effect of these missed opportunities are cumulative. Primary skills are not developed and consequently more mature ones become harder to learn. This may lead to further rejection and isolation. Play and experimenting is often all they need in order to improve in such skills as catching, bounding, aiming, throwing, batting, climbing and skipping. They are ready to learn and, given the opportunity, learn rapidly.

Physical education should take into account and help to minimise those physical limitations which occur most frequently in slow learners - poor postures and muscular inco-ordination, lack of stamina, specific physical defects. Finally physical education should take advantage of the many opportunities it will have (because the slow learners are physically nearer normal) to compensate for other limitations and to ensure feelings of accomplishment and success.

The Physical Education Programme for Younger Slow Learners

In any group of slow learners there is likely to be wide variation in physical development. Although an average for height weight, or height-weight ratio may not be significantly different from that of a corresponding normal group, the individual variations within any group are certain to be greater. These differences create a difficult problem of organisation in the physical education lessons, particularly in lower classes. In these, any particular class will have a considerable range of height, weight, physical strength, skills and over all maturity within its pupils. So it is very difficult to devise a rigid programme of physical education for the class as a whole. As in all the other areas of the curriculum, the teacher should recognise and cater to individual differences. In physical education particularly, the manifestation of unevenness of personal development will be clear and the problems associated with it highlighted. For example, on the one hand we have children whose physical growth is normal but they may be immature emotionally and socially. Because of their physique the teacher may expect them to take responsibilities and perform in group activities for which they are emotionally and socially inadequate. On the other hand, albeit in less number, we have children whose physical strength is not adequate but they may be emotionally and socially sound. Such children will probably be unable to keep up with the rest in speed, skills, rhythm and strength. It is therefore very essential for the teacher to have a good organising ability if the physical education is adequately to play its part in educational treatment.

For the younger slow learners in primary grades the following programme will form the basis of physical education lessons and activities. The programme includes.

i) Informal physical education lessons

ii) Use of rhythm

iii) Transition to participate in formal work and team games

iv) Allowing children to experiment

v) Comprehensive (or Broad Spectrum) physical education

vi) Health education as integral part of physical education.

i) Informal Physical Education Lesson

In the early stages especially at primary level, lessons should be as free and informal as possible. The teacher should encourage children to use their natural activity, e.g. climbing, walking, running, skipping, catching, throwing, and to develop other physical skills. The teachers can use apparatus such as large and small balls, bean bags, hoops, skittles, mats, skipping, balance benches, climbing frames, beams for hanging and crawling activities and targets for aiming practice. The best physical education lesson would be to allow younger children to use the gymnasium with its fixed, portable and small apparatus for a free physical activity period. It is an educational treat to observe children using the varied apparatus in multitude of ways and often with surprising ingenuity; to see the individual children's different reactions; to notice over a period of few lessons the increase in confidence, initiative and co-operativeness and the ways in which highly individualistic activity gradually develops into group activities.

ii) Use of Rhythm

In the early stages of physical education, rhythm should be made use of effectively. It is necessary that these should be uncomplicated and used in conjunction with many forms of locomotion, e.g. skipping, walking, tiptoeing, crawling and marching to the rhythm beaten on a drum or played as chords on a piano or sung by the children as they move. It is also possible to combine these rhythmic activities with music and movement to lead to simple free dance or dramatic activity. It is a good thing to include some form of rhythmic, activity in all lessons at this stage: indeed, suitably adapted for age and ability, it may be popular even with senior children, e.g. dance drama is very much stimulating and provides excellent physical and mental exercise for boys and girls of fifteen years. The younger slow learners should be encouraged to become more aware of their own bodies and what they can do. When rhythm is properly made use of the children develop interest in the physical activity and they don't feel tired very soon. Without stimulating rhythm, the physical activity may become dull and drab.

iii) Transition to Formal Work and Team Games

All the activities mentioned in the preceding paragraphs will lead to a gradual increase in control and refinement of movement and stimulate the desire to participate in more formal work and team games. The children always want to imitate the activities of their old friends and use their new skills in more traditional ways. The boy who has learned to jump over a cane supported by two skittles will want to jump on to and finally over, the box or buck. The boy who has learned how to hang on to a rope and swing will try to climb it. The boy who has acquired skill in kicking and controlling a ball will try to become a soccer player. The girl who has learned to catch and throw may like to play net ball or throw ball. In this way, the early stages prepare for later ones when more formal and controlled activities are introduced. It is quite interesting to observe how agile and accomplished many slow learning children can become when their physical development and skills are encouraged and nurtured in this way. Also, these activities provided in the early stages prepare the children for team games. Group games that let children develop rules and abide by them encourage co-operation and self-governance (Kamii and DeVries, 1980). Because pre-operational thinking is still tied to actions, the actions necessary for co-operation should be concrete and observable. For example, three legged stilts where two children stand next to each other and have their inside leg tied to a shared middle stilt require children to co-ordinate their physical movements (Goffin and Tull, 1984).

iv) Allowing Children to Experiment

There is need at all stages for allowing the children to experiment, within the bounds of safety, with exercises and games. Left to themselves children, even slow learning children invent their own exercises with the use of logs. Great ingenuity is shown in devising these exercises and the children demonstrate them to others. Also, when we allow children to experiment with exercises and games, it ignites in them the spark of creativity. It can be seen that most of the physical activities (Play and games) of the children of the present generation are quite different from those of ours. It is the resultant product of constant experimentation of children with exercises and games.

v) Comprehensive Physical Education

Physical education should not be confined to the gymnasium or hall. Games, athletics and swimming are essential components. Team games are particularly very useful for encouraging co-operation, team spirit, and social relationships generally. But the slow learning children need assistance and practice before they can become useful members of a team, and it is as well to start training in team work, perhaps in small groups, as early as possible. Around 3 to 5, children begin to engage in co-operative play in which they co-ordinate their activities, take turns, and work together to achieve a group goal (Guralnick and Weinhouse, 1984). Athletics and swimming are more individual and, therefore, have the advantage of allowing the child to compete against himself. Adventure training in the form of camping, canoeing, rambling, cross-country running and mountain climbing and fell walking where possible, is of immense value. Camping for both boys and girls not only fosters physical fitness but also introduces the children to new experiences and provides opportunities for a wide range of educational activities. The teacher can also recommend, the use of adventure or 'junk' playground, which can be a great asset to the younger slow learning children. In addition, an adventure playground provides unique opportunities for emotional release, language development and the growth of confidence and self-reliance which are very essential for slow learning children.

vi) Health Education as Integral Part of Physical Education

The physical education programme for younger slow learners must include health education. There are many incidental opportunities in physical education for helping children to appreciate how their bodies work and what are the requirements for healthy living. In the gymnasium, they should always wear appropriate clothing, be made aware of the need for good lighting, ventilation, cleanliness and tidiness, and the value of co-operation. In the changing rooms or spots attention should be paid to the care of clothing, the use of lavatories and regard for other people's property. In games and athletics the value of physical fitness should be stressed e.g. the harmful effects of smoking, unbalanced diet, over strain, and irregularities in sleep. Simple Yoga asanas may be introduced as a part of health education. Yoga asanas restore order and balance in the positive and negative currents of the body. It slows down the breath and brings about tranquillity. It calms down the nervous system and increases blood circulation. All these will build up good health.

It is not necessary that there should be a special physical education teacher for younger slow learning children who do not have a structured physical education syllabus. Even the class teacher who has had some training in physical education and who is keen and enthusiastic and aware of the aims and purposes of his teaching can do excellent work. If the teacher pays proper attention to preparation of lessons, anticipates the organisational difficulties that are bound to occur with a heterogenous group, avoids obvious dangers and makes his lesson lively, cheerful and interesting, he will be successful. It is not necessary that he should be a good performer himself but if he is able to get one child to help or give a demonstration to others that will do since that is a sound educational technique.

Teaching Physical Education to Older Slow Learners

We have a number of slow learners studying in high schools and higher secondary school. For these slow learners there are structured syllabi and there are special teachers for this purpose. The structured syllabus requires the physical education teacher to teach the lessons methodologically. Physical education for the slow learning students in high schools and higher secondary schools refers to the process of education that concerns activities which develop and maintain the human body. It comprises athletic events, team games and other related physical activities. When a student is playing a game, swimming, marching, working out on the parallel bars, skating or performing in any one of the game of physical education activities, education takes place at the same time. This education may be conducive to the enrichment of the individual's life or it may be detrimental. Whether physical education helps or inhibits the attainment of educational objectives, will largely depend on the leadership responsible for its direction.

Aims and Objectives of Physical Education to Senior Slow Learners

Aims and objectives differ from each other in the following ways.

a) An aim is the ultimate goal that we have in view while an objective is an immediate goal that we have before us.

b) An objective may form one of the steps towards realising an aim.

c) An aim is general in nature while objectives are specific in nature.

d) An aim is hardly realised, but objectives can be easily realised.

e) Aim is the final goal and it should be one and the last but objective may be numerous.

Aim of Physical Education for Senior Students

There are many authors who have defined the aim of physical education in different ways. The aim of physical education is the same as that of general education because physical education is a part of general education. According to J.P. Nash the aim of physical education is to have healthy, skillful, emotionally adjusted individuals integrated with worthwhile vocational and recreational activities in home, in community in which he lives. According to Nizon and Cozens the aim of physical education is to make the maximum contribution to the optimum development of the individuals potentialities in all phases of life.

According to J.F. Williams physical education should provide skilled leadership and adequate facilities which will afford an opportunity for the individual or group to act in situations which are physically wholesome, mentally stimulating and satisfying and socially sound. The primary aim of physical education is not to develop star athletes, winning teams or expert performance but a national vitality with character values and physical fitness. This aim is more applicable to slow learners. We have to impart physical education to them to develop their physical fitness, to develop a sense of co-operation to promote co-ordination, to become emotionally adjusted and to work for common goal. The cumulative effect of physical education activities will enable the slow learning children to circumvent their deficiencies in other social skills.

Objectives of Physical Education

The following are the primary and immediate objectives of physical education for slow learners.

i) organic growth and development.
ii) Development of neuro - muscular coordination and skill.
iii) Interpretive and intellectual development.
iv) Emotional Development.
v) Recreational competency (worthy use of leisure time)
vi) Development of correct health habits.

i) Organic Growth and Development

This objective is concerned with the building of physical power through the growth and development of various systems (respiratory, circulatory, digestive, excretory) in the body. Participation in good programmes of physical education activities will promote bodily growth, strength, endurance structurally and functionally. To achieve this every student must participate in big muscle activities involving fundamental movements like running, jumping, throwing, climbing, pushing, pulling etc. Further games and body building exercises can also contribute to the achievements of these activities. Hence physical education programme should consist of all games and sports events and other physical activities like gymnastics, celesthenics, yoga etc, These activities are very important for the slow learning children since these activities will enable them to circumvent their weakness if their slow learning is due to physical factors.

ii) Neuro-muscular Co-ordination and Skill

The nervous system controls the behaviour of human beings. This objective is concerned with the performance of a given act efficiently with ease and grace at the expense of less time and energy. Neuro-muscular co-ordination develops well only if various types of exercises are done repeatedly for a long period of time. Participation in physical activities of various types develops neuro-muscular co-ordination and skill. Development of coordination and skills makes it possible for students to participate in the activities of their choice and derive satisfaction for them. Development of these skills will have a far reaching consequences for the slow learning children who are very much in need of neuro-muscular co-ordination in their academic activities. When neuro-muscular co-ordination and skills are developed by means of proper physical education it will have a direct bearing on the performance of slow learning students in the learning activities. Therefore the physical education teacher should provide more facilities and fix a good programme of physical education which should include variety of activities in order to provide a chance for the individual to develop variety of skills.

iii) Interpretive and Intellectual Development

This objective is concerned with the adequate knowledge regarding values of physical education, rules and regulations pertaining to games and other activities. Further, this objective includes the ability of an individual to think, interpret, judge and act in a situation. Team games develop their skill in speed and accuracy. The students are activated to think and act fast. In case of football or shuttle badminton, for example, the student has to think, in a second or two, where to give the ball, how to give the ball and how fast to act. Games activities sharpen their thinking ability as well as discerning ability which will ultimately tell upon the intellectual development of slow learning children. Proper physical education programme will thus facilitate intellectual development of slow learners.

iv) Emotional Development

It is a known fact that most of the slow learners have emotional problems. Emotional development is a must for a normal human being. This emotional development can be ensured in a better way by means of physical education programme. Emotional development refers to the adjustment of the individual both to self and to others and also to the development of behaviour. Participation in sports and games and other physical activities under leaders of moral standards will develop social attitude and better behaviour and standards. The qualities of fair play, co-operation, respecting the rules and regulations, competitive spirit, sportsmanship etc can be developed through physical activities. It is more essential for the slow learners. It is in these areas where the slow learners can experience success which will boost up their self-image and foster self-confidence. This will ultimately lead to emotional development in a few years. As a result, when they leave the school they will be emotionally developed adult members.

v) Recreational Competency

Students should be encouraged to participate in physical activities for the love of wholesome play and for worthy use of leisure. Many students get into trouble or indulge in undesirable activities during their free time. Schools should provide activities to be continued during leisure and after school hours also so that students can engage themselves in some kinds of recreational activities to suit their age and strength. During leisure the students can go to the indoor stadium and they can play in the open playground after the school hours. It serves two purposes for slow learners. First, the slow learners are able to spend the time in a useful manner. Second, their isolation and rejection by age mates are reduced to a considerable extent.

vi) Development of Correct Health Habits

A good physical education programme should develop correct health habits. For children health education begins at home and it continues in schools. Physical activities are one of the agencies that promote health. Health has been defined by the world Health Organisation(WHO) as a state of complete physical, mental and social well being and not merely the absence of disease or infirmity. A sound programme of physical education and proper leadership in a wholesome environment will develop favourable attitude and habits which will form the basis of health. Getting up in the early morning, elimination of waste products, participation in physical activities, regular wash after the activities, non-participation in physical activities after food, avoidance of intoxicating drinks and tobacco, regulated diet, adequate rest etc are the correct health habits. These activities must be stressed for slow learners so that they can develop correct health habits and feel more confident and competent to perform academic activities.

The Role of Physical Education Teacher

The role of physical education teacher is significant in the all round development of slow learners. Physical education is more than physical in nature. Physical activities should more than just develop strength and fitness. They also develop high moral standards and help the students to think for themselves. Strength and fitness activities contribute to the development of one's personality. So the teacher should engage the students in team games whenever opportunity is available. Physical education also aids the students in developing the quality of honesty, courage, creativity and sportsmanship. The teacher should be an ideal model for students' emulation. Through personal example of vigorous health and personality, the physical education teacher should lead the students towards greater accomplishment.

The effectiveness of any physical education programme largely depends on the efficiency of the physical education teacher. The physical education teacher is responsible for the effectiveness of the programme. The guidance of the teacher is more important to carrying out the programme than the facilities and equipments available. Any amount of facilities and equipments will be of no use if the physical education teacher is not competent and interested in the task. He should not use any one method of teaching. He should use various instructional strategies. For slow learners the teacher should make profuse use of video from which they can learn better.

More meaningful experiences can be gained when there is a variety of activity. The teacher should therefore provide varied programmes of physical education. Through these activities the students not only learn by doing but also gain a measure of self-control and discipline and learn to co-operate with others. The teacher should be a good motivator. The teacher should motivate the students to participate in activities that are most beneficial to students. He should encourage student leadership. He should make use of the playground as a training ground for developing leadership qualities in students.

The teacher should base his physical education programme on scientific knowledge. He must accomplish the objectives by means of a scientifically formulated curriculum. Activities must be selected on the basis of scientific evidence of their worth from a study of anatomy or physiology. While selecting students for different team games and athletic events he should take into consideration the aptitude and the attitude of the students. Also he should be shrewd enough to observe who are driven by compensation mechanism and he should not fail to capitalise on them . At the same time he should not set very high goals for the students. He should provide for easy access to success so that success can lead to success.

Drill plays an important part in the learning process. The physical education teacher should use drills extensively and break units of work down into orderly progressions. The teaching emphasis must be placed on fundamentals of games and activities with each skill broken down into its component parts. He should introduce inter scholastic athletic programmes since these are very necessary to develop desirable social behaviour. He should also take the students for friendly as well as tournament matches since these will provide a better exposure to students for interaction and acquistions of social skills. He should encourage all the students, in general, and the slow learners in particular to participate in play as well as recreational activities so that the students will be able to function better in the society. Physical education provides a smooth transition to desirable social adjustment.

The physical education teacher has to shoulder the onerous task of enforcing discipline, developing good health habits and monitoring and measuring the progress made by the students from time to time. He is the teacher who is in touch with the students of all the classes. So his responsibility is of primary importance. Whatever behavioural changes he brings about in the students and whatever skills he develops in students by means of his physical education programme will influence the academic performance of the students. A resourceful physical education teacher can contribute a lot to the all round development of slow learners because it is he who extricates the slow learner most often from "his shell", instills self-confidence and makes him aware of what he is also capable of. Finally, attainment of the objectives of physical education programme will depend, to a great extent, on the leadership responsible for its direction. It is not the facilities or equipments that matter but the teacher and he must know he matters for the effective utilisation of facilities and equipments depends on the efficiency of the teacher.

Summary

Teaching vocational subjects and physical education plays a vital role in the career as well as personality development of slow learners. An effective teaching of vocational subjects can ensure a smooth transition from school life to social life. Vocational subjects are the fields in which most of the slow learners can often more easily achieve success or have it engineered for them. The vocational subjects taught in the school must be suited to the capacity of students and it should also be something which produces evidence of success by looking good or being useful.

Teaching of vocational subjects to slow learners facilitates development of habits of work, fosters positive attitude towards work and ensures smooth transition from school life to adult life.

An effective strategy of vocational instruction requires the teacher to ensure proper training environment, provide concrete step-by-step procedure and/or demonstration, plan for success, use positive reinforcement and to provide rules and regulations.

Vocational subjects serve as foundation on which the slow learners can build their futures. So the teachers, by way of effective vocational training, can provide the building blocks for their foundation. When the teachers succeed in their venture to make the slow learners self-supportive socialman, it is a service not only to the concerned slow learners but also to the nation as a whole, since it makes concrete contribution to human resource development of the country which is the need of the hour for a developing country like India.

Physical education is not a 'frill' or an "oranament" to deek with the school programme as a means of keeping children busy. Through well directed physical education programme, children develop skills for the worthy use of leisure time, engage in activities conducive to healthy living and develop socially.

Physical education should include, at all levels, training in personal hygiene and general fitness, and the development of co-operation, courage and confidence, perseverance and independence. It should provide ample opportunities for exploration and experiment in the use of physical activity and the use of skill and strength in work and play.

The physical education programme for younger slow learners at primary grades should include informal physical education lessons and use of rhythm. It should provide transition to participate in formal work and team games. It should allow children to explore and experiment. It should be comprehensive in nature comprising health education as an integral component.

It is not necessary that there should be a special physical education teacher for younger slow learning children who do not have a structured physical education syllabus. Even the class teacher who has had some training in physical education and who is keen and enthusiastic and aware of the aims and purposes of his teaching can do excellent work.

The objectives of teaching physical education to the slow learners in high schools and higher secondary schools include organic growth and development, development of neuro-muscular co-ordination and skill, interpretive and intellectual development, emotional development, recreational competency and development of correct health habits.

Physical education is more than physical in nature. Physical activities should do more than just develop strength and fitness. They also develop high moral standards and help the students to think for themselves. Strength and fitness activities contribute to the development of one's personality.

A resourceful physical education teacher can contribute a lot to the all round development of slow learners. because it is he who extricates the slow learner from his "shell", instils self-confidence and makes him aware of what he is also capable of. Attainment of the objectives of physical education will depend on the leadership responsible for its direction. It is not the facilities or equipments that matter but the teacher and he must know he matters since the effective utilisation of facilities and equipments depends on the efficiency of the teacher.

REFERENCES

Broline, D., and Kokaska, C. (1979) 'Career Education for Handicapped Children and Youth'. Merrill, Columbus, Ohio.

Brophy, J. (1981) 'Teacher Praise'. A Functional Analysis'. *Review of Educational Research*, 51, 5-32

Christie, J.F. (1980) 'The Cognitive Significance of Children's Play A Review of Selected Research'. *Journal of Education*, 162, 23-33.

Damon, W. (1983) 'Social and Personality Development: Infancy Through Adolescence'. Norton, New York.

Damon, W. (1984) 'Peer Education: The Untapped Potential'. *Journal of Applied Developmental Psychology*, 5, 331-334.

Edgar, E. (1987) 'Secondary Programmes in Special Education: Are Many of them Justifiable?' *Exceptional Children*, 53, 551-561.

Elkind, D. (1986) 'Helping Parents Make Healthy Educational Choices For Their Children'. *Educational Leadership*, 44(3), 36-38.

Fein, G.G. (1979) 'Play and Acquisition of Symbols'. In L.G. Katz (Ed) *Current Topics in Early Childhood Education*, vol 2, 195-226.

Goffin, S.G., and Tull, C.Q. (1984) 'Encouraging Possibilities For Co-operative Behaviour with Young Children'. Paper Presented at the Annual Meeting of the Southern Association for Children Under Six, Lexington, Ky.

Guralnick, M.J., and Weinhouse, E. (1984) 'Peer-related social Interactions of Developmentally Delayed Young Children: Developmental Characteristics'. *Developmental Psychology*, 20, 815-82?

Hallahan, D.P. and Kauffman, J.M. (1991) 'Exceptional Children'. Prentice Hall, Inc, Englewood Cliffs, New Jersey.

Hendrick, I.G., MacMillan, D.L., and Balow, I.H. (1989) 'Early School Leaving in America: A Review of the Literature'. University of California, Riverside.

Hoyt, K. (1975) 'An Introduction to Career Education: A Policy

Paper of the U.S. Office of Education'. Govt Printing Office, Washington D.C.

Kamil, C., and Devries, R. (1980) 'Group Games in Early Education: Implications of Piaget's Theory'. National Association for the Education of Young Children, Washington D.C.

Maslow, A. (1950) 'Self-actualising People: A study of Psychological Health'. *Personality Symposia: Symposium No.1. on Values*, 11-34. Grune and Stratton, New York.

Morsink, C.V. (1984) 'Teaching Special Needs Children in Regular Classrooms'. Little, Brown and Company, Boston.

Nafpaktitis, M., Mayer, G.R., and Butterworth, T. (1985) 'Natural Rates of Teacher Approval and Disapproval and Their Relation to Student Behaviour in Intermediate School Classrooms'. *Journal of Educational Psychology*, 77, 362-367.

Neel, R.S., Meadows, N., Levine, P., and Edgar, E.B. (1988) 'What Happens After School Education: A Statewide Follow-up Study of Secondary Students who have Behaviour Disorders'. *Behavioural Disorders*, 13, 209-216.

O'Leary, K.D., and O'Leary, S.G. (1977) 'Classroom Management: The Successful Use of Behaviour Modification'. Pergamon, New York.

Rotter, J., Seeman, J., and Liverant, S.O. (1962) 'Internal Versus External Control of Reinforcement: A Major Variable in Behaviour Theory'. In N.F. Washburne, (Ed), *Decisions, Values, Groups*, Vol 2, Pergamon, London.

Schwartz, S. (1983) 'Dealing with the Unexpected: A Situational Approach'. Wadswoth, Belmont, Cal.

Skinner, B.F. (1953) 'Science and Human Behaviour'. MacMillan, New York.

Slavin, R.E. (1985) 'Educational Psychology: Theory into Practice'. Prentice Hall, New Delhi.

Tansley, A.E., and Gulliford, R. (1962) 'The Education of Slow Learning Children'. Routledge and Kegan Paul Ltd, London.

Witkin, H.A., Moore, C.A., Goodenough, D.R., and Cox, P.W. (1977) 'Field Dependent and Field-independent Cognitive Styles and their Educational Implications'. *Review of Educational Research*, 47, 1-64.

Wolfgang, D.C., and Sanders, S. (1981) 'Defending Young Children's Play as the Ladder to Literacy'. *Theory into Practice*, 20, 116-120.

Wolman, C., Bruininks, R., and Thurlow, M. (1989) 'Dropouts and Dropouts Programmes: Implication for Special Education'. *Remedial and Special Education*, 10(5), 6-20.

Yawkey, T.D. (1980) 'More on Play as Intelligence in Children'. *Journal of Creative Behaviour*, 13, 247-258.

9 Developing Creativity and Social Competence in Slow Learners

Chapter Outline

Chapter Objectives

After reading this chapter your should be able to:

- Understand the need for developing creativity in slow learners.
- Describe the importance of creative works
- Know the teachers role in promoting creativity in slow learners
- Enumerate and describe in detail various activities meant for developing creativity in slow *Painting* learners.
- Understand the importance of developing social competence in slow learners.
- Devise programme for developing social competence in slow learners.

The educational and social limitations of slow learners are so obvious that a great deal of time and effort is devoted to ensuring that these children acquire certain basic skills (such as reading and number) and habits of behaving (social training), which have much practical value in life after leaving the school. The benefits derived from creative and expressive activities such as art, craft, drama, music, movement and dance are not usually understood properly and there is sometimes a tendency to think of these rather as relaxation after the more serious work of the school is done. But, in fact, they provide experiences which are essential for the full development of pupils.

Developing Creativity in Slow Learners

Creative work is, in essence, a form of play and it provides children with the variety of experiences needed for all-round growth as play does. Cole and Sarnoff (1980) define creativity as "activities and products invented in the interest of solving a problem". They further indicate that creativity is not an inherent trait but that it can be developed in students by teachers. They suggest that creative thought is an "interactive" process, influenced not only by the thinker's capability but also by the culture, with its tools, symbols, and conceptual systems, and by external reality. Citing the work of Jerison(1977) and Crick(1979) they point out that one's perception of the world results from one's processing of a related sample of the mass of incoming stimuli. The individual's experience, then, interacts with and contributes to the development of thinking abilities.

Creative activities are extremely important for all kinds of students, whether they are normal or sub-normal. Unfortunately, creativity is often neglected because of the one right answer orientation of most classrooms. Wassermann(1982) has expressed concern that lack of experience in problem solving, creating and imagining may cause students to become lesson-learners, excelling in the low-order cognitive tasks found in traditional text book and workbook exercises. No teacher should focus exclusively on creative activities just as no teacher should over-emphasise lower-level skills or single-right-answer responses. The needs of the students and the nature of the task should be the criteria for selection of activities and formats.

Cole and Saroff (1980) urge that students be given many opportunities to develop thinking and creative abilities through discovery learning. They suggest that the teachers should evince great enthusiasm for their subject matter. They further point out that discovery learning does not mean abandonment of direct instruction and careful organisation, and that the required degree of structure differs for individual learners and tasks. They emphasise that discovery and self directed inquiry approaches can work better only when the individual learner has enough enthusiasm, information, knowledge, and skill in the area being studied to cope well with the task of finding and solving problems in the subject matter area (p. 40). It envisages that the slow learners should be taught knowledge and skill before they are provided with opportunities for self directed enquiry.

Many of the experiences through which a classroom teacher could help students to develop creativity would be classified as enrichment. They are extensions of the regular curriculum, which allow slow learning students to explore topics in greater breadth or depth than would be possible for the whole class. The essence of creativity development seems to be to provide learning experiences that enable the students to learn strategies, principles or concepts rather than isolated facts. Cole (1969) has suggested that teachers use process curricula that recognise that learning is essentially a creative activity (p. 253). These materials are designed to allow the students to be more active in learning. The child becomes a seeker, an observer, organiser, recorder, communicator, rule deriver and tester (p. 253). Cole and his colleague J. Merrell Hansen (1972) established that modified classroom programme can promote creativity and problem solving through divergent thinking.

Importance of Creative Work

Developing creativity in slow learning children is the primary task of the teacher. Every individual has a unique skill or quality which is markedly different from that of others. There are various creative works such as music, art, modellings drama painting etc which can be effectively and properly made use of in our instructional strategy to bring out the the uniqueness in the individual to the surface. Once this task is satisfactorily accomplished by the teacher, the process of making him a self-supportive social being becomes easier. It is therefore very important to teach creative work to slow learners so that they can make interesting manifestation in some creative work or the other. The freedom, activity and satisfaction of creative expression are often the means by which the slow learning child achieves balance and harmony in his process of growth. When the child achieves these, even partially, he is more able and ready to learn. Teaching of creative work to slow learners is of vital importance on three grounds. They are:

i) Acceleration of emotional growth.

ii) Stimulation of creative thinking.

iii) Promotion of other learning.

i) Acceleration of Emotional Growth

When creative work is taught there is a relaxed, happy atmosphere of classrooms and the children are encouraged and helped to find some means of expression. This provides evidence of personal and emotional growth. Creative and expressive activities are very useful to slow learners which enable them gradually to unfold and to 'let themselves go'. As they do so they not only gain in confidence but also become more capable of participating in life at school and more generally alert and responsive. In the creative works many slow learners find opportunities for achievement and success to counteract their loss of confidence and sense of inadequacy. Many slow learning children are able to achieve success, or have it contrived for them, in one or other of the creative activities. On this foundation, other successes, in academic subjects and other areas, can be based. Above all, it is a valuable compensation for failures and difficulties in other aspects of school work. Apart from this, the creative works provide relief and relaxation which the children obtain from touching and handling materials, from moving about and doing. Even we experience this relaxation after periods of effort or frustration and difficulty, when we achieve release from tension by means of games, hobbies or the vicarious emotional experiences of film and novel. It is for this reason that backward children like slow learners should be provided with creative work in the classroom. Formal work should be closely and genuinely linked with creative work.

In every school there are some slow learners whose emotional and personal difficulties mark them out as difficult or problem children. They range from children whose emotional difficulties are expressed in an active and aggressive way to those who are extremely apathetic and withdrawn. The teacher has primary responsibility for dealing with these problems as he has for specific learning difficulties in basic subjects. Creative and expressive activities are perhaps the chief components of what may be termed a therapeutic curriculum. Pent-up feelings of hostility or frustration find a safe outlet in creative and expressive activities. The fact that such outlets are achieved in a situation watched and controlled by a tolerant teacher seems to make emotional release all the more effective. It fosters emotional stability and finally leads to emotional growth.

ii) Stimulation of Thinking

Creative work is not only concerned with emotional aspects of growth but also it involves thinking as well as feeling. The child who models, paints or dramatises some aspect of his experience is certainly learning more about it. It makes him more observant, and he thinks about what he observes and becomes ready to interpret similar experience later. He assimilates and organises his impressions in expressing what he has experienced. Slow learners are more limited than normal children in verbal expression and there is greater need for them to have alternative means of expression. Art stimulates intelligence and it compels the child to see properly and then to express his thoughts in a form that is tangible and precise. Even drawing should be looked upon primarily as a form of speech. The simple and spontaneous drawings of young children serve just this purpose. In his drawings of people, houses, books, cars and trains, he is going back over what he has observed about them and learning their essential features. In making pictures about stories he has been told or about events he has witnessed or taken part in, the child is familiarising himself with them. It is a form of learning for which the old teaching tenet, 'expression checks impression' is applicable.

Thinking is also involved in the choice and use of materials. Media attributes can be made use of effectively for this purpose. The teacher can provoke purposeful thinking if he can design the creative work as an extension of work in some other aspect of the curriculum. One of the significant characteristics of slow learners is their poor concentration. They are often distractible, and lacking in persistence as mentioned in our earlier chapter. The quality of concentration is related to level of intelligence but there are such factors as interest, and expectation of success or failure which are also influential. Within limits, the ability to concentrate is learnt in the repeated experience of absorbing and satisfying activity. Play in general, and creative work in particular, provide conducive conditions for the development of this trait. Materials and occupations which are suited to the child's level of ability and to his interests can often sustain attention for surprisingly long periods. Many slow learners seldom enjoy ample play opportunities. This laguna can be made up by creative work which ignites the spark of thinking critically and creatively.

Promotion of Other Learning

Slow learners are in general rather more clumsy in both fine and large movements. It is due to poor motor coordination, creative work has an additional value of improving motor coordination. Poor coordination is the resultant product of basic neuro-muscular weakness combined with lack of practice and exercise and its effects are often cumulative. There is a tendency on the part of children to avoid what they can not accomplish easily, especially as they grow older and become more aware of their limitations compared with other children. Slow learners need more of those activities which can improve coordination. Art and craft movement and dance are among such means of helping slow learners. When the teacher encourages creative activities which arise naturally in connection with other work it will lead to incidental learning in learning to share materials and tools, and to look after them, learning to co-operate with others and to experience the satisfaction of group participation. Also this will provide adequate opportunity for development in talking about what is going to be done and how they are going to do it. There will be significant mean gains in vocabulary from following instructions. Children become more aware of the qualities of beauty in form and colour, movement and sound through creative work. In this, even the attractiveness of the whole school environment plays an important role.

Above, all, it is to be noted that these activities often help to bring about good-teacher child relationships through mutual participation in an enjoyable and satisfying experience singing, acting or making together. Moreover, there is another advantage that the creative work leads to a greater understanding of the child since the child's expressions often reveal what experiences he has had, what he made of them and how he feels about them. These creative activities provide ample opportunities for the teacher to observe the child in a new light. This understanding is essential in teaching all the children but it is especially very necessary when the teacher is dealing with slow learners.

The Teacher's Role

Succees of creative work programme depends on the personal involvement and full participation of the child. This naturally raises the question of the extent to which the teacher should give help and make suggestion. In the first place, the teacher contributes by providing the children with the required materials and in the second place he gives them help and guidance about how to use the materials. Sometimes there is a proclivity to interpret that the teacher's contribution is not significant and the teacher plays a passive role while the class gets on with self-expression. But, it is not a correct interpretation. It is very clear that without teacher's help with techniques of handling different materials there can be no better means of releasing and facilitating expression.

The teacher should have a proper understanding of the children's development in order to be aware of the uses to which children are likely to put materials at different stages. The cue for advice often comes from the children themselves. For example, at early stages of development children are satisfied with their schematic representations of the human figure, but there comes a stage when they are dissatisfied and want to make their drawing 'more like'. It is when the teacher can help, not by merely telling them how to do it but by drawing their attention to the proportions and details about which they are dissatisfied. It is not necessary for sketching suggestion on the board because it will be slavishly copied by the children. It is always better to encourage children to observe and find their own way of drawing or painting. There are always children who have no confidence in their own ability and need rather more help to get started. For such children the teacher should provide some new medium about which they have not had the chance to develop unfavourable attitudes. It often happens that some limited and unobtrusive help by the teacher establishes a feeling of success and achievement which enables a child to go ahead without help. The criterion of successful intervention by the teacher is whether the child is enabled to work more freely and spontaneously afterwards.

Another major contribution of the teacher is to ensure that children develop some ideas to express. As children grow older there should be discussion of wider environment, bringing in not only the perpetual favourites - fire engines, trains, supersonic planes - but also topical news - explorers, space travel etc. The teacher should not only make suggestions but also he should ensure an atmosphere in which children feel encouraged to express themselves. The teachers can better provide that atmosphere if they realise well that it is the process of creating, not the results, that matters most. Perhaps most important of all are the enthusiasm and inspiration of the teacher.

Art and Craft

Art activities for slow learners should be part of their total educational programme. This makes the art experience more meaningful, and it also aids the students in integrating classroom lessons. Before planning an art programme the teacher must consider what the learners can tolerate as well as their past experiences and their present interests and skills. It is important not to exceed the learner's lowest tolerance level. It is less important to be concerned about the learner's ability level. We have got a wide range of materials and activities but selection should be determined by the interests, capacities and previous experience of the individual children.

Considerations for the Development of Art Activities

Art activities are very important for all the students in general and slow learners in particular. There are various considerations for the development of art activities. Some of them are:

a. Art activities enable the student's to recognise colour, line and design, and help to develop body image.

b. Art activities increase student's abilities to perceive themselves in their environment.

c. Art works encourage sensory growth.

d. Art works provide ample opportunities to develop social relationships with peers and adults in initiating and completing art activities.

e. Students develop skills in the proper use of the different art media, which will aid in the development of fine and gross motor skills.

f. Arts works foster creativity and initiative within the student's limitations.

g. Art activities enable the students to develop the perceptual skills that are necessary in all academic achievements.

h. Art works help in developing the skill of thinking more clearly.

Art work is markedly different from busy work which is mainly used to keep the hands active while the mind remains passive. The student must be in control of materials, tools, ideas and emotions in expression to engage in any form of art work. When slow learners are engaged in art work these things happen to them. This is nothing but an indication that thinking processes are taking place.

Art Activities for the Slow Learners

Many are the art activities that can be implemented for the slow learners in the mainstreamed classroom. The most common of these include paper activities, crayon, chalk, painting, printing, modelling and drama. By introducing any or some of these art works in the curriculum, the teacher can positively aim at developing the creativity of the slow learners in course of time.

i) Paper Activities

It is the most common as well as feasible art work. Paper is a simple material that can be white or coloured, plain or decorated. It is easier to cut paper along a straight line. It is therefore convenient to begin simple art activities by using the four basic shapes i.e. a circle, a square, a triangle and a rectangle. Paper activities serve as the starting point for art activities.

The teacher should provide the students with pieces of construction paper. Most of the construction papers start out by being rectangles from which we proceed to get a square by folding the paper in two on a diagonal so that one of the sides matches the bottom of the paper. The folder triangle will form one-half of the square, and if there is any extra paper it should be cut away. The teacher can draw squares on the board and divide them with drawn lines; one can be symmetrical and the other off-centre. The teacher can ask students which one they like and why. After that the teacher can add sets of lines to both squares, such as making sixteen equal boxes on one and a variety of rectangles on the other. Even though it is a simple activity, it builds confidence because there is no pressure to draw something. Also, it is an excellent activity to develop the skill of using a ruler.

Then comes circle which is the next shape for an art activity. Here the teacher should start with a square and find the centre point by crossing the diagonals. Then the circle can be constructed. From this the students can understand how closely the square and circle are related. The teacher can instruct the students to divide the square into equal boxes and the boxes can be filled with circles to develop interesting designs with different coloured crayons.

The teacher can instruct the students how to make some simple cutting so that they can make triangles by folding the square on the diagonal and cutting the line. Each triangle can be folded in half and cut into rectangles which again folded can be cut into smaller squares, and so on.

Basic shapes cut from construction paper can be put together to make figures, vehicles, buildings etc. according to the ideas developed by the students. The students just need some guidance to get started. In case of slow learners they need extra guidance to begin the creative processes.

ii) Crayons

The crayons is the most widely used of the art media in schools.

It is available in assorted colours. It is important to note that crayon work has many possibilities, especially when it is combined with other art media. The teacher should instruct the students to make preliminary sketches for crayon picture with white crayon instead of pencils. This helps minimise frustration that is experienced by trying to make a blunt crayon colour minute details of a pencil sketch. Also, by using pieces of crayons instead of whole ones distractions can be eliminated. This does away with the possibility of crayons breaking or the need for peeling down paper covers. The students should be instructed to keep the broken crayons in boxes or cans. He should also encourage students to use the crayons boldly and to colour shapes from inside out instead of outlining the shape first. Some students may quickly colour in one or two shapes and insist that they have completed. Such students should be provided with effective visual motivation. Crayon resist, crayon batik, crayon tapa, marbling with crayon, crayon engraving are some of the creative activities which can be carried out with crayons.

iii) Chalk

Chalk is an easily available material which can be used for creative activites. Chalk comes in different colours and can be used effectively for developing bright pictures. It is also easier to work with chalk on construction paper that has been dampened. The students should apply chalk to the paper without the preliminary drawing, and free design and colour should be emphasised. It is also possible to preserve chalk drawings if they are sprayed with clear fixative outside the classroom. Chalk activities as well as crayon activities are very useful to younger slow learners since these develop in them creative thinking and motor co-ordination.

iv) Painting

Tempera powder paint of good quality is rich in colour and easy to mix, and it covers very well. Painting activities require more preparation, storage, and clean up than crayon art, but the results that we get are worth the effort. The following points are very useful to plan painting activities for the slow learning children. The students can use discarded half-pint wax milk cartons as containers for tempera paint. After it has been mixed, they can be resealed with clips or tape to prevent drying, so they will be ready for the next session. There should be a large brush for each container. If the brushes are too long, about three inches of the handles can be cut off to make them easier for young students to manipulate. The table should be covered with old newspapers and discarded shirts should be used as paint smocks when possible. The teacher should instruct the students who have not had the opportunity to paint before, how to wipe the excess paint off their brush against the lip of the container. They should be reminded to return brushes to their container before using another colour. The teacher should allot enough time for all phases of the activity, such as preliminary sketches, colour choices, and design. There must be occasional exhibition of painting works of students and discussions of the displayed works. There are various different art activities that are fun when working with tempera paint. Some of these activities are:

a) Blowing paint through straw
b) Stencil Painting
c) Portraits
d) Finger Painting.

a) Blow Painting

Blowing paint through straw can be a creative activity. Here the student drops bloks of paint onto a piece of paper and moves the paint around on the paper by blowing through straws. In this manner the student can make his own design according to his imagination and creative thinking. After the student develops a design there must be a discussion about it.

b) Stencil Painting

Stencil painting is another interesting creative activity. The student should cut familiar or abstract shapes from wax-coated freezer paper. He should then attach a stencil to the background paper with doubled-over-tape, and paint over the edge with a brush or the sponge. This will result in a shape with colours around it. The stenciling can be continued with different colours, making overall designs for wrapping paper or any type of decoration.

c) Portrait

If the teacher can properly motivate the students, the portrait can be a great job. It can be a self portrait or of another student in the classroom. The teacher should motivate portrait painting as fun and help alleviate frustration that builds up because 'I can't draw or it doesn't look good'. The teacher must encourage students to make self-portrait by using many methods. It will provide opportunities to get a spontaneous portrayal that is astounding in its clarity. Self-portrait collages can also be made using cut-up construction paper of different colours. Another fun activity is that the teacher can ask the students to draw their self-image lifesize on a piece of folded white kraft paper, either whole body or head or shoulder, using crayons for the features and colours needed.

d) Finger Painting

It is a creative activity which is enjoyed by all students, even the students who do not want to get their hands dirty also like this activity. This activity requires elaborate preparation and planning. The student must have paint shirts, spaces adequately covered with news papers, and a plan for distributing water, paint, and completed papers before the activity begins. Finger paint paper is glazed on the painting side and the students should write their names and date on the dull side before they begin. The paper should be wet completely with a wet sponge and smoothed to get rid of wrinkles or air bubbles. The students should place a heaping spoonful of paint on the paper and begin. The teacher should demonstrate to students how to use fingers, parts of hands, finger tips and fingernails to get different effects. It is very important to provide motivation and also to discuss the paintings as they develop. After completing the work, the student should hang the wet painting on a line to dry or place on floor space covered by newspapers. Though this activity requires good cleaning up practices, the effort is worth the excitement generated by the final product.

v) Printing

Printing is a creative activity which has a magical appeal to most students because of the element of surprise generated by the negative print. The teacher can restrict print making activities to simple procedures. Though there are many ways of printing, the simplest printing is with common materials such as vegetables, fruits, sponges, bars of soap or paraffin, and clap stamps. These materials can be cut or incised to print interesting shapes for a repetitive pattern. Vegetables or fruits can be cut in half or potatoes and carrots can be incised to print interesting shapes. The surface to be printed on should be coated with tempera paint. The simplest way to do this is to make a stamp of tempera - or ink - moistened paper towels. The printing can be done on different kinds of paper, but coloured construction paper will be the most effective medium for combining the colours of the printing with the background.

a) Monoprints:

The teacher can encourage students to make monoprints. Monoprints are transfers of paintings made of tempera or finger paintings. The process involves the following steps.

a. The student should use finger paints on glazed paper to make a finger painting.

b. The student should place any kind of paper to be printed on top of the wet finger painting.

c. The student should then rule gently but firmly over back of the printing paper.

d. When the student lifts the print, the negative print appears. For varietythe students can use materials such as string, tooth picks leaves, grasses, sawdust, torn or cut pieces of paper, and paper or plastic lace. These materials can be arranged on the wet finger painting for second and third prints.

b) Linoleum Block Prints

It is a kind of Print that can be used for making greeting cards or special days or for decorative holiday displays. The required materials include a rubber brayer, a set of cutting tools, linoleum blocks, inking surface, and water based printing ink. The students should cut the blocks using their ideas. They should do the actual printing, cutting the proper sizes of the paper, making envelopes if necessary, and learning how to roll the brayer into the water based ink and then rolling it onto the linoleum block. The student should give firm pressure to print the inked block onto paper. Thus creative activites can be generated in a wide variety of ways in printing.

vi) Modelling

Modelling is a creative activity which children enjoy very much, and various ways of doing this should be used from time to time. Plasticine that has been kept pliable can be a good introudction but it has its own limitations. It tends to lead to small models which are hard to work and does not provide the best practice in coordination. Clay is a more useful as well as satisfactory material to use at all ages. This usually comes in powdered form that needs to be mixed with water. It is easy to work, responding and yielding easily to pulling and pushing with hands. Animals provide a great motivation for reproduction in clay and four legged animals are suggested for first ventures because they stand more easily. The teacher should provide assistance and motivation for students working with clay so that they can enjoy the creative experience to the fullest. Slip (watered clay) can be used to smooth areas and also to get rid of cracks. When the clay model is thoroughly dry, it can be painted with tempera paint, which makes a permanent smooth finish.

Modelling with wire makes an interesting change but is much more difficult since it requires a clearer idea of the nature of the material and what can be done with it. Even so, some slow learners have used it quite successfully in making aeroplanes insects and animals. Wire is frequently used as a frame work on which a surface is built up with bandage or strips of paper and plaster, the model being finally painted. A collection of wire models i.e. animals, insects, aeroplanes etc. made in this way gives immense satisfaction to children.

The students can make use of a collection of scrap materials for making models. Cardboard boxes, match. boxes, spools and reels, packaging material and so on, can be used to build up trains, ships, lorries and houses. The students can make individual models or they can construct group models of streets, villages, harbours and castles to illustrate centres of interest.

Boys are fond of using wooden boxes and timber off-cuts for making models in which they find satisfying woodwork.

vii) Drama

Besides promoting language development, drama has immense educational value in a wider setting. It is to be remembered that all creative works have an intellectual content since it is the result of the child's awareness of and thinking about his experience. Drama, as a means of fostering personality development, should be emphasised in any programme intended to promote creativity in children. Experienced teachers of backward children realise that with many children the emotional development is often as retarded as the intellectual development. Peter Slade defines drama as "doing of life" and it can do much to minimise the difficulties, both personal and social, which arise from emotional retardation and disturbance.

The aims of dramas are numerous. Some important aims are enumerated here.

i) Drama can be effectively used to develop personality through spontaneous dramatic activity. A teacher watching children at play can realise how characteristic is their love of make-believe and dramatic play. The teacher can observe the fundamental and dynamic part which emotion, movement and rhythm play in their activities. The teacher may be struck by their imagination and by their complete absorption in dramatic play as it arises spontaneously in the absence of self-consciousness. Creative drama should be based on these forms of play and develop from them. It thus forms out of, and meets the psychological needs of the child as an individual and as a member of a team. In fact, it is child-centred. It serves as an integral part of the school's programme for child development.

ii) Another important aim of drama is to provide opportunities for the imagination to develop through improvisation, for the development of increasing sensitivity and appropriate reaction to the environment. In drama the teachers can encourage children to use their imagination in both real life and imaginary situation. For example, the teacher can ask the students to show them what they would do if a wild animal entered the room, how they would feel if they were lost in a wood or if a snake crawled over them, or if they had lost money given for mother's shopping etc. The teacher can make use of rhythm(on a drum or tambourine) and music to suggest dance forms, animal movements, dramatic situations and emotional states.

iii) Another aim of drama is to provide opportunities for emotional re-education and for the improvement of social behaviour. Many backward children like slow learners are socially deprived since they have been wrongly handled in their up-bringing. They have been denied opportunities for normal play. In many cases their lives have been almost devoid of love, affection and security. They have not experienced feelings of success and self-esteem, and have had little chance to build up happy social relationships and ideas of acceptable behaviour. Drama can be of use so as to give children who need it the opportunity to 'live through' their early years.

When the teacher gives opportunity for slow learners to compose their own plays it provides outlets for their aggressiveness, negativism, destructiveness and feelings of antagonism towards authority and other children. Drama activities enable even the most ego-centric students to develop strong group feeling. Sociometric surveys made at the beginning and the end of a term's drama sessions have revealed the benefts which are derived from drama work. The dominant, histrionic leader becomes less dominant, the isolate begins to make contact with the group. The withdrawn and fearful child gains considerably because his bottled-up aggression is brought out into the open. He is no longer afraid of his aggressive impulses since they are accepted, and he gradually becomes more relaxed and enters the team. (Tansley and Gulliford, 1962).

iv) Drama can also be used to enrich and make more meaningful other areas of the curriculum. Drama in all its forms becomes an essential part of the educational process since it involves the principle of 'learning by doing'. There are ample opportunities in history, geography, religious education, arithmetic and reading when simple dramatisations can make learning more exciting and vivid. Our reading programme for slow learners should make use of dramas extensively. The teacher can instruct children to make up plays about the stories they have read or to improvise on the situations which make up the themes of the books. Their feelings, impressions and observations in drama are transferred to other forms of expression.

How to use Creative Drama for Slow Learners

a) Movement and Mime

Movement and mime should form the starting point in introducing drama to slow learners. The teacher should therefore begin with movement and mime. The first thing the teacher should concentrate on is the art of relaxation complete relaxation. Suitable music can be a great help in inducing relaxation and a peaceful atmosphere. Every lesson must end with a period of relaxation (a de- Climax) so that the children leave the place calm and peaceful eventhough the de-climax may have been immediately preceded by a noisy 'playing up' scene. In a group of lessons the teacher should work through the whole range of emotions. The teacher should be dramatic in the descriptions of situations. Suppose the teacher creates a situation like this: 'Imagine you are in a dark room; it is very dark. The door begins to open slowly-it creaks a little. Can you hear it? Look can you see something at the door?' This provides ample opportunities to express a variety of emotions love and hate, fear, pain happiness, friendships, disgust, suspense, contentment, surprise, indifference, being accepted or rejected. The students will evince varied responses enormously. The withdrawn children may not show much excitement or willingness to use large movements. To start with practice in miming small movement will be helpful. With teacher's encouragement and inspirations improvement takes place quickly and the lessons become exciting and interesting. Demonstrations by students and the growing relationships between teacher and pupils expedite the progress.

b) Dance Drama

The next step is applying movement and mime to simple dance drama. Dance drama is a useful starting point since it suggests a variety of moods and range of movements. It has several rhythms, and its quiet beginning, tremendous climax followed by de-climax, together with its story arouse children's interest and emotions. Some editing of music on records is often needed if expression is not to flag. Rhythms on percussion instruments can be used at this stage, these primitive rhythms give children much pleasure and stimulation.

c) Application of Techniques to Play-making

At this stage, the teacher should instruct how to apply the above techniques to the beginnings of play-making. For this purpose the teacher can use subjects such as family situations, visits to the sea side or the country, to the circus, exploring in the jungle and acting other familiar scenes. For a greater effect with more withdrawn children sound effects either recorded or made at the time will be helpful. For example we need train and aeroplane noises, explosions, thunderstroms, street sounds and the like to make situations more realistic lighting effects are also useful. By this time the children are ready to dramatise the whole or parts of well-known stories. The teacher should emphasise movement and expression of feelings but should not hold back spontaneous speech. Too much attention to speech has to be guarded against however lest it inhibit the expression of the whole child in movement and action. There are various stories for young children which can be acted out. The teacher should allow the whole group to mime the various characters in a story before asking them for suggestions for role playing.

d) Composition of Plays

Composition of plays almost entirely by children is the final stage in this development of dramatic activity. There is little use for the acting of scripted plays leading to a performance although reading plays within the reading ability of the pupils is enjoyed. Acting scripted plays leads to an artificial performance lacking the genuineness of real dramatic movement. The new play should begin with a discussion in which the preliminary plot is developed and the roles are temporarily allotted. The first scene must be then worked out and acted. After that discussions should continue again. Alterations and modifications should be agreed upon; suitable sound effects, lighting, music and simple properties should be planned and obtained. Then the play will ultimately evolve. In this way, a single play can take as long as one term to complete. Some teachers may be reluctant to attempt this type of drama because of lack of knowledge or experience. However, it does not require any knowledge of Theatre or any previous experience of acting. What is more important is an understanding of children and a willingness to follow the children's lead in the dramatic realisation of their imaginations. Teachers using drama in this way can improve teacher-child relationships which can, in turn, resolve many disciplinary problems.

Developing Social Competence in Slow Learners

Preparing students for continued education, adult responsibilities, independence, and employment have always been the goals of school education. Most students complete high school and find jobs, enter a vocational training programme, or go to college without experiencing major difficulties of adjustment. Dropout and unemployment rates are far too high for all youths, especially in economically depressed communities, but the outlook for students with disabilities may be even worse (Handrick, MacMillan, and Balow,1989; Wolman, Bruininks, and Thurlow, 1989). Many drop out of school, experience great difficulty in finding and holding a job, do not find work suited to their capabilities, do not receive further training or education, or become dependent on their families (Edgar, 1987; Neel, Meadow, Levine and Edgar, 1988).

Zetlin and Hosseini (1989) have noted in their case studies that learning handicapped young adults are anxious and frustrated by the uncertainty of their future. They have no clear course that they are following; rather, they move around from part-time job to part-time job from class to class, from school to school (p 411). It emphasises the need for developing social competence in slow learners so that their transition from school life to adult life can be smooth and successful.

A smooth and successful transition to adult life is difficult for any adolescent. Students find many different routes to adulthood, and it would be foolish on the part of the teacher to prescribe a single pattern of transition. Our primary aim is to provide the slow learners with the special assistance that will help them achieve the most rewarding, productive, independent and integrated adult life possible. We can not achieve this goal just by assuming that all adolescents and slow learners will need special transition services or that all will achieve the same level of independence and productivity. One of education's great challenges in the 1990's is to devise an effective array of programmes that will meet the individual needs of students on their paths to adulthood.

Training and experience at home and school will play a vital role in developing the qualities needed for a satisfactory adjustment to life after leaving the school. The primary aims of education for slow learners are development of desirable personal behaviour, the capacity for proper human relationships and social responsibility. These particular aims are, of course, applicable at all levels of education but they assume greater difficulty in making satisfactory adjustments at home, school and work. Their poorer endowment and achievement make it more difficult for them to obtain recognition and esteem in socially desirable ways. Their difficulties in thinking may make it harder for them to be self-critical and to anticipate the outcome of their behaviour. Their earlier unsatisfactory social experiences may have bred attitudes and ways of behaving which make their adjustment precarious. To give a few examples, the over protected child may have difficulty in adapting to the give-and-take of group activities; the neglected child may not be able to form good relationship with others; emotional disturbance may result in irresponsible behaviour or anxieties about making social contacts. The teacher teaching slow learners should therefore pay special attention to ensuring the development of the qualities needed for successful adjustment to post school life and in overcoming or minimising some of the personal problems that can lead to failure. The characteristics needed by the slow learners leaving the school may be considered under two heads. They are:

i) Personal Qualities

ii) Social relationships.

i) Personal Qualities

The slow learners should have acquired, by the time they leave the school, good standards of personal hygiene, in the mental as well as the physical sense. They should have developed habits of personal cleanliness, a liking for physical activity and a desire to keep fit and healthy. This is where the vocational education and physical education are very helpful. They should have reached a stage of maturity at which they are capable of the independent management of their affairs. They should be able to organise their leisure activities and be self-sufficient so as to avoid lonliness and boredom; to realise and auapt to the difficulties of new situations; and to appreciate the importance of such qualities as punctuality, persistence, reliability, self-criticism, friendliness and cheerfulness. This is where the art, craft and drama activities will hold good. In short, all these personal qualities required for social competence can be developed by means of proper vocational and physical education and art and drama activities. The slow learners must be able to understand their limitations and to match their aspirations to their abilities.

ii) Social Relationships

The slow learners when they leave the school should appreciate the importance of getting along with other people and of acting towards them in ways which will be considered fitting. They should be ready to learn from their superiors and to meet their reasonable demands, to listen to and act upon the advice of more knowledgeable people and to reject undesirable suggestions. They should be sufficiently sensitive to the reactions of other people to avoid rejection by being too persistent in his demands for attention and friendship, and to avoid over compensatory behaviour such as showing off, boasting and lying. In work situations, the school leaving slow learners should be able to endeavour to keep a suitable job, to budget wisely and save adequately. If at all they happen to change their jobs, it should be for good reasons like greater opportunity, more security, better health conditions and not for such reasons as increased wages without prospects, to work with a friend, to be nearer home or because of personal inadequacies and an inability to get along with other work people.

Research Base

A few follow up studies have been made to assess whether the backward children leaving the school match up to these requirements. These studies point out that a large percentage are employable and provide a useful source of unskilled and semi-skilled labour. Hargrove (1954) reports that out of 440 school leavers 337 were fully employed. Collman(1956) in a follow up study of 98 school leavers from residential schools and 125 from day schools between 1949 and 1952 states that 72 percent were wholly or partly successful at work, 16 per cent were failures and 12 percent were unemployable. If the unemployables were excluded 69 percent were completely successful. Alkinson (1957) followed up 45 leavers from a boys' residential school and considered that 89 percent had settled satisfactorily in work Twenty nine boys were in unskilled work, 12 in semi-skilled work and 4 were unemployable. Jones (1957) followed up 59 boys who left a mixed residential school between July 1952 and July 1955. Seventeen boys had been certified, 5 had left before the statutory leaving age and 37 were at work of the last group, 26 were followed up in detail and Jones states that one became unemployable for health reasons, 5 had had more than two employers and more than half changed their jobs within three months of leaving the school. Collman(1956) gives the following figures in connection with his failure group:

IQ	40-49	50-59	60-69	70+
Percentage of Employment failures	22	12	18	12
Percentage of Unemployable	48	12	4	6

Causes of Failure at Work

The above studies suggest that main causes of failure are:

1) Irresponsible behaviour arising from emotional disturbance and temperamental instability. This irresponsibility usually manifests itself in lack of persistence, susceptibility to monotony, inability to put up with necessary frustrations, disinterestedness, resulting in unpunctuality, poor work habits and apathy.
2) Lack of adequate supervision and guidance at home.
3) Lack of understanding on the part of employers and, in particular, of immediate superiors. The slow learning adolescents do not readily adapt to changes and the transition from school to work can be very difficult. These adolescents may have difficulty in understanding or remembering instructions, they may find the speed of work too much for them or they may find the the apparently simple processes difficult to grasp. Changes in the routine, the necessary making of new social relationships with more normal people who may not appreciate the problems of slow learners, and the removal of support from school make adjustment difficult. Because of these causative factors some slow learners miserably fail at work.

Importance of Developing Social Competence in School

It has been already mentioned that certain personal qualities and social relationships are very much needed by the slow learning adolescents to make a satisfactory adjustment to post-school life. It is therefore one of the important tasks of the school to develop these qualities, but this can not be achieved only in the last year or two at school. Social competence is the resultant product of a long process of development, the foundation of which is laid in the work done in the junior classes and consolidated and extended as children grow older. The schools should provide such an environment that children can live and grow in it successfully. They must be able to learn from it, desire and develop acceptable attitude and modes of behaviour from their experience in it, and eventually realise that it is helping them to prepare for independence in post-school life. In organising the school programmes to these ends, the following should be taken into considerations.

(a) Children do not develop these qualities at uniform rate. They develop these required qualities at different rates. Age and intelligence must be considered in setting standards of school behaviour and personal competence. Variations in these can occur because of the students' previous experiences at home and school. The students' constitutional make up and their physical development also play a significant role.

(b) Social re-education will be necessary for some children. This is not easy because it is very difficult to change previous attitudes and forms of behaviour. This is particularly true of over-demanding behaviour which has previously been successful.

(c) The above considerations indicate that there must be certain amount of flexibility in the standards of behaviour and in the approach to children. A specific pattern should not be imposed, it must develop as the majority of children in the class are becoming ready to act up to it. Sometimes a child's individual activity may be contrary to what is desirable but the school should accept that it is a necessary part of his attempts at adjustment. The teacher should regard his behaviour as his way of meeting a felt need, perhaps as an emotional release. The teacher should understand the need and try to make required arrangement for meeting it, and for avoiding the repetition of unacceptable behaviour in connection with it. For example, a child may sometimes deface his reading and exercise book and this may be his way of relieving frustrations arising from educational demands which he is incapable of meeting. The teacher should ensure remedy for this by adjusting the difficulty of the work.

(d) Social education must be viewed as an integral part of the whole educational process in play, in school work, at home. The teacher should arrange the school programme in such a way that each child should be able to grow in personal awareness and develop feeling of confidence, self-esteem and self-reliance. Many children do not have the privilege of playing and working with others, either because mother has not allowed them or because they have been rejected by the peers. It is not possible for children to learn to play and work with others in just a few days. They also need to go through the stages that normal children usually go through. First they play more or less on their own, then they play next to another child albeit not in active co-operation and only later will they make more active contact with each other. That is why the slow learners need time for informal activities or play throughout the primary school, as well as continued opportunities for group activities throughout their school life. Just because the slow learners need an individualised approach in teaching of basic subjects it does not mean that all work should be individualised. Group work is essential in areas like art, drama and practical subjects to gain experience in working and in planning together. For older slow learners there should be a balance between such group work and individual work so that the children can learn to work by himself with the minimum supervision. They should have good personal relationship with the teacher in the school since they may have had little experience of the give-and-take of good relationships in their home life.

e) The attitudes and relationships within the school are also very important. Slow learning children can learn more about the art of living together when they are educated in an atmosphere of friendliness, consistency and respect for other than from repeated moralising and exhortations. There must be a good relationship between the headmaster and the teachers and between the teachers and students.

Procedures to Develop Social Competence in Slow Learners

Research evidences indicate that failure of slow learners as adult members of the society is largely due to weakness in character and personality, and inability to meet the demands of new situations. The teacher should look on every child as a potential school leaver. He should plan his educational programme for slow learners in such a way that it should develop those qualities and attitudes which will lead to successful participation in all spheres of post-school life. An educational programme which aims at developing social competence in slow learners should include the following procedures:

- i) Introducing Vocational education, and art, craft and drama.
- ii) Pre-vocational training.
- iii) Group discussion
- iv) Educational visits
- v) Individual assignments.
- vi) Educational first-aid
- vii) Post-school management.
- viii) Job placement.
- ix) Further Education

i) Introducing Vocation Education and Art, Craft and Drama

Teaching of vocational subjects plays a vital role in the career as well as personality development of slow learners. An effective teaching of vocational subjects can ensure a smooth transition from school life to social life. Vocational subjects serve as foundation on which the slow learning adolescents can build their futures. So the teachers, by way of effective vocational training, can provide the building blocks for their foundation. Vocational subjects are the fields in which most of the slow learning adolescents can often more easily achieve success or have it engineered for them. There is nothing which works like success; and success leads to success. Similarly art, craft and drama activities not only foster the creativity of slow learning adolescents but also promote such physical qualities and social relationships that are very essential for developing social competence.

ii) Pre-Vocational Training

The school should concentrate on pre-vocational training of school leaving slow learners since these students, whether they go to college, or for vocational training, or directly into the job market, can profit from appropriate pre-vocational training. It is already seen that failure of slow learning children in post-school life is due to weakness in personality and inexperience rather than due to low intelligence and lack of skill. It is therefore essential that the training programme should include the following:

a. The arrangements of visits which show the school leaver a variety of working conditions.
b. Introducing the pupils to new experiences similar to those he will be likely to meet in post-school life.
c. Training in specific aspects of working life such as interviews, form-filling, details of wage slips, changing jobs, estimation of travelling time, factory rules, and the way a factory works.
d. Advice on how to choose leisure activities and how to make good relationships with others and opposite sex.
e. Guidance about fitting in at home. School leaving children will have to meet difficulties of new situations at work and so they should not have any adjustment problems at home.
f. Personal budgeting.

iii) Group Discussion

Informal and friendly discussions are very essential for developing social competence. It should be ensured that even quieter withdrawn children are also given a chance and that the more outgoing, talkative children do not dominate the discussion. It may be difficult in the early stages to get the members of the group to relax and talk, or to be sufficiently serious. However, if interesting topics related to the present and past experiences of the children are chosen discussion can be stimulated and difficulties can be overcome. The first discussions should usually deal with the children's present problems and status and with their ideas about various aspects of school life. They can be encouraged to discuss school organisation and methods of improving treatment or discipline.

Whenever possible, discussion should be followed by some first hand experience. It is, therefore, important to integrate the programme of discussions with that for educational visits. Before the visit the teacher should give information about the type of work they will see, the working conditions, and a simple description of the manufacturing process they will see. Each visit should be followed by discussion during which the children can analyse their impressions. The post-visit discussions also serve an important purpose. They bring up many of the problems and need situations which the school leaver may have to face in his post-school life. There should be a focussed group discussion on working life and conditions because economic efficiency and job satisfaction are very important in the making of satisfactory post-school adjustments. It is to be noted that social competence also includes adjustment at home and in the wider community. Group discussion should therefore include such topics as relationships in the home, choice of friends, club activites and personal budgeting.

iv) Educational Visits

Educational visits play a predominant role in acquiring first hand informations about things, places and people. Educational visits should be an integral part of any pre-vocational scheme and of preparation for adult life. Some teachers think that it will suffice if they take the school leavers to works which specialise in processes which they are likely to carry out, or in which first class working conditions obtain. But what is more important is that they should see skilled work in progress in order to help them appreciate their own limitations. It is essential that they should gain some experience of all types of woking conditions-noisy, quick, dirty, clean, indoor, outdoor, and in large and small firms. In short, educational visits enable the slow learners to understand better what is what and how to cope. The better understanding and progressive selfconfidence ensured by the educational visits are the marked mile stones in the development of social competence of slow learners.

v) Individual Assignment

We can not aim at developing social competence without making the slow learning children capable of independent action and of working without direct supervisions. Our eduational programme should aim at the development of these two skills by the slow learners require more intensive and practical training. So a programme intended to promote social competence should include individual assignments designed to develop self-confidence, initiative, a willingness to ask for advice and information, and an ability to meet new situations without strain. These assignments should be devised so as to provide experiences in shopping, travelling, using the telephone, estimation of time and distance, the carrying out of requests and the following of directions.

The principle of easy to difficult should be followed in assigning individual assignments. First they should be trained up in the use of telephone. Once they are proficient in using the phone, they should follow a scheme of graded assignments which involve various activities such as using a public transport, making of a telephone call and estimating about travelling. Assignments should also include performing tasks such as finding an address, obtaining an article from a shop, buying stamp or postal orders, finding prices of clothes, foods, hairdressing, shoe repairing, obtaining pamphlets and brochures, and details about bus or train times. But the assignments should be arranged in a graded manner. Grading of assignments must be adapted to individual differences as well as to meet the needs of its own population. By the time all these assignments are successfully completed by the school leaves he will have developed those social skills that are most required for adult life in the society.

vi) Post-School Management

The pre-vocational training plays a vital role in enabling the slow learners to meet the problems inherent in the transition from school to work. Even then, further help and supervisions are necessary for most of the slow learners because the slow learning children will move from a society which has been geared to their individual needs, and in which they have been taught and guided by trained personnel, into one which probably expects standards of achievement without regard to individual differences. In school they had teachers who understood them and whom they could respect and lean upon but in the post-school life they have no one like that. Earlier they were in a group which consisted of individuals with some what similar inadequacies and feeling to their own. But in the post-school life they have to meet, in an extremely different setting; the demands of a more mixed group. These demands may accentuate their feeling of inadequacy; loneliness and frustration and make apparent to others his general immaturity. That is why post-school management becomes a must for slow learning children. This scheme should be designed so as to provide readily available aids to vocational, social and personal adjustment.

vii) Job Placement

Getting a suitable job for the slow learning adolescents is the first step towards eventual adjustment. Most of the slow learners find for themselves some jobs or other since they usually do not go for higher education. However, it is not placement that matters but job satisfaction. To achieve this, the teachers may be consulted in the matter of job placement for slow learners. Task according to aptitude should be the governing criterion. Placement should take into account the school leaving adolescent's strengths, weaknesses, interests and wishes, and parental attitudes.

Wherever possible, parents should be consulted about their children's employment since their co-operation and understanding are vital. Many parents themselves need guidance as to how to help their children to adjust to their work. The teacher should apprise the parents of how to ensure punctuality, independence, self-criticism, cheerfulness and willingness to take a job. They must be able to advise the young adults what to do when a job seems unsuitable. They must know how and when to offer encouragement and how to help over financial matters. It should be made clear to the parents that changing jobs for financial gain is not always the best thing in the long run and they should accept the young adults as they are, but without undue complacency. Where there is parental co-operation in this way the slow learning young adults will do well in their jobs.

viii) Further Education

Some slow learning young adults are capable of further intellectual growth and leaving after leaving the school. Such adolescents become more sensitive to the felt needs of life and become more ready to accept help. For instance, although their poor learning rate and limited intellectual capacity may not be a marked handicap in their employment, they do sooner or later realise that further education is essential for promotions at work and to feel adequate in social situation. Such young adults join distance education or further education courses and they complete the course at their own speed if not within the stipulated duration. Distance education now offers many job-oriented diploma and certificate courses for the benefit of such young adults and age is no bar for admission to these courses. So these young adults, while in job, can join their job related courses and attain better professional competence. It also develops their skill in language and communication which are very essential for attaining better social competence. The young adults in cities can avail the evening college facilities in this regard. Further education can thus promote not only professional competence but also social competence of slow learners.

Summary

Developing creativity in slow learning children is the primary task of the teacher. Every individual has a unique skill or quality which is markedly different from that of others. There are various creative works such as music, art, modelling, drama, painting etc which can be effectively and properly made use of in our instructional strategy to bring out the uniqueness in the individual to the surface.

Teaching of creative work to slow learning adolescents is of vital importance on three grounds. It accelerates the emotional growth of slow learning adolescents. It stimulates their creative thinking besides promoting other learning.

Success of a creative work programme depends on the personal involvement and full participations of the adolescents. The teacher has to ensure these two requirements to make his creative work programme fruitful. The teacher should not only make suggestions but also ensure an atmosphere in which the slow learning adolescents feel encouraged to express themselves. The teacher can better provide such atmosphere if they realise well that it is the proccess of creating, not the results, that matters most. Perhaps the most important of all are the enthusiasm and inspiration of the teacher.

Art activities for slow learners should be part of their total educational programme, since it makes the art experiences more meaningful and it also aids the students in integrating classroom lessons.

Besides promoting language development, drama has immense educational value in a wider setting. Drama can be effectively used to develop personality through spontaneous dramatic activity. Drama provides opportunities for the imagination to develop through improvisation, for development of sensitivity and appropriate reaction to environments. Also it provides opportunities for emotional re-education and for the improvement of social behaviour. Drama can also be used to enrich and make more meaningful other areas of the curriculum.

Preparing students for continued education, adult responsibilities, independence and employment have always been the goals of school education. So there is a greater need for developing social competence in slow·learning adolescents so that their transition from school life to adult life can be smooth and successful.

Research evidences indicate that failure of slow learners as adult members of the society is largely due to weakness in character and personality, and inability to meet the demands of new situations. The teacher should look on every child as a potential school leaver. He should plan his educational programme for slow learning adolescents in such a way that it should develop those qualities and attitudes which will lead to successful participation in all spheres of post-school life. An educational programme which aims that developing social competence in slow learners should include procedures such as introduction of vocational education and creative works, pre-vocational training, group discussion, educational visits, individual assignments, post-school management, job placement and further education.

REFERENCES

Atkinson, E.J. (1957) 'Post-school Adjustment of Educationally Sub-normal Boys'.

Cole, H., (1969) 'Process of Curricula and Creativity Development'. *The Journal of Creative Behaviour,* 6, 243-259.

Cole, H., Hansen, J.M., and Parsons, D. (1973) 'Enhancing Creativity Through Classroom Differences to Encourage Individual Differences'. University of Kentucky, Lexington, Ky.

Cole, H., and Samoff, D. (1980) 'Interactive Creativity: Explorations of Basic Meanings and their Implications for Teaching and Counselling'. Paper Presented at 26th Annual Creative Problem Solving Institute, State University College, Buffalo.

Collman, R.D. (1956) 'Employment Success of ESN School Ex-pupils in England'. *The Slow Learning Child,* Vol. 3, No. 2.

Crick, F.H. (1970) 'Thinking About the Brain'. *Scientific American* 24', 219-232.

Edgar, E.(1987) 'Secondary Programmes in Special Education'. Are many of them Justifiable?' *Exceptional Children,* 53, 555-561.

Hallahan, D.P., and Kauffman, J.M. (1991) 'Exceptional Children'. Prentice-Hall, Englewood Cliffs, NJ.

Hargrove, A.L. (1954) 'The Social Adaptation of Educationally Subnormal School Leavers'. National Association for Mental Health.

Hendrick, I.G., MacMillan, D.L., and Balow, I.H. (1980) 'Early School Leaving in America'. University of California, Riverside.

Jerison, H. (1977) 'Evolution of the Brain'. In M.C. Wittrock (Ed) 'The Human Brain'. Prentice-Hall, Englewood Cliffs, N.J.

Joes, D.J. (1957) 'A Study of the Problems and Needs of Boys who Left a Residential School For ESN Children'.

Morsink, C.V. (1984) 'Teaching Special Needs Students in Regular Classrooms'. Little, Brown and Co, Boston.

Neel, R.S., Meadows, N., Levine, P., and Edgar, E.D. (1988) 'What Happens After Special Education: A Statewide Follow-up Study of Secondary Students who have Behavioural Disorders'. *Behavioural Disorders,* 13, 209-216.

Tansley, A.E., and Gulliford, R. (1962) 'The Education of Slow Learning Children'. Routledge and Kegan Paul Ltd, London.

Wassermann, S. (1982) 'The Gifted Canit Weigh That Giraffe'. Phi Delta Kappan, 63, 6261.

Wolman, C., Bruininks, R., and Thurlow, M. (1989) 'Dropouts and Dropout Programmes: Implications for Special Education'. *Remedial and Special Education,* 7(2), 49-55.

Zetlin, A.G., and Hosseini, A. (1989) Six Post-school Case Studies of Mildly Learning Handicapped Young Adults'. *Exceptional Children,* 55, 405-411.

10 Research on Slow Learners

Chapter Outline

Chapter Objectives

The chapter furnishes the abstracts of the research works done on slow learners. After reading this chapter you should be able to:

- Understand the nature of research and educational research
- List out the needs for research on Slow Learners.
- Gain an insight into the research works done recently
- Know the thrust areas where researches are warranted on slow learners or with reference to slow learners.

What is Research?

John W. Best defines research as "the systematic and objective analysis and recording of controlled observations that may lead to the developments of generalisations, principles, or theories, resulting in prediction and possibly ultimate control of events". According to him "research is considered to be the more formal, systematic, intensive process of carrying on the scientific method of analysis. It involves a more systematic structure of investigation, usually resulting in some sort of formal record of procedures and a report of results or conclusions".

In the words of Wayne Courtney "research, ideally, is the careful unbiased investigation of a problem, and based, so far as possible, upon demonstrable facts and involving refined distinctions, interpretations and usually some generalisations. The Webster's International Dictionary gives a very inclusive definition of research as "a careful critical enquiry or examination in seeking facts or principles; diligent investigation in order to ascertain something".

D. Slesinger and M. Stephenson in the Encyclopaedia of Social Sciences define research as the manipulation of things concepts or symbols for the purpose of generalising to extend correct or verify knowledge, whether that knowledge aids in construction of theory or in the practice of an art. Research is directed towards solution of a problem. It may attempt to answer a question or to find out a relation between two or more variables.

What is Educational Research?

Travers states that educational research is that activity which is directed towards development of a science of behaviour in educational institutions. The ultimate aim of such science is to provide knowledge that will permit the educator to achieve his goals by the most effective methods. Educational research is the process of applying the scientific method to the solution of educational problems. It is the method of obtaining objective solutions to the problems encountered in the theory and practices of education.

It is the process of arriving at empirically verifiable principles or generalisations about educational theory or practice. We may say that whenever the scientific method is used for obtaining solutions to problems encountered by educational theoreticians or practitioners, this activity may be described as educational research.

Need for Educational Research

"The secret of our cultural development has been research, pushing back the areas of ignorance by discovering new truths which, in turn, lead to better ways of doing things and better products". — John W. Best.

"We pass through research from subjectivity or personal experience to objective validity and universal applicability".

— Robut R. Rusk.

"Research is perhaps the only assurance we have that a discipline or a profession will not decay into meaningless scraps or dogmatic utterances".

— Bernard Mehl.

1. We know how research helps us in solving the various problems that we encounter in the field of education in scientific manner. The findings of different investigations enlighten us as to how best we can administer education, how best we can provide instructional material to our pupils and how best we can teach and evaluate their progress. Hence the need for research.
2. Research is needed for devising new technique of teaching which would adequately motivate the learners and help them in the acquisition of knowledge, skills and attitudes.
3. The ultimate end of research is the advancement of knowledge. Educational research would provide us with more and more knowledge about the pupils we have to teach, methods of instruction, curriculum, evaluation, administration etc.
4. Education should keep pace with the social changes that are continually taking place and the changes we effect in education should be based on research.

5. Research becomes essential because of the dynamic nature of education.
6. Research promotes better understanding of the teaching learning process.
7. Destiny of a nation is being shaped in her classrooms. So research should be the base for all the planned changes in the field of education.
8. Research leads to adaption to new techniques and methods.
9. Research economises effort and increases efficiency.
10. Above all, research promotes educational reforms.

Need For Research on Slow Learners

Perhaps the most difficult problem of classroom organisation is dealing with the fact that students come into class with different knowledge skills, learning rate and motivation. This problem requires teachers to provide appropriate levels of instruction. Teaching a class of thirty students or even a class of ten is fundamentally different from one-to-one tutoring because of the inevitability of student-to-student differences that affect the success of instruction. Teachers can always be sure that if they teach one lesson to the whole class, some students will learn the material more quickly than others. In fact, some students may not learn the lesson at all because they lack important prerequisite skills or are not given adequate time (because to give them enough time would waste too much of the time of those students who learn rapidly). Recognition of these instructionally important differences leads many teachers to search for ways of individualising instruction, adapting instruction to meet students' different needs, or grouping students according to their abilities (Slavin, 1986).

Slow learners are those students who are unable to cope with the work normally expected of their age group. They are the students who are unable to do the work normally expected of their age group. They are the students who are unable to do the work of the class in which they are placed or even the class below that. These slow learners constitute such a considerable percentage of student population that they can not be ignored. Children of today are the future citizens and they are going to be the pillars of the country. Hence it is essential to ensure that each pillar is as strong as the other. Moreover the very fact that the slow learners do not respond satisfactorily to the ordinary school curriculum and to the usual methods and procedures of the classroom teaching warrants a special instructional strategy for them. This makes the role of research significant.

Effective teaching in any subject depends largely upon the introduction of newer methods of instruction. There is a growing need for trying out newer methods of instruction and establishing their effectiveness in teaching. Now-a-days a teacher can not depend on any single method of teaching. The teacher has to try out several innovative methods to present the content to students. When they are taught by innovative methods, the students are able to understand the concept, principles and content in an effective manner. It envisages the need for research to be undertaken in this regard.

Although much has been achieved in this field of education, there are many opportunities for experiments and research. Throughout we have been constantly aware of the need for further investigation of the learning, thinking and adjustment of slow learning children so that teaching method can be precisely planned to suit their needs (Tansley and Gulliford, 1962).

Above all, human resource development should be at the focus of any research effort for a developing country like India which has abundant human resources. In the Indian system of education, it is observed that the human resources teachers and learners are under developed and perform less than their capabilities. The learners are under developed in the sense that they are not achieving in tune with their capabilities. Even some of the most efficient teachers are not adequately equipped to identify and guide the under achievers, low achievers and slow learners to reach their optimum levels. As a result, the institutions in turn are not able to send their products into the society as fully developed learners. To ensure this we need researches to be undertaken to find out newer methods of instruction for these backward students and to establish their effectiveness in Indian classroom environment.

Researches on Slow Learners

Though any research on backward children may have far reaching implications, only a few studies have been conducted so far in India. Stella (1993) has established the effectiveness of CAI with special reference to under achievers. Reddy, and Ramar (1994, 1995, 1996) have established the effectiveness of multimedia based modular approach in teaching, science, maths and social science to low achievers. Soundararaja Rao and Rajaguru (1995) have established the effectiveness of Video assisted instruction in teaching science to slow learners. Reddy and Ramar (1996, 1997) have verified the effectiveness of ÇAI, Video instruction, modular approach, multimedia instructional strategy, and multimedia based modular approach on the achievement of slow learners in various subjects. A brief summary of each of the above experimental studies on slow learners is presented below under appropriate sub-heading.

1. *An Experimental Study on Effectiveness of Video Assisted Instruction On Achievement of Slow Learners*

Soundararaja Rao and Rajaguru (1995) studied "effectiveness of video assisted instruction on the achievement of slow learners". The major objectives of the study were:

i) To investigate the effectiveness of video assisted instructions on the achievement of slow learners in learning science concepts.

ii) To make a comparative study of the achievement of slow learners in terms of the following variables: sex difference, socio-economical difference, management of school, parents' educational status and family size of slow learners.

iii) To study the relationship between achievement of slow learners and their intellectual capacity.

After analysis, the study gave the following conclusions:

i) The slow learners of control and experimental groups were alike in immediate retention. But female slow learners of video assisted instruction group performed better in immediate retention than conventional learning group.

ii) Irrespective of the type of schools managed by different bodies, the slow learners of those groups were alike in immediate retention.

iii) The socio-economic status had impact on immediate retention of slow learners in learning science concepts through video assisted instruction.

iv) The video assisted instruction facilitated male and female slow learners to have better retention even after the lapse of one month period.

v) The socio-economic status had impact on retention test with regard to experimental group slow learners. On the other hand, the remaining factors like parents' educational status and family size have least impact on retention test.

vi) The male and female slow learners in control and experimental groups were alike in intelligence test.

vii) The slow learners of Government schools and private schools were alike in intelligence test.

viii) The socio-economic status and parents' educational status had least impact on intelligence of control and experimental group slow learners.

ix) The intellectual ability of slow learners was positively correlated with post-test and retention test. The correlation between post-test and retention test was also positive.

2. *Effectiveness of Multimedia Based Modular Approach in Teaching English to Slow Learners.*

Reddy and Ramar(1996) conducted this experimental study with two objectives in view (i) to develop multimedia based modules for VIII Std English subject and (ii) to measure the effectiveness of multimedia based modular approach with special references to slow learners. Two matched groups of slow learners were constituted for the purpose of this experiment and a normal group comprising average and above average students was also formed in order to assess how far multimedia based modular approach enabled the slow learners to cope with normal students. The control group was taught through traditional lecture method while the experimental group was taught through multimedia based modular approach.

The experiment was conducted for a period of thirty working days. At the end of the experimental period, a post-test was conducted to the slow learners of the experimental group, the slow learners of the control group and the students of the normal group. After a lapse of two months, a retention test was conducted to measure the retention of the students. The responses given by these three groups in the three tests formed the vital data required for the analysis.

Findings and Conclusions

1. There was not significant difference between the pre-test and post-test mean scores of the control group slow learners taught through traditional lecture method. Though their performance was better in the post-test, they could not make any significant difference.
2. There was significant difference between the pre-test and the post-test mean scores of experimental group slow learners when English subject was taught through multimedia based modular approach. Further, their achievement was higher in the post-test than in the pre-test

   Moreover, an analysis of rate of progress made by both control group and experimental group throws light on the effectiveness of the multimedia based modular approach in teaching English to slow learners. From a meagre mean score of 18.6 in the pre-test, they could gain an impressive mean score of 35.2 in the post-test, which is almost double the pre-test mean score. But, the control group slow learners could not make significant mean gain in the post-test. This vouchsafes the advantage of multimedia based modular approach over the traditional lecture method with special reference to slow learners.
3. There was significant difference between the post-test

mean scores of control group slow learners taught through traditional lecture method and the experimental group slow learners taught through multimedia based modular approach. Further, the achievement of experimental group slow learners was higher than the achievement of control group slow learners.

Moreover, the rate of progress made by the experimental group slow learners was higher than that of the control group slow learners. In terms of percentage, the rate of progress shown by the experimental group slow learners taught through multimedia based modular approach was 89.2 per cent while the rate of progress made by the control group slow learners was 12.37 per cent. The variation in the rates of progress made by both the groups is the resultant product of implementation of multimedia based modular approach and it vouches for the effectiveness of multimedia based modular approach with special reference to slow learners.

4. There was significant defference between the post-test mean scores of control group slow learners and the normal group students. Further, the achievement of normal group students was higher than the achievement of control group slow learners

   The mean value (21.8) obtained by the control group slow learners in the post-test reveals that they could make a meagre mean gain only and they could not narrow down the gap between them and the normal group students. It means that the traditional lecture method could not enable the slow learners to cope with normal students.

5. There was significant defference between the post-test mean scores of experimental group slow learners and the normal group students. The achievement of normal group students was higher than the achievement of experimental group slow learners.

   However, a critical analysis of mean values avowed that the experimental group slow learners significantly improved their acheivement after the experiment.

Moreover, the multimedia based modular approach enabled the experimental group slow learners to cope with normal students to a great extent. The narrowed down gulf of difference between both the groups bears testimony to the effectiveness of the multimedia based modular approach.

6. There was no significant difference between the post-test and retention test mean scores of each group.

However, a critical comparison of the retention test mean scores with that of post-test makes some interesting revelations. Both control group and normal group taught through traditional lecture method could not improve upon their post-test mean score in the retention test. There was a decline in the mean score in both their cases whereas the experimental group slow learners could improve upon their post-test mean score in the retention test. Moreover, the mean difference between the pre-test and post-test scores of experimental group slow learners reflects the volume of new additional informations acquired by them at the time of post-test. This fast learnt informations could be properly processed in their minds and kept in memory storage even for a period of two months without loss or distortion. This enhanced retention power may be attributed to the effectiveness of multimedia based modular approach. In terms of acquisition and retention of new informations, it is the experimental group slow learners who have excelled the other two groups students. It substantiates that the multimedia based modular approach can facilitate better learning and promote longer retention.

3. Relative Effectiveness of Video Instruction in Teaching Science and Social Science to Slow learners

Reddy and Ramar (1996) undertook this experimental study to assess the 'relative effectiveness of video instruction in teaching science and social science to slow learners. The main findings of the study were:

i) The Control group slow learners showed significant difference between the pre-test and post-test mean scores when they were taught through traditional lecture method. Further, their performance in the post-test was better than their performance in the pre-test.

ii) There was significant difference between the pre-test and post-test mean scores of experimental group slow learners when the subjects were taught through video instruction. Further, their achievement was higher in the post-test than in the pre-test. Moreover, the rates of progress made by the experimental group slow learners signified the relative effectiveness of video instruction in teaching two different subjects i.e. science and social science. The rate of progress shown by the experimental group slow learners in science was 94.4 percentage while the rate of progress shown in social science was 88.17 percentage. It implies that though the video instruction was effective in teaching both the subjects, it is more effective for science than for social science.

iii) There was significant difference between the post-test scores of the control group slow learners taught through traditional lecture method and the experimental group slow learners taught through video instruction. Further, the achievement of experimental group slow learners was higher than the achievement of control group slow learners. Moreover, an analysis of rate of progress made by the control group slow learners and the experimental group slow learners brought to light the effectiveness of video instruction. The rates of progress made by the experimental group slow learners taught through video instruction were 94.4 percentage in science and 88.17 percentage in social science subject whereas the rates of progress shown by the cont[illegible] group slow learners were 11.81 percentage in science subject and 12.37 percentage in social scienc[illegible] subject. This vouchsafes the advantage of video instruction over the traditional lecture method.

iv) There was significant difference between the post-test scores of control group slow learners and the normal group students. Further,the achievement of the normal group students was higher than the achievement of control group slow learners. The mean values obtained by the control group slow learners revealed that, though they had made progress by traditional lecture method, they could not narrow down the gap between them and the normal group students. It means that the traditional lecture method could not enable the control group slow learners to cope with normal students.

v) There was significant difference between the post-test scores of the experimental group slow learners and the normal group students. The achievement of normal group students was higher than the achievement of experimental group slow learners. However, a critical analysis of mean values signified that the experimental group slow learners significantly improved their performance after the experiment. In terms of rate of progress, it was the experimental group slow learners who had shown a better rate of progress than the normal group students. Video instruction enabled the experimental group slow learners to cope with the normal students to a considerable extent. The narrowed down gulf of difference between both the groups highlighted the effectiveness of video instruction.

4. Effects of Video Instruction on Achievement of Slow Learners in Mathematics

Reddy and Ramar (1996) conducted this experimental study to measure the effectiveness of video instruction in teaching maths to slow learners. The study concluded the following:

Findings and Conclusions

1. The control group slow learners could not show any significant difference between the pre-test and post-test scores when they were taught through traditional lecture method.
2. There was significant differences between the pre-test and the post-test mean scores of experimental group slow learners when they were taught mathematics through video instruction. Further, their achievement was higher in the post-test than in the pre-test.

3. There was significant difference between the post-test mean scores of control group slow learners taught through traditional lecture method and the experimental group slow learners taught through video instruction.

   Further, the achievement of experimental group slow learners was higher than the achievement of control group slow learners. Moreover, the rate of progress made by the experimental group slow learners was higher than that of the control group slow learners. The variation in the rates of progress made by both the groups was the resultant product of video instruction and it vouches for the effectiveness of video instruction as a method of teaching.

4. There was significant defference between the post-test mean scores of control group slow learners and the normal group students. Further, the achievement of normal group students was higher than the achievement of control group slow learners.

   The mean value (19.4) obtained by the control group slow learners in the post-test revealed that they could neither make a significant mean gain nor could they narrow down the gap between them and the normal group students. It means that the traditional lecture method could not enable the slow learners to cope with normal students.

`5. There was significant difference between the post-test mean scores of experimental group slow learners and the normal group students. The achievement of normal group students was higher than the achievement of experimental group slow learners

However, a critical analysis of mean values signified that the experimental group slow learners significantly improved their achievement after the experiment. Moreover, the video instruction enabled the experimental group slow learners to cope with normal students to a considerable extent. The narrowed down gulf of difference between both the groups testified to the effectiveness of video instruction.

5. Effectiveness of Computer Assisted Instruction in Teaching Science to Slow Learners.

The main objective of this experimental study conducted by Reddy and Ramar(1995) was to develop CAI software for science subject of std VIII and to assess its effectiveness with special reference to slow learners. Keeping the above main objective in mind, the following specific objectives were framed.

1) To find out whether there is any significant difference between the pre-test and post-test mean scores of the slow learners in the control group.
2) To assess whether there exists any significant difference between the pre-test and post-test mean scores of the slow learners in the experimental group.
3) To find out whether there is any significant difference between the post-test mean scores of the experimental group and the control group.
4) To assess whether there exists any significant difference between the post-test mean scores of the slow learners in the control group and the students in the normal group.

After analysis the study arrived at the following results:

1) The control group slow learners showed significant difference between the pre-test and the post-test mean scores when they were taught through traditional lecture method. Further, their performance in the post-test was better than their performance in the pre-test.
2) There was significant difference between the pre-test and the post-test mean scores of experimental group slow learners when science subject was taught through CAI. Further, their achievement was higher in the post-test than in the pre-test.
3) There was significant difference between the post-test mean scores of control group slow learners taught through traditional lecture method and the experimental group slow learners taught through CAI. Further, the achievement of experimental group slow learners was higher than the achievement of control group slow learners.

Moreover, the rate of progress made by the experimental group slow learners was higher than that of the control group slow learners. In terms of percentage, the rate of progress shown by the experimental group slow lerners taught through CAI was 126% while the rate of progress made by the control group slow learners was 18.75%. This variation in the rates of progress made by both the groups was the resultant outcome of CAI and it vouches for the effectiveness of CAI with special reference to slow leaners.

4) There was significant difference between the post-test mean scores of the control group slow learners and the normal group students. Further, the achievement of normal group students was higher than the achievement of control group slow learners.

   The mean value (22.8) obtained by the control group slow learners revealed that through they had made progress (from 19.2 to 22.8) by traditional lecture method, they could not narrow down the gap between them and the normal group students. It meant that the traditional lecture method could not enable the control group slow learners to cope with normal students.

5) There was significant difference between the post-test mean scores of the experimental group slow learners and the normal group students. The achievement of normal group students was higher than the achievement of experimental group slow learners. However, the gap between both the group was reduced to a great extent. This can be ascribed to the effectiveness of CAI.

6. Impact of Modular Approach on Achievement of Slow Learners in Social Science

Reddy and Ramar (1996) conducted this experimental study to measure the effectiveness of modular approach with special reference to Slow learners and also to assess how far modular approach enables the slow learners to cope with normal students. The study was undertaken for the following reasons.

Need for the study

The slow learners lack concentration. So they can not concentrate on the instructional presentation for or more than 30 minutes. In modular approach a single unit is divided into three to four conceptual sub units. Each sub unit constitutes the subject content for development of one module. The duration of each module is 20 to 25 minutes only. So the slow learners will be able to concentrate on the concept. Also it caters to the short span of attention of the slow learners.

A learning module is a self contained and self instructional package dealing with a single conceptual unit or subject matter. It can be used in any setting, convenient to the learner and the learner can complete the module at his own pace. It may be used individually or in small learning groups. In this way modular approach accommodates instruction to individual differences. Here, what matters most is the mastery of the subject, not the time. So, the modules are very suitable to the students and they are more effective for slow learners.

One of the most frequent complaints about slow learners is the weakness of their memory. Of all the problems that hamper educational progress, the most frequent is a weakness in what may be termed long-term memory. Slow learners need to go over the material more times before it is fixed in their mind, and more frequent revision is required to prevent forgetting. The efficiency of the initial learning is important as well as actual retention and recall. Modular approach takes care of these problems by providing frequent revision and repetition in each module.

The slow learners are very poor in abstract thinking. It is because they are unable to understand the relationship between things. They are slower to perceive and use possible association. Meaningful associations are of great importance not only for comprehension but also for prolonged retention. The learning materials presented in the module for each objective, the project work and the practicum incorporated in the learning module enable the slow learners to surmount the problems of abstract thinking and to understand the possible association which will, ultimately, tell upon their retention.

It is a fallacy to think that just because the slow learners are limited in intelligence, they can only learn by rote memorisation. They also can make meaningful learning where there is concrete presentation of subject matter. Slow learners must understand as much as they can of what they are learning, and then they need more repetition, revision and practice to ensure retention. Modular approach takes care of concrete presentation of subject matter by incorporating necessary diagrams, sketches, pictures, worksheets, examples, dimensional drawings etc. in the learning material at appropriate places. Also, modular approach provides for the required review, repetition, and revision by highlighting the main points in learning materials, various tests and in recapitulation and summary. In provides for practice in project work and practicum. Thus, in many ways, the modular approach proves to be suitable for slow learners.

Objectives of the Study

The main objective of the study was to develop modules for social science subject of Std VIII and to assess their effectiveness with special reference to slow learners. Keeping the above main objective in mind, the following specific objectives were framed.

1. To find out whether there is any significant difference between the pre-test and the post-test mean scores of the slow learners in the control group.
2. To assess whether there exists any significant differences between the pre-test and post-test mean scores of the slow learners in the experimental group.
3. To find out whether there is any significant differences between the post-test mean scores of the experimental group and the control group.
4. To assess whether there exists any significant difference between the post-test mean scores of the slow learners in the control group and the students in the normal group.
5. To find out whether there is any significant difference between the post-test mean scores of the slow learners

in the experimental group and the students in the normal group.

Findings and Conclusions

1. The control group slow learners showed significant difference between the pre-test and the post-test mean scores when they were taught through traditional lecture method. Further, their achievement in the post-test was better than their achievement in the pre-test.
2. There was significant difference between the pre-test and the post-test mean scores of experimental group slow learners when social science subject was taught through modular approach. Further their achievement was higher in the post-test than in the pre-test.
3. There was significant difference between the post-test mean scores of control group slow learners taught through traditional lecture method and the experimental group slow learners taught through modular approach. Further, the achievement of experimental group slow learners was higher than the achievement of control group slow learners.

   Moreover, the rate of progress made by the experimental group slow learners was higher than that of the control group slow learners. In terms of percentage, the rate of progress shown by the experimental group slow learners taught through modular approach was 94.4% while the rate of progress made by the control group slow learners was 16.36%. The variation in the rates of progress made by both the groups was the outcome of implementation of modular approach and it vouches for the effectiveness of modular approach with special reference to slow learners.
4. There was significant difference between the post-test mean scores of control group slow learners and the normal group students. Further, the achievement of normal group students was higher than the achievement of normal group students.
5. There was significant difference between the post-test mean scores of the experimental group slow learners

and the normal group students. The achievement of normal group students was higher than the achievement of experimental group slow learners.

However, a critical analysis of mean values evinced that the experimental group slow learners significantly improved their achievement after the experiment. Moreover, the modular approach enabled the experimental group slow learners to cope with normal students to a great extent. The narrowed down gulf of difference between both the group testified to the effectiveness of the modular approach.

7. Effectiveness of Multimedia Instructional Strategy in Teaching Science to Slow Learners.

The present experimental study was undertaken with two objectives in view (i) to develop multimedia packages for VIII Std science subject, and (ii) to measure the effectiveness of multimedia instructional strategy with special reference to slow learners. Two matched groups of slow learners were constituted for the purpose of this experiment and a normal group comprising average and above average students was also formed in order to assess how far multimedia instructional strategy enabled the slow learners to cope with normal students. The control group and the normal group were taught through traditional lecture method while the experimental group was taught through multimedia instructional strategy. The obtained results showed that the multimedia instructional strategy was more effective than the traditional lecture method in teaching science and it enabled the slow learners to cope with normal students to a considerable extent.

Suggestions For Further Research

1. In the above studies, the effectiveness of a single medium in teaching a single subject has been assessed. Further studies can be undertaken to assess the effectiveness of the same medium in teaching other subjects as well.
2. Relative effectiveness of different media in teaching a particular subject can also assessed by undertaking appropriate experimental studies.

3. Studies can be undertaken to measure the effectiveness of mastery learning strategy on the achievement of slow learners as suggested by Bloom (1976). Similarly the impact of additional instructional time on the achievement of Slow Learners can also be verified by research studies.
4. A survey study can be undertaken to probe into the causative factors of slow learning.
5. Separate experimental studies can be undertaken to assess the effectiveness of peer tutoring, parent tutoring and adult tutoring with special reference to slow learners.
6. A survey study can be made to assess the extent of job placement provided to slow learning adolescents.
7. Separate studies can be undertaken to assess how for vocational education and physical education provide for smooth transition from school life to adult life.
8. Case studies can be undertaken to assess the success / failure of slow learners in post-school life.
9. Survey study can be attempted to study the role played by the slow learners in later life in education of their children.
10. The suggestions made herein are not comprehensive and the scholars can undertake many more researches considering the problems they encounter in the teaching learning process.

Summary

Educational Research is the process of applying the scientific method to the solution of educational problems. It is the process of arriving at empirically verifiable principles or generalisations about educational theory or practice.

Education should keep pace with the social changes that are continually taking place and the changes we effect in education should be based on research.

Only a few experimental studies have been conducted on backward, students in general, and slow learners in particular. All the survey books published so far by the NCERT have no study on slow learners. Only recently Reddy and Ramar have done some worthwhile studies in this regard. All these studies subtly point out that media attributes are a must in any special instructional strategy devised for slow learners.

Relative effectiveness of different media in teaching different subjects may be assessed. Effectiveness of mastery learning strategy with special reference to slow learners can also be assessed. Also, a separate study may be attempted to study the effectiveness of additional instructional time on the achievement of slow learners. The suggestions made are not comprehensive and many more researches can be attempted by the scholars considering the problem they are confronted with.

REFERENCES

1. Reddy and Ramar (1995) 'Effectiveness of Multimedia Instructional Strategy in Teaching Science to Slow Learners'. Department of Education, Alagappa University, Karaikudi.

2. Reddy and Ramar (1995) 'Effectiveness of Computer Assisted Instruction in Teaching Science to Slow Learners'. Department of Education, Alagappa University, Karaikudi.

3. Reddy and Ramar (1996) 'Relative Effectiveness of Video Instruction in Teaching Science and Social Science to Slow Learners'. Paper Presented at the Third National conference on Development of Educational Technology, Bharathithasan University, Dec. 27, 28, 1996.

4. Reddy and Ramar (1997) 'Effectiveness of Multimedia Based Modular Approach in Teaching English to Slow Learners'. *Journal of ICCW, April, 1997.*

5. Reddy and Ramar (1997) 'Impact of Modular Approach on Achievement of Slow learners in Social Science'. Department of Education Alagappa University, Karaikudi.

6. Reddy and Ramar (1997) 'Effects of Video instruction on Achievement of Slow learners in Mathematics'. Department of Education, Alagappa University, Karaikudi.

7. Soundararaja Rao and Rajaguru (1995) 'Effectiveness of Video Assisted Instruction on Achievement of Slow Learners'. *Journal of Educational Research and Extension,* Vol. 32, No. 2, Oct. 1995.

INDEX